a. Hawkins

D1524040

ALDABONAZO

Inside the
Cuban revolutionary
underground

1952–58

Aldabonazo

Inside the Cuban revolutionary underground

1952–58

A PARTICIPANT'S ACCOUNT

Armando Hart

Pathfinder

NEW YORK   LONDON   MONTREAL   SYDNEY

Edited by Mary-Alice Waters

Copyright © 1997 by Armando Hart Dávalos
Copyright © 2004 by Pathfinder Press

ISBN 0-87348-968-3
Library of Congress Control Number: 2003114346
Manufactured in Canada

First edition, 2004

COVER AND PHOTO PAGES DESIGN: Eric Simpson
COVER PHOTO: University students march in Havana, April 6, 1952, to protest
Fulgencio Batista's U.S.-backed coup the previous month. In this first street
demonstration against the dictatorship, the students symbolically buried
Cuba's 1940 constitution annulled by Batista. Armando Hart is in front row,
center, holding up a copy of the constitution. Raúl Castro is carrying the
Cuban flag. (*Bohemia*)

Pathfinder

www.pathfinderpress.com
E-mail: pathfinderpress@compuserve.com

PATHFINDER DISTRIBUTORS AROUND THE WORLD:
Australia (and Southeast Asia and the Pacific):
    Pathfinder, Level 1, 3/281-287 Beamish St., Campsie, NSW 2194
    Postal address: P.O. Box 164, Campsie, NSW 2194
Canada:
    Pathfinder, 2761 Dundas St. West, Toronto, ON M6P 1Y4
Iceland:
    Pathfinder, Skolavordustig 6B, Reykjavík
    Postal address: P. Box 0233, IS 121 Reykjavík
New Zealand:
    Pathfinder, P.O. Box 3025, Auckland
Sweden:
    Pathfinder, Domargränd 16, S-129 47 Hägersten
United Kingdom (and Europe, Africa, Middle East, and South Asia):
    Pathfinder, 47 The Cut, London, SE1 8LF
United States (and Caribbean, Latin America, and East Asia):
    Pathfinder Books, 307 W. 36th St., 10th floor north, New York, NY 10018

TO FIDEL CASTRO RUZ,

> *whose conscience contains*
> *all the ethical values*
> *and political wisdom*
> *that the 20th century has lacked.*

TO MY U.S. GRANDFATHER,
FRANK EDMUNDO HART BALOT,

> *who represented for me*
> *the people of the United States.*
> *Born in Georgia,*
> *during the 1870s he came to Cuba,*
> *where he raised a family*
> *and lived until 1960.*

Contents

Armando Hart

Born in Havana in 1930, Armando Hart Dávalos entered the University of Havana in 1947, where, as a member of the Orthodox Party Youth and the Federation of University Students, he became involved in political struggles against the corruption of the Authentic Party regime and its subservience to Washington.

Following Fulgencio Batista's U.S.-backed coup in March 1952, he joined the Revolutionary National Movement (MNR) led by Rafael García Bárcena and became one of its leading cadres. When García Bárcena was arrested in April 1953 on charges of conspiracy, Hart gained national prominence as the defense attorney for the MNR leader.

Subsequently, Hart worked to reorganize the MNR on a national level. Arrested in October 1954 for planning actions of sabotage, he was released the following month.

In June 1955 Hart was a founding member of the July 26 Movement and its National Directorate. He played a central role in organizing the new movement and in preparing to launch the revolutionary war against the Batista regime in 1956.

He participated in the November 30, 1956, Santiago de Cuba uprising timed to coincide with the *Granma* landing, and was one of the national organizers of the July 26 Movement's urban underground, known as the *Llano* [plains]. The underground gave vital support to the Rebel Army in the Sierra Maestra and carried out propaganda and sabotage actions against the regime, leading the Civic Resistance Movement as well as opposition fronts of workers and students.

Arrested and jailed in April 1957, he escaped in July and was named national coordinator of the July 26 Movement following the July 30 murder of Frank País. In mid-November 1957 he went to the Sierra Maestra for political consultation with Fidel Castro and other leaders of the Rebel Army. As he was leaving in January 1958 to resume his regular activities in the Llano, he and two other July 26 Movement leaders were captured and imprisoned. His life was spared due to the swift action and publicity campaign of the July 26 Movement. He spent all of 1958 in jail. In the second half of the year he was sent to the Isle of Pines prison, where hundreds of political prisoners were incarcerated.

When Batista fled Cuba in the early morning of January 1, 1959, the prison authorities refused to release the political prisoners. Hart and other leaders of the July 26 Movement organized the political prisoners to seize the compound and then take control of the entire Isle of Pines.

Arriving in Havana January 2, Hart was named minister of education in the revolutionary government a few days later, and held that responsibility until 1965. He directed the mass literacy campaign of 1961, which taught a million Cubans to read and write, eliminating illiteracy in countryside and city across the island.

In 1961 Armando Hart became a member of the National Directorate of the Integrated Revolutionary Organizations (ORI) and was part of the national leadership of the United Party of the Socialist Revolution (PURS) that replaced the ORI. When the Communist Party of Cuba (PCC) was formed in 1965, Hart became a member of its Central Committee. He was the party's organization secretary in 1965–70, and in 1970–76 was its first secretary in Oriente province. He has been a member of the Communist Party Central Committee since 1965 and was a member of its Political Bureau from 1965 through 1991.

When the Ministry of Culture was created in 1976, Hart became minister, remaining in that post until 1997, when he became the founding director of the Martí Program. Since 1997 he has also been president of the José Martí Cultural Society. He is a deputy to the National Assembly and a member of the Council of State.

He is author of numerous essays, articles, books, and pamphlets on culture and cultural policy, history, and social development. These include *La cultura en el proceso de integración de América Latina* [Culture in the fight for Latin American unification]; *Del trabajo cultural* [On cultural work]; *Cambiar las reglas del juego* [Changing the rules of the game]; *Cultura en Revolución* [Culture in revolution]; *Cubanía, cultura y política* [Cubanhood, culture, and politics]; *Mi visión del Che desde los '90* [My vision of Che in the 1990s]; *Perfiles* [Characteristics]; *Poner en orden las ideas* [Putting ideas in order]; *Una pelea cubana contra viejos y nuevos demonios* [A Cuban fight against old and new demons]; *Cuba e Iberoamérica* [Cuba and Latin America]; *Hacia una dimensión cultural del desarrollo* [Toward a cultural dimension of development]; *Cuba, raíces del presente* [Cuba: roots of the present]; *José Antonio Saco, Félix Varela y Antonio Maceo: ética, cultura y política* [José Antonio Saco, Félix Varela, and Antonio Maceo: ethics, culture, and politics]; *La cultura de hacer política* [The culture of doing politics]; *Discursos y artículos; Indagaciones desde la epopeya* [Investigations since the feat]; *Una interpretación de la historia de Cuba desde el 2001* [An interpretation from 2001 of Cuba's history]; *Cultura, ética y política* [Ethics, culture, and politics]; *Martí y Marx, raíces de la Revolución cubana* [Martí and Marx: roots of the Cuban Revolution]; *Cómo llegamos a las ideas socialistas* [How we came to socialist ideas].

For his writings and work he has received numerous awards and distinctions, both in Cuba and internationally.

Publisher's preface

The simultaneous publication in English and Spanish of Pathfinder's edition of *Aldabonazo: Inside the Cuban Revolutionary Underground, 1952–58,* brings this account of the victorious struggle to overthrow the U.S.-backed dictatorship of Fulgencio Batista to significantly new and broader audiences.

Written by Armando Hart, one of the historic leaders of the Cuban Revolution, *Aldabonazo* is now accessible for the first time ever to English-speaking readers. In Spanish, the book, which has been out of print for half a decade, is again available not only in Latin America and Spain, but for the first time to the large and ever-growing audience of Spanish-speaking readers in the United States, Canada, and elsewhere around the globe—wherever the whiplash of capital has accelerated the emigration of those who possess nothing to live by but the sale of their own labor power.

More than five decades ago, Armando Hart emerged as a leader of the young generation of students and working people who burst into history as they took to the streets in opposition to the 1952 military coup d'état in Cuba that installed one of the most brutal dictatorships Latin America had yet experienced. The Centennial Generation, as they became known, refused to

Mary-Alice Waters, president of Pathfinder Press, is the editor of *New International,* a magazine of Marxist politics and theory. She has edited more than a dozen books of interviews, writings, and speeches of leaders of the Cuban Revolution.

15

accept or compromise with the tyranny and corruption that marked political life in Cuba. They asserted not only the right but the obligation of the Cuban people to rise in armed insurrection if need be to bring down a bloody, illegitimate regime that had usurped power by force. And they set out to forge a revolutionary movement capable of achieving their aims.

Aldabonazo—which in Spanish means a sharp, warning knock on the door—became a rallying cry of that generation of youth who risked their lives in defiance of the military regime. What distinguished them from the various bourgeois political parties and associations that opposed the Batista dictatorship was not primarily words, but deeds. Without fear of consequences for themselves, or political hesitation over where the struggle might lead, they fought for what they believed was right and refused to settle for less.

Fewer than seven years later, under the leadership of Fidel Castro, the July 26 Revolutionary Movement and its Rebel Army led the workers, peasants, and revolutionary-minded youth of Cuba to victory. Some 20,000 had paid with their lives by the time Batista and his henchmen fled the country on January 1, 1959. A new revolutionary government was installed with the jubilant support of the overwhelming majority of the Cuban people. Armando Hart was the first minister of education in that government.

Aldabonazo takes us into this history from the perspective of the cadres who with courage and audacity led the struggle waged by the urban underground, known in the political vocabulary of Cuba as the *Llano* (plains). The book joins other titles published by Pathfinder over the last decade, among which are:

• Ernesto Che Guevara's *Episodes of the Cuban Revolutionary War, 1956–58*, and Teté Puebla's *Marianas in Combat*, each of which tells pieces of the story from inside what was known as the *Sierra* (mountains), recounting the experiences and lessons of the Rebel Army forces of the July 26 Movement based in the Sierra Maestra mountain range of eastern Cuba;

• Víctor Dreke's *From the Escambray to the Congo*, which

incorporates experiences of the student-led forces of the Revolutionary Directorate and the guerrilla war in the Escambray mountains of the central region of Cuba; and

• *Making History: Interviews with Four Generals of Cuba's Revolutionary Armed Forces,* which recounts the experiences of Enrique Carreras and José Ramón Fernández, both military officers who helped lead anti-Batista conspiracies within the armed forces, as well as the stories of Néstor López Cuba and Harry Villegas *(Pombo)* who fought in the Sierra.

Hart's narrative of his own political trajectory and experiences in the revolutionary underground draws extensively on and ties together a rich, even dizzying, collection of letters, circulars, articles, and manifestos interspersed throughout the pages of this book. Hart himself participated in drafting many of these documents, each written in the heat of the struggle. A good number of them are published for the first time in *Aldabonazo.*

Through Hart's account we begin to understand more fully and accurately the day-by-day political struggle waged by the forces that came together in 1955 under the leadership of Fidel Castro to form the July 26 Revolutionary Movement, named for the date of the 1953 assault on the Moncada military garrison in Santiago de Cuba that marked the opening of the popular insurrection against the dictatorship. We follow the men and women of the July 26 Movement as they work to develop their political program; as they struggle, through action and debate, to win the leadership of the revolutionary vanguard; as they take advantage of every opening to intervene in the broad political ferment, exposing the empty posturing and pretensions of the traditional bourgeois opposition parties; and as they clarify questions of strategy and tactics debated not only among the revolutionary cadres of the Llano and of the Sierra, but throughout the anti-Batista opposition.

Above all we come to appreciate the leadership capacities of Fidel Castro as he pulls together and politically orients the revolutionary cadres coming from diverse origins and experiences—

exemplified by men and women like Armando Hart and his brother Enrique, Celia Sánchez, Frank País, Haydée Santamaría, Ñico López, Vilma Espín, and Faustino Pérez—to name but a few of those whom we meet and begin to know in these pages. We watch the core of the national leadership of the July 26 Movement in the Llano emerge, grow and recover from the blows of repression, and transform themselves in the course of the struggle.

As Hart puts it in his epilogue, "Revolutions are not a stroll through beautiful meadows and gardens, where men march without difficulty or anguish. A process of change is filled with both, and multiplies them. History does not move in a straight line. Contradictory situations generate passions that are full of human conflict and mark revolutionary conduct." Those were the leadership challenges they met and surmounted.

We see how the men and women of the July 26 Movement fought to forge a *disciplined* organization of cadres whose goal— as explained in the leadership's 1957 "Circular No. 1 to the membership," printed here—was "a) To overthrow Batista through popular action, [which] is not the same as just overthrowing him," and "b) To consolidate the revolutionary instrument to ensure the fulfillment of the revolution's program, also through popular action, [which] is not the same as simply creating a new party."

Along this course the July 26 Movement and Rebel Army not only led the working people of Cuba to bring down the dictatorship and establish the first "free territory of the Americas." They opened the road to the first socialist revolution in our hemisphere as well. For the first time since the Bolsheviks under Lenin led the workers, peasants, and soldiers of the tsarist empire to power in October 1917, a leadership of the toilers unpoisoned by the degeneration of the Russian Revolution emerged on the world stage, bypassing obstacles and creating new possibilities for struggle. A quarter century of revolution in the Americas ensued—from the Southern Cone through the Andes, to Central America and the Caribbean. The liberation of southern Africa became a reality.

Therein lies the root of the implacable hatred of the U.S. rulers for the Cuban Revolution and for those who led—and lead—it. Therein lie the reasons why for more than forty years Washington has never for an instant ceased attempting to punish the Cuban people for their audacity, to force them into submission. And why imperialism has failed.

*

Aldabonazo is not an "inside story" or a polemic. "My aim was not to investigate what was done badly, or what could have been done, or what should have been done better," Hart writes in his epilogue. "The main interest of this book lies in showing some fundamental elements of a historical thread that should not be forgotten, and that can serve as an important point of reference to better understand how the fabric of the Cuban Revolution was woven and, more broadly, to comprehend the second half of the twentieth century."

It is in that spirit, too, that Pathfinder publishes this new edition of *Aldabonazo*. The book is of interest not only, or even primarily, for historical reasons, as important as they may be. The Cuban Revolution in all its rich complexity is a vital, living part of the present and future struggles of Our America, and the world. The better we understand how that revolution was led to victory, the better prepared we will be to emulate its example and meet the challenges posed by the social and political explosions that will shape the twenty-first century.

*

Ernesto Che Guevara, the Argentine-born leader of the Cuban Revolution, told an international youth congress in Havana in July of 1960, "If this revolution is Marxist . . . it is because it discovered, by its own methods, the road pointed out by Marx."

For more than forty years, one of the most persistent themes of the left-liberal spokespersons for the U.S. ruling class has been the examination and reexamination of what could have been done, what should have been done to prevent (or can yet be done to reverse) the mighty social revolution in Cuba. A revolution that swept away not only North American propertied interests but their Cuban counterparts as well, and established a new class—the working class—in power.

A mythology has been cultivated and widely disseminated, especially by a layer of individuals who supported the struggle against Batista but recoiled from the deep social revolution that accelerated as that struggle advanced, assuring its victory. Among these individuals were men and women of whom Hart says, "they aspired to be more than what they could be in the revolution. They were moved by resentment."

That mythology, in the version popular among liberals in the United States, holds that deep political differences existed between the leading cadres of the Sierra and Llano, with the latter being more "democratically" inclined. If only the U.S. government had acted differently, they argue, then somehow the leaders of the Llano, not Fidel Castro and the commanders of the Rebel Army in the mountains, would have emerged as the political leadership of the Cuban people after Batista was overthrown. The subsequent history of Cuba, and indeed the twentieth century, would have been different.

Hart addresses this mythology directly and indirectly throughout the pages of *Aldabonazo*, exposing the fallacies in which such arguments are rooted. "Outside the country," he writes, "a tale has been woven about how our whole struggle could have moved toward a bourgeois revolution. I invite anyone who believes this to consider the consequences of the implementation of our entire program. Enactment and strict enforcement of laws implementing the constitution of 1940 alone meant totally opposing the interests of the domestic oligarchy and imperialism. Suffice it to say that this constitution provided for the abolition of the large landed estates."

While he himself came from the family of a prominent Havana magistrate, "the social composition of the most representative leadership cadres and rank-and-file combatants was not bourgeois," Hart notes. "They came from the working masses, the middle layers (mostly of modest means), the poor peasants, and the unemployed." The reader need only review the content of the circulars, letters, and declarations printed here, issued from the beginning of the revolutionary war in 1956 onward, to realize the accuracy of Hart's statement that they "illustrate the social and profoundly radical character of the revolution from its formative years." They offer "proof that we were marching toward a confrontation with imperialism, and that the idea of social revolution had taken root among the combatants of the July 26 Movement."

The majority of cadres of the July 26 Movement fighting in the Llano as well as the Sierra underwent a profound transformation as they put their lives on the line day after day, determined to transform their world. They emerged as different people, molded by these experiences and by the social realities they shared with the men and women in the mountains and fields, from whom they learned, and with whom their future was fused. Whatever ideas each individual held to begin with, those ideas evolved, matured, became clearer, more proletarian, as the revolutionary struggle deepened. Moving from city to mountains, and sometimes in reverse, as a significant number of cadres of the Llano did, brought greater homogeneity in political character and revolutionary priorities to the leadership core. As Faustino Pérez, Hart's close comrade-in-arms, puts it in a letter to Hart included in these pages, the "Sierra is a savior. It has saved the revolution from being annihilated, and it saves sick spirits from death. . . . [It] detoxifies, encourages, heals, restores, revitalizes."

The cord that has bound the leadership of the Cuban Revolution together for more than five decades is none other than their commitment to that "profoundly radical" social program, first presented in *History Will Absolve Me*, Fidel Castro's courtroom defense speech at his trial for leading the July 26, 1953, assault on the Moncada garrison. That program became flesh and blood in the trenches of battle to bring down the dictatorship and to prevent the fruits of victory from being stolen once again by the masters of the empire to the north.

✱

Aldabonazo was first published in Cuba by Editorial Letras Cubanas in 1997. In 1998 the Spanish publishing house Libertarias Prodhufi brought out an edition under the title *Cuba: Roots of the Present.*

Pathfinder's edition, prepared in collaboration with the author, reorganizes materials contained in the earlier publications, incorporating them into the narrative in a more integral way. Readers, especially those for whom much of the rich revolutionary history of Cuba is relatively unknown, will be aided by the extensive chronology and glossary, edited with generous help from a number of knowledgeable collaborators in Cuba, but for which Pathfinder alone bears editorial responsibility.

The historic photos and graphic illustrations of the underground publications of the 1950s that appear in these pages are also reproduced in large part courtesy of Armando Hart, who provided them from his own collection or helped make them available from other archives.

The preface to the U.S. edition by Eliades Acosta, director of the José Martí National Library of Cuba, is an especially welcome contribution. It joins the valuable preface to the original Cuban edition by Roberto Fernández Retamar, director of *Casa de las Américas,* and himself a combatant of the Centennial Generation.

The initial translation into English was provided by Olimpia Sigarroa. Editing of the translation and preparation of the glossary, chronology, and annotation were the work of Michael Taber. The Spanish-language text was prepared by Luis Madrid.

Scores of volunteers from countries around the world, all part of the Pathfinder Printing Project, eagerly contributed their time and abilities to translate, format, proofread, index, prepare the photo pages and maps, assemble the digital production files, and assure delivery of the final printed product.

Above all, special appreciation is due to Eloísa Carreras, whose alert editorial contributions, diligence, and good-natured collaboration from Havana were indispensable to the quality and accuracy of this edition.

Most important, of course, without the close attention, keen interest, and generous allotment of time of the author himself, this new edition of *Aldabonazo* would not have been possible.

NOVEMBER 2003

Preface to the U.S. edition

BY ELIADES ACOSTA MATOS

One of the erroneous interpretations of the Cuban Revolution
that has shown the greatest resiliency and been disseminated
most broadly is that the revolution was a total accident. It is
portrayed as the product of irresponsible improvisations by its
leaders both in their thinking and actions, as well as their con-
cretization of policies. As if a process that has set millions of
Cubans into motion—something unheard-of heretofore in our
nation—could be the product of chance or the act of some Ma-
chiavellian genius hunting for opportunities.

This line of thinking was put forward in writing a few months
back by one of the exponents of the postmodernist wing of the
Cuban counterrevolution:

"Cuban socialism can be thought of as a device, a masterpiece
of advanced social engineering that has been imported by a country of low technological—read political—development. It is a
device that came with user instructions but without the original blueprints. . . . There is no doubt in my mind that even
among the top Cuban leadership, the knowledge of how to use

Eliades Acosta Matos has been director of the José Martí National Library of Cuba since 1997. He is author of the books *Los hermanos
santiagueros de Martí* [Martí's Santiago brothers]; *El árbol de la discordia* [The
tree of discord]; *El Siboney de los cubanos* [The Cubans' Siboney]; *El 98: la
guerra que no cesa* [1898: the war that doesn't end]; and *Los colores secretos
del Imperio* [The secret colors of the empire].

this device and of its workings has always been a matter of intuition."[1]

From the very beginning of the struggle against the Fulgencio Batista dictatorship and then after the triumph of January 1, 1959, Dr. Armando Hart Dávalos has been a member of the "top Cuban leadership" referred to above. Utilizing unassailable evidence in the form of documents—many never before reprinted—*Aldabonazo* refutes not only this clever argument of the right (both the Stone Age and postmodern varieties) but also the naive interpretations (either due to ignorance or laziness) coming from a section of the left. That is why this book has such great historical value. It is indispensable reading for those wishing to thoroughly understand, without cosmetics and without mediators, the essence and freshness of a revolution that has already been in power forty-five years.

Revolution is a process and a concept that has today been banished from the politically correct dictionaries of the global era. And if use of the word is sometimes allowed, it's solely to describe the glamorous worlds of the stock market, fashion, or the technologies of Silicon Valley. Time and again it has been said that revolutions are part of the barbaric, irrational, and violent stage of human history. That they're aberrations leading to deviations from society's evolutionary course. That revolutions mark the triumph of selfish methods by sinister groups seeking to rise in society. So thoroughly have the enemies of the Cuban Revolution convinced themselves and others of these arguments that they wind up looking pathetic and ridiculous each time they predict its fall, unable to explain how it has survived amid so many shipwrecks.

These enemies of revolutions are organically incapable of understanding history—its chain of cause and effect; the eternal interplay of subjective and objective factors; the existence of classes, class interests, and class struggles, which can be felt

1. Prieto, José Manuel: Presentation of the November 2002 issue of the Mexican magazine *Letras Libres*, Guadalajara International Book Fair.

today more than they were two hundred years ago. To this incapacity we must add the decay of global conservative thought. Partially blinded by their conjunctural dominance (a war booty looted from the ruins of the European socialist experience and the history of the people's struggles), these forces are full of pompous proclamations of pseudo-emancipation. As a result, they are incapable of freeing themselves from trite commonplaces and moving beyond them. Their smug ineptness prevents them from understanding the new awakening in lands they thought "pacified" and immune to change. They cannot comprehend the social processes taking place today in Venezuela, Brazil, Bolivia, Ecuador, Argentina, Mexico, Nicaragua, and El Salvador—to cite countries in Latin America alone.

To parody these adversaries, one might well say that the globalized and neoliberal world under U.S. government hegemony is the shortest and surest road to rebuilding the left, to the triumph of popular revolutions, to the construction of genuine socialism. Tomorrow the people will have to thank the International Monetary Fund, for example, more than the Comintern or Red Army for bringing to maturity the conditions necessary for the triumph of their cause. And more than the writings of Marx, Trotsky, or Mao, they will run up against the obvious failure of the preachings of ideologues masquerading as writers, in the style of Mario Vargas Llosa or Guillermo Cabrera Infante (to stay in the realm of Latin America here too).

The first U.S. edition of *Aldabonazo* is thus appearing at just the right moment. Not only will it demonstrate the ideological, popular, and humanist coherence of those in Cuba who first risked their lives and have since devoted every minute of their existence to the cause of the Cuban people—for justice, rights, freedom, and democracy for all, not just the privileged elites. *Aldabonazo* will also be in the very front lines of the ideological battles looming on our continent and the rest of the world against those who now try—with arguments we are more than familiar with—to dismiss and demonize the developments that are taking place in the region.

Strictly speaking, the postmodern revolutions, as Fidel Castro said not long ago, "will not be like the Bolshevik revolution or even the Cuban Revolution." Nonetheless, the traditional adversaries of revolution, those who are rushing to expunge the word from political life, dictionaries, and the media, will find it disquieting that revolutions continue to occur nonetheless with rigorous punctuality—even if in different garb and using different slogans—as they have ever since the milestone events that burst forth against the monarchies of England and France. Can postmodern globalized thought explain this? Can they do so without the vainglorious quotes from Derridá, Foucault, or Popper—brilliant literary figures, perhaps, but useless for resolving the problems of hunger, disease, violence, corruption, and illiteracy in Latin America? Can it be achieved by appealing to formulas and concepts of the developed world, by invoking the sacrosanct terms "liberty," "democracy," and "human rights"—as if that is sufficient to resolve all of humanity's problems, like the miracle elixir our grandmothers used for treating indiscriminately all their various ailments?

Aldabonazo is also a defense of a world outlook rooted in the political creativity of genuine revolutionaries, the product of analyzing the real conditions at every moment. And it is done in the best spirit of the teachings of José Martí. It is a courageous vindication—in times of shameful acts of renegacy and capitulation—of faith in the people, in the revolutionary capacity of the masses, and in the unavoidable necessity of the masses' educated, active, and conscious participation in social processes and struggles.

As if all this were not enough to make Armando Hart's book special, *Aldabonazo* is also a moving ode to radical political solutions, using the poetry of an entire lifetime given over to the struggle for principles. And I am not afraid to use the words "radical political solutions," because according to the author's conception—which is also part of the essence and significance of the Cuban Revolution's political philosophy—being radical, as Martí said, does not mean advocating violence. Rather it means going to the root of social ills and applying the measures required, based on their magnitude and scope: not demagogic or populist palliatives, not illusory solutions for bleeding bodies and battered lives. But true and lasting solutions, coming from the people themselves, for the humiliated and slighted, who are always the majority. And also for their children.

If there is anything many protagonists of the Cuban Revolution have rightly been reproached for, it is not having taken the time—amid many tasks and the battle for the nation's survival and its social aims—to write down what they lived through and the ideas they hold. One of those who has fully carried out this other duty to the country has been Armando Hart, as can be seen in the recent publication of the first volume of his bibliography, prepared by Eloísa Carreras.[2] Anyone who has a chance to read his writings—and *Aldabonazo* is a good example—will appreciate the author's clarity and passion, and will not be able to remain indifferent to his honesty and the beauty of his prose.

To sensitive and demanding readers, I particularly recommend that they read some of his letters to family members, such as the one written from the underground on January 4, 1957, and above all, the letter of April 1958 written from jail to console his family upon learning of the death in the course of the struggle of his brother Enrique. Rarely has the generous giving of a young revolutionary's life for the sake of others been expressed with greater precision and nobility, exemplified by the idea that it is possible to "die of life" itself, as the author says at the end of that letter.

Barely ninety miles from the Florida coast, Cuba, its revolution, and its people continue to be an enigma for the majority of people in the United States, yet an enigma to which they are drawn. In no small measure, the blockade and the hostile media campaigns waged in the course of ten U.S. administrations have helped spark interest among many people to know at first hand

2. Carreras, Eloísa, *Biobibliografía de Armando Hart Dávalos: 1990-2000*. Havana: Sociedad Cultural José Martí, 2000.

what did happen and what is still happening on this island located so close to their nation's southern border. When books such as *Aldabonazo* are read by people in the United States, I'm sure they will find that Cubans such as the author share the same aspirations for justice, honesty, freedom, and patriotism that they do; the same attachment to the most noble ideas, to peace, and to life itself. It will open the bridge of comprehension and mutual understanding that we need so much.

In this sense, this book can also be an *aldabonazo*—a knock on the door—of the conscience of readers in the land of Lincoln and Whitman, whom Cubans respect so much.

HAVANA, OCTOBER 2003

Preface to the Cuban edition

BY ROBERTO FERNÁNDEZ RETAMAR

When the main actors in our Ten Years War of 1868–78 wrote about that struggle, their stories were described by Max Henríquez Ureña as "history narrated by its creators." Explaining the origin of these writings, he said: "The actors who not only lived through the events but helped create them come to testify before history as witnesses of a process in which they had been actively involved." They reconstruct "for posterity incidents in which they participated, and which ultimately became part of their own lives."

The same could be said of other events in Cuba, notably the new stage of the war that began in 1895 and, in our century, the attempted revolution of the 1930s. These great endeavors became successively more radical in their goals, but remained linked by strong ties, since each aimed at enabling the nation to become master of its own fate and achieve social justice. The War of Independence was thwarted in 1898, and in 1935 "the revolution went adrift" (as Raúl Roa graphically observed)—in both cases because of U.S. imperialist interference. But this only

Roberto Fernández Retamar has been director of the journal *Casa de las Américas* since 1965. An internationally renowned poet, essayist, and educator, his works have been published in numerous books and compilations since 1950.

united these processes more tightly around a common purpose: affirmation of the country, rebelliousness, and moral integrity. On each occasion, "history narrated by its creators" would again provide us with testimony.

The book now in the reader's hands is a clear demonstration.

Its author, Armando Hart, is himself an outstanding example of those in Cuba today who with good reason are called "historic" compañeros, that is, those who witnessed the very emergence of the revolutionary process that came to power in 1959. Such is the authority with which he has written this work, which is aptly described by the words of Henríquez Ureña quoted above. Echoing these words, Hart writes in the present volume, "For me, everything was related to, everything was an integral part of the great revolutionary and historical task we had ahead of us. *Nothing in my life was alien to this.*" (Emphasis added— RFR) That is what readers of this book will feel. At one and the same time it evokes the drama of a single human being during an intense period, and reflects this period with all its risks, pain, hopes, and grandeur.

The period in question is, of course, the years that immediately preceded the now famous decade of the 1960s, that is, the years preceding the triumph of the Cuban Revolution. Neither this decade nor the revolution itself can be properly understood without knowing how they came to be. These formative years have been the object of much speculation, which often reveals an inadequate grasp of the facts, not to mention distortion born of prejudice. In these pages, Hart makes an essential contribution to understanding them correctly.

Here facts are portrayed transparently and free of prejudice. The author, whose life contains a surprising amount of daring, danger, and adventure (in the best sense of the word), nonetheless steps aside to give the floor to history unadorned. Even the personal documents contained are but arrows shot toward that history. The author's reflections have no other aim than explaining actions. The magnitude of these actions and the mark they made explain the reverberations this work will undoubtedly have.

"A country stymied to its political core"—that is how José Lezama Lima described Cuba on the eve of the 1950s. This country, which the United States had converted first into a militarily occupied land and then into a protectorate and neocolony, with the complicity of servile local leaders devoted to the most shameless corruption, hit bottom on March 10, 1952, when Fulgencio Batista carried out his coup d'état. But "God's handwriting is straight, following twisted lines," as the Portuguese proverb tells us. The repudiation of that ignominious act ended up awakening the citizenry, kindling a new spirit, and generating new leaders, the greatest of whom was—and is—Fidel Castro. Armando was counted among these leaders, and one of his great merits was to have quickly recognized Fidel's indisputable and ever-creative leadership.

Prior to the initiating action of 1953 that tried to storm the heavens, Armando had been politically active under the guidance of an honorable man, Professor Rafael García Bárcena. He paints a noble portrait of García Bárcena (as well as other figures, all of whom merit the prominence given to them here—it is enough to recall the name of Faustino Pérez). Hart is the first to show how García Bárcena was linked, through his unique book *Rediscovering God,* with those who many years later put forward Liberation Theology. García Bárcena was certainly a precursor. And although his book was very difficult to understand when it appeared (1956), that is the usual fate of precursors.

Nevertheless, this well-intentioned and courageous philosopher could not be the one to lead the vast, ever-changing insurrectional movement that the country required. The attacks on the Moncada garrison in Santiago de Cuba and the Carlos Manuel de Céspedes garrison in Bayamo showed that Fidel was emerging as just such a leader. Hart already knew and admired him. They had met in the ranks of the Orthodox Party, founded by Eduardo Chibás, which, under the slogan "Honor against money," was to sink roots among the vast majority of the Cuban people. Despite Chibás's gesture of self-sacrifice in 1951 (his dramatic "final *aldabonazo*"), it was essentially this party that was the target of the coup d'état of March 10, 1952. And from the youth wing of this party emerged those who assaulted the Moncada garrison in 1953 and the nucleus of what was to become the powerful July 26 Movement, which numbers Hart among its initial and ongoing leaders.

There is no need to belabor the point, since he describes the process clearly in these pages. It would be just as useless to analyze the hundreds of episodes we encounter in this book, episodes closely related to the dialectic of the Sierra and the Llano in the anti-Batista struggle. I wish to make an exception, however, with regard to one particularly noteworthy point. Referring to documents prepared for public distribution right after November 30, 1956, while waiting for the *Granma* to reach Cuba, Hart explains:

> These documents are proof that we were marching toward a confrontation with imperialism, and that the idea of social revolution had taken root among the combatants of the July 26 Movement. . . .
>
> Outside the country, a tale has been woven about how our whole struggle could have moved toward a bourgeois revolution. I invite anyone who believes this to consider the consequences of the implementation of our entire program.

Further on, Hart adds, "The social composition of the most representative leadership cadres and rank-and-file combatants was not bourgeois." On the contrary, they "came from the working masses, the middle layers (mostly of modest means), the poor peasants, and the unemployed." Such comments validate the correctness of what Hart says in the epilogue:

> In November 1959, in a complex discussion taking place in the Council of Ministers [Hart was then Minister of Education—RFR], I stated my position: "To understand Fidel one has to bear in mind that he is promoting the socialist revolution

34 / ROBERTO FERNÁNDEZ RETAMAR

starting from the history of Cuba, Latin America, and the anti-imperialist and universal ideas of José Martí."

Further:

I became a Fidelista because Fidel has been capable of defending and bringing into being, with dignity and talent, the ethical and democratic principles contained in this patriotic tradition.

Nothing could sum up this vibrant and honest book better than these words. "This patriotic tradition" remained alive in a country that, after fighting thirty years for its independence, saw it snatched away by a new foreign power, one that inaugurated modern imperialism with its 1898 intervention. In this country the antidictatorial struggles for redemption by men such as Mella, Martínez Villena, Guiteras, and Pablo de la Torriente had merged with the now inseparably combined streams of indigenous social thought and internationalist conduct. José Martí embodied that tradition to the utmost, and the Centennial Generation, which came of age a century after his birth in 1853, found in this tradition its intellectual inspiration, its moral foundation, and its basic driving force. Armando Hart was an outstanding member of that generation, and his book will contribute to an accurate understanding of it. *Aldabonazo* thus helps us understand the roots in which our present is anchored—a present that leads, notwithstanding current difficulties, toward a future that, if genuine, can only be one of victory.

HAVANA, OCTOBER 7, 1997

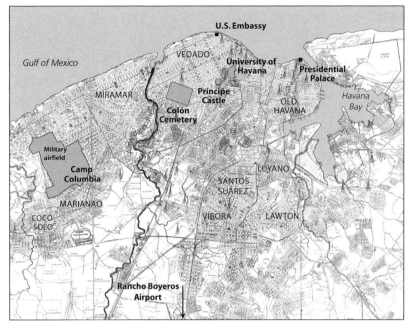

Gulf of Mexico

U.S. Embassy

VEDADO

University of Havana

Presidential Palace

MIRAMAR

Príncipe Castle

Colón Cemetery

OLD HAVANA

Havana Bay

Military airfield

Camp Columbia

LUYANÓ

SANTOS SUÁREZ

MARIANAO

COCO SOLO

VÍBORA

LAWTON

Rancho Boyeros Airport

Havana 1952–58

3 kilometers

2.5 miles

EGO DE AVILA

CAMAGÜEY

CAMAGÜEY

VICTORIA DE
LAS TUNAS

HOLGUÍN

MAYARÍ

O R I E N T E

BAYAMO

MANZANILLO

YARA

PALMA SORIANO

SIERRA MAESTRA

GUANTANAMO

SANTIAGO DE CUBA

U.S. NAVAL BASE

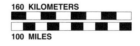

160 KILOMETERS

100 MILES

Cuba 1952–58

ALDABONAZO

Inside the Cuban revolutionary underground

1952–58

Acknowledgments

Above all, it is to the people of Cuba and the vanguard Centennial Generation, leading actors in this great event, that I express my gratitude. Appreciation is also due to:

The Council of State Office of Historical Affairs, founded by Compañera Celia Sánchez, and the José Martí National Library, for the facilities they offered me to carry out the preliminary research.

The group of editors at Pathfinder, represented by Mary-Alice Waters, who from the very first believed in the importance of publishing a book such as this in the United States, and put their painstaking care and professionalism at our disposal to make this project a reality.

Graciela Rodríguez (Chela), who zealously kept many of these papers in my personal archive.

Luis Buch and Héctor Rodríguez Llompart, for their valued contributions to the text.

Enrique Oltuski, for his careful review of the manuscript in English.

Jorge Renato Ibarra and Jorge Lozano, for their contributions to the chronology and glossary.

Aracelis García Carranza and Julio Domínguez García, for their complicity.

Armando Hart
Eloísa Carreras
HAVANA, OCTOBER 2003

Foreword

I began writing this account at the end of the 1970s. In 1991 Eloísa Carreras, my wife, began to analyze and investigate these "papers," and in the end she suggested to me how to write the present book. Without her obstinate insistence, I could not have reconstructed it in this form. We worked together to create the memoirs that I now present to you.

In everything I write, I always bear in mind the political realities before me. I am inspired not by a desire to meditate but by the goal of tackling and understanding concretes.

The events I relate cover essentially my passage through the underground struggle. I lived these events twenty-four hours a day, giving no thought to anything else. I have not described every last detail, and there are thus gaps and omissions.

My experiences during this period blend in my memory. To present you with a list of events in strict chronological order would be an obstacle to reaching a satisfactory conclusion. For that reason, even when I mention dates, my focus remains the broad panorama.

Although I'm not a historian, I have a passion for this history. In these pages I present you with the reasons I adopted the Cuban Revolution as my life's purpose.

It would be impossible to understand the revolution's subsequent development and the possibilities that opened up for its rapid radicalization without bearing in mind the transformation that occurred in Cuba as a consequence of the revolutionary action of the July 26 Movement.

In this volume, I outline the personal traits of a group of comrades in arms, to whom I render tribute. I also include letters, circulars, and other documents that help illustrate the social and profoundly radical character of the revolution from its formative years.

During the period covered by this story, the representatives of the traditional political parties, though aligned in opposition to the tyranny, lost every possibility of leading the popular movement and representing the country. The leadership passed definitively to Fidel Castro and the revolutionary movement initiated at Moncada.

In the 1950s my life entered into this history. I arrived at this entry point by following a line of ideas and sentiments that I identify with the memories of childhood. From my earliest days, the notion of justice and the search for equilibrium were very deeply rooted in me. I combined these values and convictions with an ethical sense transmitted by my family, school, and Cuba's cultural tradition, which reached its high point in José Martí. To me, everything started out as a moral question.

Having made these observations, I now begin my account of the period in which I became a Fidelista.

Chapter 1

Background

The Cuban nation, forged over 150 years, was shaped by individuals and deeds that left a rich legacy of heroism, sacrifice, and lessons. This country grew and became strong in the struggle for humanity's universal utopia.

From the late eighteenth and early nineteenth centuries, the Cuban soul was stirred by the beginnings of a national consciousness that took form as an unshakable patriotism, by an unbounded love of liberty, later deepened in combat and war, and by a thirst for knowledge and culture expressed in a sharp, universal vision.

Since then, Cubans have had our hearts set on the homeland of Cuba, the homeland of America, and the homeland of humanity. This fact is key to understanding the magnitude and acuteness of the enormous contradictions we have had to face.

Economic forces hostile to our country found expression in political, social, and cultural currents. In order to safeguard their dominance, an extraordinary economic power—first Spanish colonialism and later U.S. imperialism—relied, as a last resort to safeguard its hegemony, on the apparatus of violence furnished by professional armies of the colonial or imperialist power and of the Cuban oligarchy.

Cuba has encountered enormous obstacles on the road to development free of foreign interference. Ever since colonial times, this has demanded great firmness in defending the nation's independence.

In the late eighteenth and early nineteenth centuries, the old colonialism then in existence was altered by reforms that we identify with Francisco de Arango y Parreño. These measures, however, were caught in a contradiction: they facilitated the black slave trade. This fact is crucial in explaining why the goal of separation from Spain did not succeed at the beginning of the nineteenth century. By shaping Cuba's social stratification, slavery led to the subsequent radicalization of the independence movement.

Between 1791 and 1825 slavery expanded dramatically. By that latter date blacks made up 56 percent of Cuba's population. This alarmed the landowners, who feared the emergence of a movement such as the one that led to the independence of Haiti. In the course of eighty years, the ratio of Cuba's exploited to its Spanish population increased decisively. Between 1791 and 1868, the overall population grew from 272,000 to 1,350,000.

Those originally from Spain, who had arrived in Cuba to hold military, administrative, or commercial posts, had no deep roots on the land. Over the course of several generations, a large portion of their descendants became a working population holding lesser positions in agriculture, administration, and services.

Political trends in the nineteenth century can best be characterized in terms of the stance each of these trends took toward slavery and the goal of independence.

In 1868 the revolutionary war was launched by educated layers of the Creole landowner class, particularly those in the eastern part of the country, who were the most harmed by the colonizing power's protectionist policies.[1]

In La Demajagua and Guáimaro, the democratic ideal that had emerged in the cultural arena became linked to the abolition of slavery. Since that time this link has given the Cuban national ideology a markedly social character. After the setback at Zanjón, this process took even more radical form through the Baraguá Protest.[2]

Then came Martí, the Fertile Truce, the Cuban Revolutionary Party, Baire, and the reconstruction of the Army of Liberation, which together permanently imprinted the interests of the exploited masses on Cuba's national identity.

Indeed, the revolution born October 10, 1868, is unique in its synthesis of politics, ethics, and culture.

Lengthy, fierce battles forged sentiments that sparked the first and most important expression of solidarity: the identification between whites and blacks, between Creoles and immigrants, as components of the nation. That was the starting point for the country's unity.

The fact that we were the last colony to achieve liberation from Spanish rule forced us to carry out a long struggle, one influenced by the fight against U.S. expansionist aspirations.

Maceo's fears and Martí's concerns were confirmed in reality. The country that carried out a revolution in 1895 found its development sidetracked, its freedom restricted, and its sovereignty curtailed. Our liberation movement's collision with U.S. expansionist development resulted in the Platt Amendment and the handing over of our wealth to the insatiable greed of a rapidly growing U.S. capitalism.

These conditions gave birth to an improvised and artificial bourgeoisie, the result of a parasitical economy conceived to exploit the nation.

1. For Creoles, see glossary, which contains information on many individuals, historical events, and terms that appear throughout the book.
2. For information about Cuba's 1868–78 and 1895–98 independence wars, as well as the revolutionary upsurge of 1933–34 and other historical events referred to throughout the book, see the chronology.

Three facts blocked the emergence in Cuba of a bourgeoisie that could carry forward the national ideal:

- The Spanish monarchy, whose antiquated political system remained shackled to the most backward medieval ideology, could not come to terms with the Cuban reformers, who might conceivably have produced a force to advance a national bourgeois culture.

- Beginning in 1868 those bourgeois sectors less committed to Spanish interests, less dependent on them, and more stifled economically—located mainly in the eastern region—opted for a radical solution to the social contradictions produced by slavery and Cuba's colonial status. Their more advanced representatives—heirs of Félix Varela's stand in favor of independence and the abolition of slavery—made common cause with the oppressed masses during a long process that included a thirty-year war of liberation.

- The military and political intervention of the United States, and the subsequent seizure of Cuba by this world power, blocked forever the possibility that after independence a bourgeoisie could emerge and develop that was capable of expressing the genuine Cuban ideal.

During the 1920s and 1930s, the patriotic aspirations of the nineteenth century were revived and carried forward by anti-imperialist and socialist currents that sought a broadly based popular democracy. Pro-independence political ideas linked up with those of the revolutionary generations of the twentieth century.

Carlos Baliño had worked beside Martí in the revolutionary clubs of Key West, Florida. As the story goes, the Apostle told Baliño that a revolution was not what was made in the forests and hills; rather, it was what would be realized in the republic. Baliño succeeded in transmitting the Master's message to Julio Antonio Mella.

We remember Enrique José Varona for his great intellectual and moral stature. The evolution of Varona's ideas shows how democratic and radical ideas matured and sank deep popular roots in the nation's culture.

Several events and processes shaped Cuban political life during this period: the rise of ABC;[3] the revival of José Martí's revolutionary ideas, which had been forgotten or discounted in the first two decades of the century; the growth of anti-imperialism; the influence of the October Revolution; the founding of the Communist Party of Cuba in 1925; the emergence of the Student Directorate in 1927 and again in 1930; the creation, after Rafael Trejo's murder, of the Student Left Wing; and the development of a popular movement that culminated in the general strike of August 1933 and the overthrow of Machado's tyranny. Machado's downfall, however, took place only after U.S. intervention, in what became known as Ambassador Benjamin Sumner Welles's brokered deal. It was Welles, with the support of the army's high command, who ended up imposing Carlos Manuel de Céspedes as president.

On September 4, 1933, the Sergeants' Revolt took place against the army high command. They then created, in alliance with the students and professors, a provisional government headed by Ramón Grau San Martín. The interior secretary and secretary of war and the navy was Antonio Guiteras Holmes, whose radical measures marked this government with a certain revolutionary character. That provisional government, known as the Hundred Days Government, was overthrown in January 1934 by Fulgencio Batista, who from that moment on placed his services at the disposal of the U.S. embassy.

Guiteras came to be the highest symbol of the revolution's radical program. He founded a revolutionary organization, Young Cuba, and was then murdered by the tyranny's henchmen on May 8, 1935, while attempting to leave the country in order to return with an armed expedition.

---

3 An underground organization that grouped together broad layers of the middle and upper classes of bourgeois society and carried out subversive actions against the Machado tyranny. After 1933 it became a center-right party and gradually disappeared due to the loss of its political space. [AH]

The rise of internationalist sentiment was concretized during the late 1930s by the legions of fighters who joined the struggle to defend the republic in the Spanish Civil War[4]—exemplified by the revolutionary leader Pablo de la Torriente Brau, who was killed in that struggle.

In 1939 the working class, which had played a decisive role in the revolutionary struggles of the previous decades, organized the Confederation of Cuban Workers (CTC) under the leadership of Lázaro Peña and the Communists, who were always the natural leaders of the trade union movement.

By the mid-1930s, however, the revolutionary upsurge that began in the 1920s had exhausted its chances of achieving its goals. A new period began, characterized by new forms of U.S. neocolonial domination.

A few years later, all the country's political forces took part in a peaceful political process that led to the Constituent Assembly of 1940. That assembly was an equilibrium between two weak forces: the old order, which lacked the strength to impose its will, and the revolution, also too weak to prevail. The 1940 constitution marks the furthest limit of political thought achieved through national consensus up to the middle of the century; that's its historical significance. Going one step further would have meant opening the way to a socialist program. The constitution's weak point was that it could not be put into practice, due to the prevailing economic conditions and subordination to foreign domination.

The 1940 constitution stands as the necessary starting point for any inquiry into Cuban law or political culture during that period. It is the historical culmination of a process launched at the time of Mella and the Student Directorate.

In the first years of the cold war, the regime unleashed repression against the union movement, ousting Communists by decree from the leadership of the CTC. On January 22, 1948,

4. Some 800 Cuban volunteers fought against the fascist forces in the Spanish Civil War.

one of the country's principal working-class leaders, sugar worker Jesús Menéndez, was murdered by an army officer. This act sparked universal protest among the people.

Corruption penetrated every pore of the Cuban political system, rendering it incapable of responding to the challenges facing the country. Eduardo Chibás, rooted in the revolutionary tradition of the 1930s, advocated political action against the immorality that corroded every stratum of the old society. His slogan "Honor against money," and his symbol of a broom to sweep away the decay suffocating the country, shook the nation, particularly its youngest layers.

Chibás delivered his last speech on August 5, 1951, during his Sunday radio program, and he concluded it in dramatic fashion by shooting himself. This was his final appeal:

> Compañeros of the Orthodox Party, forward! For economic independence and political and social liberty! Let us sweep away the thieves in government! People of Cuba, rise up and walk! People of Cuba, wake up! This is my final *aldabonazo* [knock on the door]!

He died on August 16 and his body lay in state in the Aula Magna of the University of Havana. No place could have better emphasized the significance of his ideas and struggle. A broad spectrum of the country's political and social leaders met there. As I reached the top of University Hill, I saw before me an immense crowd of people filling San Lázaro Street, Julio Antonio Mella Plaza, and the steps to the university. The arms of the Cuban people carried the coffin. During the long march to Colón Cemetery, the crowd kept growing. The procession followed L Street to 23rd Street and proceeded from there to 12th Street, and from that corner to the final destination.

I'm proud to recall that I had the honor of being one of those Cubans who walked alongside Chibás to his final resting place. A long list of speakers eulogized that great leader of the people.

Whatever historical analysis we may make of the Cuban

People's Party (*Ortodoxos*) and its heterogeneous membership, and above all whatever our evaluation of the Orthodox Youth, we can say for certain that Chibás's program focused on the very essence of Cuba's spiritual history: the ethical question.

To gain an understanding of the most advanced ideas found among the gigantic mass of Orthodox Party supporters, it's important to remember that the Centennial Generation emerged from its youth section. There is a document that provides a historical source for examining the conceptions then prevailing among different groups of young members of the Cuban People's Party. I'm referring to the Manifesto of the Orthodox Youth, published in 1948 under the title, *The Ideological and Political Thought of Cuban Youth*, which was socialist in direction.

From that starting point, the Orthodox movement, with its ethical program, gave rise to a political movement with a social dimension. Historically, Chibás's "final knock on the door" proved to be not only a call to fight the corruption of public life, but also a resounding warning to the country's economic and social system.

This clarion call remained unheard and unheeded. The door to reaction, represented by forces in the military, was opened. In rejecting those forces, the road was also opened to revolution, and to retaking the tradition of Martí, which since the 1920s had been intertwined with socialist thought.

The death of Chibás created a political void that was seized on by Fulgencio Batista, who carried out his coup d'état on March 10, 1952.

Bourgeois currents that had grown up in the shadow of imperialism fell into a sharp contradiction. The most reactionary among them supported the tyranny, in alliance with a lumpen layer that had spawned Batista and that constituted the backbone of the armed forces.

The bourgeois forces ousted from political power in 1952, who to some degree maintained democratic aspirations, could not rally officially to the tyrannical regime, since it had removed them from public life. Had they done so, they would no longer have been democrats and would have fallen into the worst ignominy in the eyes of the people. As a social layer, however, these bourgeois forces were too weak to offer a revolutionary solution. Given the corruption of public life, the enrichment of their leading figures, and their vacillation and surrender to U.S. imperialism, they were unable to undertake the task of restoring bourgeois democracy.

Given this state of affairs, students and workers burst upon the political arena as an independent force in defense of the constitution of the republic.

Chapter 2

University Hill

From March 10, 1952, to July 26, 1953, the Hill, home to the University of Havana, was transformed into the country's most important revolutionary political center in the struggle against the Batista tyranny. This development reflected the role played throughout our history by youth and the most progressive strata of Cuban intellectuals. Even when active supporters of an insurrection were only a minority, they reflected a broad climate rooted in the general situation and in the tradition of university struggle, which put a rebellious stamp on the student movement.

I had entered the University of Havana Law School in the 1947–48 academic year. Although always interested in history, sociology, and philosophy, I decided to study law because I saw this as a way to give expression to my calling—the struggle for justice.

That was the time of the famous events in Havana's Orfila neighborhood. During Grau San Martín's second presidency (1944–48), gangsters had taken command of several police precincts and were using their official positions of authority to advance their turf battles.[1]

One of the groups had obtained a court order to arrest its opponents, but ran up against resistance, and a bloody slaughter ensued. I listened on the radio to a live account of the Orfila battle.

The head of the army, who was abroad, sent orders that tanks be used to halt the gang battle being waged within the police force. The "honorable" president of the republic folded his arms and did nothing.

※

During my university years I became active in politics as a member of the Law Students Association. Batista's coup took place in my last year of studies, while I was vice president of the association. From that moment on, my academic training enabled me to defend and legally justify the use of violence by the masses against this criminal act, on the grounds that it was a violation of constitutional principles.

Batista's seizure of power through military sedition led us to draw up a Declaration of Principles of the Federation of University Students (FEU), urging that a struggle be organized to restore democracy and the constitution of 1940.[2]

In addition, on behalf of the Law Students Association, we sent a letter to the Court of Constitutional and Social Guarantees demanding that the government established on March 10 be declared illegal.

After the coup, no one in the university could openly support Batista with impunity. No sensible person would have done it. Whoever might have attempted to do so would have enjoyed no political influence, since Batista was a symbol of crime and usurpation. Even when moral corruption, confusion, and ideo-

1. See glossary, Gangsterism.
2. See page 66.

logical deviation were at their peak, one could not be a follower of Batista inside the university movement. Consistent with this tradition, students from all over the country were actively engaged in opposing the coup.

The causes of this vehement rejection of the tyranny lie in the historical and social framework that led the Cuban Revolution's most outstanding figures of this century to begin their first political battles linked to the university and the student movement—Julio Antonio Mella, Rubén Martínez Villena, Antonio Guiteras, Eduardo Chibás, and Fidel Castro, to name some outstanding examples.

These figures, of course, achieved their historical stature by coming down from University Hill, joining the people, and taking their place at the head of the revolutionary movement.

On the very morning after the coup, the leadership of the FEU—an organization that had rejected the corrupt government of Carlos Prío Socarrás—visited the Presidential Palace and offered its support to the constitutional president against this illegal action. That gesture was fruitless, however, because this pusillanimous ruler possessed neither ideals nor principles that could serve as a basis for confronting the coup. After receiving the FEU leaders, he immediately fled to the Mexican embassy and requested asylum.

Given the prevailing corruption, the discredited character of the overthrown government, the broad rejection of Batista, and the absence of a national opposition leadership, for several months University Hill became the focal point of political activity.

On March 10 hundreds of students and workers assembled at the university. We placed microphones and powerful loudspeakers on the roof of the old Alma Mater Bookstore and delivered fiery harangues, one after another, against oppression. We had no weapons. Our method was civic protest to express our indignation about what had occurred.

Opposition to corruption, gangsterism, and to a certain extent imperialism, tended to predominate. Many of us were strongly influenced by the nationalist and progressive ideas of Guiteras; many held left-wing views carried over from the revolutionary tradition of the 1930s. There was great respect for figures such as Raúl Roa and Rafael García Bárcena, among others.

Those who had gone to fight to defend the Spanish Republic at the end of the 1930s won the admiration of Cuban university students. After democracy was overthrown in Spain, some intellectuals could have come to teach at the university, but the old academic hierarchy, out of petty jealousy, did not want us to learn from such worthy teachers.

There were great conspiratorial comings and goings. These began to be organized formally in the offices of the FEU and other university facilities. Weapons were kept there, and students went there to learn how to use them. Through these offices passed thousands of persons, many of whom later became heroes and martyrs. The first expressions of the anti-Batista struggle came from the university. Hundreds of workers, intellectuals, and members of the middle classes gathered there seeking to unite in waging an insurrectional struggle against the tyranny.

The leaders and activists of the student movement were limited politically in their understanding both of insurrection and of the country's social and economic problems. This, however, should not blind us to the key point: the University of Havana was one of the main arenas where the insurrectional struggle against the tyranny incubated. Not a single major leader of the FEU gave in to Batista.

*

During the first days of April 1952, I took part in the most significant political event carried out by students during that period: the oath of allegiance to the constitution of 1940. This constitution was the last in the country's long legal history prior to the revolutionary triumph. The movement initiated in the university to swear allegiance to the overturned constitution was the first public action repudiating the dictatorial regime, and it was the starting point in the struggle opening up across the country.

It all began with the organization of a huge rally of students and workers who, stepping off from the university steps, advanced up San Lázaro Street until they reached the Martí Forge.[3]

I held to my chest the text of the defiled constitution and marched together with the other FEU leaders at the head of that crowd. Raúl Castro carried the Cuban flag and held it aloft. We were able to reach the Forge without interference from the police.

Hated as he was by the people for his dictatorial and criminal rule, Batista, in one of his great hypocrisies, nevertheless always tried to present himself as a democrat. His base of support was in the military, those who since September 4, 1933, had held the highest positions of command, and he also enjoyed the backing of imperialism and its interests in Cuba. Secure with these defenders, he let the "boys" from the FEU have their rally; afterwards he would figure out a way to handle the situation "politically."

And so it would have been, had not a heroic resistance arisen against the ambition of this lumpen layer to assume despotic power. The Cuban students, with their tradition of militant antidictatorial struggle, rejected everything Batista's regime represented.

The campaign around the oath of allegiance to the constitution grew into a broad and influential political movement, embracing many of the country's educational institutions. It even won the participation of several representatives of the political parties of the time, some acting on conviction and others because they felt compelled to. Even the Cuban congress, dissolved

3. The Martí Forge is a monument-museum, inaugurated in January 1952, at the site in Havana where José Martí, as a prisoner jailed for pro-independence activities, did forced labor in a stone quarry.

by the coup, managed to meet and authorize public resistance to the regime that had illegitimately seized power.

※

Another important event of those days revolved around the "University on the Air," a radio program founded and conducted by Professor Jorge Mañach.

The program's participants included the most eminent figures of Cuban intellectual life, who gave lectures on topics of cultural importance touching on the life and spiritual history of the nation. The audience could ask questions and discuss with the lecturers. Long before March 10, in fact, I had regularly attended the show's Sunday afternoon airings.

From the first Sunday of 1952, a professor had been giving a series of lectures analyzing Cuban history since independence, that is, over the previous fifty years.

Following the coup, the sessions were filled with young people who sensed an opening to express their ideas, concerns, and worries. University students poured into Radiocentro's Studio 15, posing questions that in essentially cultural language laid bare the regime's illegal and immoral character.

On Sunday afternoon, May 4, 1952, while Professor Elías Entralgo and secondary school teacher Gerardo Canet were giving lectures, Batista's thugs arrived and struck with brutal violence. I was beaten during that incident, as were Faustino Pérez and other compañeros.

Two or three days later, when I arrived at a law school lecture hall, I was greeted by applause—an event of great political significance for me. Afterwards, a warm tribute was paid to all the injured. This had been the regime's first brutal action after the coup d'état. The initial victims of the tyrant's fury were the university students.

In assaulting the "University on the Air," the government struck out against culture, because it could not permit students to make known their revolutionary message, even at educational gatherings where academic niceties were observed. Later, during seven years of horrors, crimes, and outrages of all types, such actions against the students and the people occurred frequently.

The FEU, for its part, organized a number of events and political mobilizations during those weeks. Among them were an assembly on May 20, 1952, addressed by Jorge Mañach, and a rally on August 12, when an immense crowd filled the university steps to repudiate the dictatorship.

✷

In the middle of 1952, I graduated from law school. After taking my last examination, I left for Mexico City as the FEU representative to an international oratorical gathering organized by the Mexican newspaper *Universal*. I gave an address in the Palace of Fine Arts denouncing the prevailing situation in Cuba. On my return, as I arrived at the Havana airport, the police were waiting for me. While searching my belongings, they seized several books I had with me that they considered illegal—university texts on social theory.

✷

In October I bid farewell to the compañeros of the FEU with the following letter:

UNIVERSITY OF HAVANA,
OCTOBER 17, 1952

To the president and members of the FEU
at the University of Havana

Dear compañeros:

Having left the enrolled student body of the University of Havana and relinquished my post in the Federation of University Students [FEU], I wish to send you from the depths of my heart a farewell message. Together with you, I contributed to raising

Cuban youth to the place of honor they presently hold in the struggle to defend the republic against those who have trampled on civil liberties. On March 10 of this year, these forces disrupted the legal rhythm of the state by overthrowing a government that—however much I as a student leader had criticized it and as a citizen had openly fought it—nonetheless in the last analysis represented constitutional legality.

I do not know to what degree the fiftieth-anniversary FEU[4] will engrave its name in history. This will depend in large measure on whether the central leadership of the student movement succeeds in maintaining control of the revolutionary movement now in formation. This movement's historical mission is to create a government whose cleansing actions will take aim at not only the criminals of March 10, but also at all the economic, social, and above all cultural causes of the barracks coup.

Our immediate mission has been to awaken the dormant faith of the Cuban people in its youth. Our fundamental task has been to lay bare present-day conditions through a powerful campaign of political opposition to the illegal regime. I sincerely hope, however, that your work will be able to go beyond these limits. May you not only achieve these goals, but also succeed, as circumstances permit, in offering practical formulas that definitively embrace the democratic ideal damaged by the treason of those who attacked Guardpost 6.[5] I sincerely hope that you will step forward, together with the country's most radical elements, to make the national revolution a reality. I wish this for the sake of the university and for your own sake. Bear in mind that no individual, no force can hold back the revolutionary process that is being born. The social forces in action may be turned aside or set back, but they will never be wiped

4. A reference to the fiftieth anniversary of Cuba's independence from Spain in 1902, under the U.S. military occupation.
5. The March 10 coup started when Batista and his supporters entered by a guardpost and captured the Columbia military base in Havana.

out. Cuban society is inevitably headed toward a deep convulsion.

Whether this confrontation takes place earlier or later, and what form it takes, will depend on the Federation of University Students and all of today's Cuban youth. But take place it inevitably will due to social forces that cannot be controlled. I hope we will be able to carry it through to Cuba's benefit. I hope we may be able to steer the revolution down the road of modern doctrines of civil law. I hope that our aggrieved homeland's future will grant us the consolation of contributing in some way to achieving the great historical destiny our people have deeply sought for more than a century. For all these reasons, and for the victory of these ideals, I'm reminded of the words I offered September 30 in the Aula Magna: "determination, courage, and unity."

Although I am now formally obliged to relinquish the leadership post in the student movement that my school bestowed on me, I will of course never neglect my sacred duty as a Cuban to the homeland. I need not tell you that I will continue fighting not only to oust the regime of usurpers, but also for the final victory of the political and social ideas of the Generation of the Fiftieth Anniversary.

In this regard I place myself at the disposal of the university youth that you lead for everything that may be of use to Cuba. I cherish the notion that I will soon be able to contribute to the success of these goals. The hopes of our people are at stake; the will of our nation inspires our acts. There is thus no reason to hold back from the greatest sacrifices.

With great anticipation, I await your orders as a citizen, recalling the first lines of the National Anthem.[6] I remain, with

6. Cuba's National Anthem, written during the 1868–78 independence war, goes as follows: "Hasten to battle, men of Bayamo / For the homeland looks proudly to you. / You do not fear a glorious death, / because to die for the country is to live. / To live in chains / is to live in dishonor and ignominy. / Hear the clarion call. / Hasten, braves ones, to battle!"

affection and comradeship as always,

Armando Hart Dávalos

EX-VICE PRESIDENT OF THE LAW
STUDENTS ASSOCIATION

❋

The various occurrences of 1953 were linked together by invisible and unifying threads of the type that enable diverse events to make history.

On January 15, students met to protest the desecration by Batista forces of a bust of Julio Antonio Mella—founder of the FEU and of the Cuban communist movement. During this demonstration, Rubén Batista Rubio, an architecture student at the University of Havana, was fatally wounded by the police. After protracted suffering, he died on February 13. His funeral the following day was a large, militant demonstration of repudiation of the regime. Álvaro Barba, at that time FEU president, gave the eulogy for our compañero, the first martyr of the fight against the tyranny.

Months earlier, however, at a May 1 commemoration at Colón Cemetery of the September 1951 police killing of Carlos Rodríguez, Jesús Montané had introduced Fidel to Abel Santamaría. The two immediately began to work together to win recruits and conduct propaganda for a decisive course of action against the regime.

At the demonstration of January 28, 1953—the centennial of the birth of José Martí—the university-based movement of civil and political protest took on a new character, thanks to the role of Fidel Castro and this group of compañeros who had been organized around his orientation and initiatives. This time, the nearly five thousand students and workers did not descend University Hill empty-handed: they came equipped with the means to defend themselves and strike back. San Lázaro Street was lit up by their burning torches, symbols of the liberty that was theirs to conquer.

Had the police moved against the demonstration, a vanguard force was present, equipped with the means to counterattack. This proved unnecessary, because on this occasion the police did not resort to political repression.

This march was a symbolic forerunner of what the Centennial Generation would produce for history. There was much comment at the time on how the contingent led by Fidel demonstrated a level of organization and a capacity for action that distinguished it among the student and popular masses.

❋

On April 5, 1953, Professor Rafael García Bárcena, supported by many student and youth groups, organized the first post-coup attempt at insurrection.

I had been working with the professor for some time. On November 27, 1952, I participated with him at a meeting in the Milanés Theater in Pinar del Río that condemned the regime and paid tribute to the medical students executed in 1871.[7]

Rafael García Bárcena, a member of the 1930 Student Directorate, had been greatly influenced by the Sergeants' Revolt of September 1933. He placed his hopes in action by members of the army who were dissatisfied with Batista, together with university youth.

An honest man, a patriot of democratic and anti-imperialist convictions, a Christian, and a poet, he is regarded as one of the most important Cuban philosophers of that time. In his book *Redescubrimiento de Dios* [Rediscovering God], he strives to find the relationship between scientific progress and his religious beliefs. From the cultural point of view, García Bárcena was a descendent of Félix Varela's line of thinking, with ideas similar to those of the advocates of Liberation Theology in Latin America today.

He was a devoted follower of Martí. He had fought against

---

7. See chronology.

Machado and Batista in the 1930s and 1940s, and he had opposed the corrupt governments of Grau and Prío. He was an intellectual leader with revolutionary positions. Immediately after the coup, he began organizing the Revolutionary National Movement (MNR) at the University of Havana. The MNR's immediate goal was to overthrow the dictatorship, and it sought to provide an uncorrupted, anti-imperialist response to the barracks coup.

We believed at the time that García Bárcena had some support in the army ranks, because during the time of constitutional rule he had been a teacher at the Higher Academy of War. This opinion, however, was not grounded in fact.

On April 5, hundreds of students and youth gathered in different places with the aim of attacking the Columbia military garrison in Marianao, Havana, through Guardpost 13. This event came to be known as the Easter Sunday Conspiracy. But the police carried out a broad roundup that foiled these plans. They seized Dr. García Bárcena at the home of Eva Jiménez Ruiz.[8]

I was one of García Bárcena's closest collaborators, and he chose me to be his defense lawyer. It turned out that the trial received wide publicity. García Bárcena was strongly urged to choose lawyers to represent him who had long experience and a high professional reputation. I was then only twenty-two years old and had just graduated from the university. Nonetheless, the head of the MNR was adamant in his refusal to accept any other lawyer.

The trial took place at Príncipe Castle, since they did not want to move it to the old Provincial Courthouse.

Charges had also been arbitrarily filed against other opposition leaders. In a room in the Príncipe prison, transformed into a court of "justice," we defended the right to conspire against Batista and denounced the illegal character of the regime. That was what my client wanted—he had no intention of utilizing legalistic arguments. His goal was to utilize the proceedings to

8. A courageous combatant who worked with the professor. [AH]

put the tyranny on trial politically. That's why he chose me as his defense attorney.

During the oral arguments, I addressed the court over the course of a session and a half. I had not prepared a written text, but my notes were complete enough that I was later able to reconstruct the address. I tried to demonstrate to the court that the charges against Bárcena had not been proven, even though the historical fact is that plans did exist to take Columbia by storm. My presentation to the court was simply the reasoning of a lawyer who rejects the veracity of charges for which there is no legal proof. What's more, the charges referred to acts that had not in fact taken place. There were therefore ample grounds to refute the charges in oral argument.

My address presented quite extensive legal arguments based on legislation then in force. But for me that aspect was not the most important. The heart of the matter was political principle, in particular the right to rebellion and the nature of political crime. I emphasize this to make it clear that from March 10 on, wide layers of Cuban youth, myself among them, defended the legal right to insurrection against the tyranny as an inalienable principle. Moreover, a reading of the speech makes it clear that there was at that time a broad political consensus in society that we had the right to forcibly overthrow the government established by the March 10 coup. This was a reflection of the masses' state of mind.

The magazine *Bohemia*, in its "In Cuba" section, published an extensive report under the title "Urgency Court," which explained the events and the trial itself. The article concluded by quoting me and commenting on my role as the professor's defense attorney.[9]

The trial finished at the end of May 1953, and García Bárcena was sentenced to two years in prison. It was one of the rare occasions when I acted as lawyer, and I am pleased with the rights I defended.

9. See page 69.

Two years later, when Fidel Castro formed the July 26 Movement after his release from prison on the Isle of Pines, many MNR members like myself were won to take part actively in its struggle against the government.

The chain of events described here serve as a prologue to a great event that changed the course of Cuban history: the heroic action at Moncada. From then on, the leadership of the anti-Batista movement passed into the hands of Fidel.

Declaration of principles of the Federation of University Students

March 1952

This declaration, which was published in *Bohemia* March 23, 1952, was issued four days after Fulgencio Batista's March 10 coup d'état. It was signed by the presidents and vice presidents of the student associations for each of the colleges of the University of Havana.

> *"The students are a bulwark of liberty and its strongest army."*
>
> —JOSÉ MARTÍ

The Federation of University Students, fully conscious of its responsibility and historical mission at this critical moment, announces to the public the fundamental points underlying its current stance and future actions.

1. Our unblemished and upright stance in these dark hours for Cuba allows us today to raise our voice on behalf of the people. We are again the standard-bearers of the nation's conscience. The dramatic circumstances that the homeland is experiencing impose difficult and hazardous duties upon us. We have not bothered to

measure the magnitude of the consequences. We are ready to do our duty calmly, responsibly, and firmly. University Hill continues to be the bastion and hope of Cuba's dignity.

2. Now and always it is worth spelling out: ours is a pure force. We do not defend the interests of any political party or any particular group. We defend only the rule of the constitution, popular sovereignty, and civic decency. Consistent with the tradition bequeathed by our heroes and martyrs, we fight arbitrary acts and excesses, no matter where they come from. We always remain at our post.

3. We will not give in to force or bribes. We will fight tirelessly for the reestablishment of the constitutional regime. Because of the stability of its democratic institutions and its social, economic, and cultural progress, Cuba had been the pride and banner of the peoples who share our language and spirit. Without the sovereign functioning of public powers and without political and civil liberties in full effect, the republic is a farce. The barracks coup of March 10 has placed our homeland behind an iron curtain in the Americas.

4. We cannot resume academic labors as long as the rights of citizens have not been fully safeguarded. Free and quiet cultural life is incompatible with the violence typical of a military regime. Those who have infringed laws without a second thought should not demand of us that we respect them.

5. We oppose the March 10 military coup because it destroyed the republic's essence and its reason for being at this stage of its development. The democratic structure established in the 1940 constitution that was created by the people's own determination has been consecrated at the ballot box. Twenty years of sacrifice, vigilance, and effort have been lopped off with a single blow.

6. We warn the leaders and legislators of the political parties that history will judge severely those who would seek to legalize an illegal situation under these circumstances. By doing so they would betray the memory of the founders, the rule of the constitution, the people's trust, and the cause of democracy.

7. We call on the people not to let themselves be dragged along by the usual provocateurs into a useless massacre that would serve

only to justify outrages under the pretext of pacification.

8. Cuban students will maintain their respect and reverence only for the symbols that the *mambises* brought us,[1] soaked in blood, from the battlefield of freedom: our national anthem, our coat of arms, our flag with the solitary star. Never more than in the present circumstances do those symbols have such historical meaning. We want a republic free of foreign interference and national falsification.

9. In this hour of trial when traitor apostles and false prophets renounce all that they preached for many years, we announce our unbreakable opposition to the barracks regime established by Fulgencio Batista. Our mothers gave birth to free children, not slaves. No one suffers like they do, in the depths of their shattered hearts, in days such as these in which the Sword of Damocles hangs over each of us. But we are certain that they will bravely urge us to fight for Cuba's liberty so that tomorrow we may live without shame. They know, as we do, that it is preferable to die on one's feet than live on one's knees.

10. Unity is again the watchword of the day. This is not the moment for vacillation, lobbying, or compromises. The homeland is in danger, and we must honor our country by fighting for it. From the unconquered Hill—neither defeated nor persuaded to give in— we call on all parties, organizations, and genuinely democratic groups to close ranks with us in this beautiful crusade for the exclusive benefit of the republic. We urge all students, workers, peasants, intellectuals, and professionals to raise their voices together with ours, which is the voice of the people and therefore the voice of God. We call on everyone to discuss the situation and organize a plan of struggle that will lead us to the reestablishment of the republic's democratic structure and the sovereign validity of the constitution of 1940.

11. People of Cuba: this uncontaminated and bold voice is the echo of your very own. Commemorate in a worthy manner the fiftieth anniversary of the founding of the republic by fighting for

1. See glossary, *Mambí*.

liberty, law, and justice. Have absolute faith in us. The Federation of University Students neither gives in nor sells out.

UNIVERSITY OF HAVANA,
YEAR OF THE 50TH ANNIVERSARY,
ON THE FOURTH DAY OF THE TREACHEROUS BARRACKS COUP

Álvaro Barba, Quino Peláez, Julio Castañeda,
Orestes Robledo, Agustín Valero, Segismundo Parés,
Andrés Rodríguez Fraga, Antonio Cisneros,
Antonio Torres Villa, Eduardo Sabatés, Edelberto Cué,
Ismael Hernández, Vilma Garrido, José Hidalgo Peraza,
Aurora Cueva, Juan Mena Ortiz, Pedro García Mellado,
Ramiro Baeza, Armando Hart, Armando Prieto,
Mario Chaple, José A. Echeverría

Armando Hart's courtroom defense of Rafael García Bárcena

May 1953

This news article on the trial of the leader of the Revolutionary National Movement (MNR), charged with organizing an armed uprising against the dictatorship, appeared in the "In Cuba" section of *Bohemia*, May 24, 1953.

If anyone doubted the competency of a lawyer so young (he only recently walked down the university steps with his degree under his arm) to assume such an important defense, he was mistaken. There was Armando Hart, fully earning the trust his client had placed in him. Not only did he touch on the trial's formal aspects, he also analyzed something much deeper than the proceedings of a trial like this: García Bárcena's political views and the ideological content of the movement he headed. . . .

"Your Honors," he began, "what is important for me at this moment goes beyond criminal law: it is devotion to a body of ideas, friendship, admiration of a man, and affection for a teacher. . . . This is the most significant trial historically since March 10, when the rule of law was toppled. Since then what has been enshrined are outrages, violence, and torture committed against men of honor. I do not say this to be theatrical, but because of the deep drama coming out of the events of April 5."

He continued:

"We are not just standing before public opinion today. We are standing before the very history of Cuba, which this court must respond to when issuing your verdict. I hope you will not issue it using the same historical lens through which José Martí and the students of 1871 were tried and convicted during colonial days, but rather with a broad criteria of state policy. There is a higher legal end to serve. What is before you in this trial is an entire judicial interpretation of state power, which you represent and must defend."

Hart stated categorically that all Cuban political thought revolved around the idea that, by virtue of specific sociological laws, sooner or later there would be a struggle for power. He pointed out how the Congress of the Republic itself, through a Joint Resolution, decreed a national mobilization to fight the March 10 regime. He then evoked the origins of the Cuban nationality, the struggle of political ideas during the second half of the nineteenth century, the "necessary war" preached by Martí in opposition to Montoro's compliant autonomism.[2]

With emphasis, he stated:

"García Bárcena chose the thesis of José Martí. If you convict him, you are convicting, in a certain sense, the political ideas of the Apostle!"

2. See glossary, Autonomism.

Later Hart made a biographical sketch of his client. Revolutionary, academic, philosopher, poet. Pointing to him with his index finger, he stated:

"This is the man against whom the public ministry has called for applying the provisions of the law against gangsters!"

And turning ironically to Zayas:

"I recall when the prosecutor came before this very court to raise, as a matter of honor, that Orlando León Lemus *(El Colorado),*" should be acquitted, terming him a clean and pure revolutionary."

Further he stated:

"García Bárcena was the only one to denounce, long ago, the fact that Batista was conspiring and planning an attack against the democratic institutions of government. . . . Here is an article published in *Bohemia* in July 1951 titled, 'Is the PAU [Batista's United Action Party] preparing a revolt?" García Bárcena is not before you because of acts he committed as an individual. Judge him as an interpreter of an idea!"

It was 11:30 a.m. Having exhausted the political side of the debate, Hart began to take up the report of the prosecutor. If previously his tone had been that of a fiery speech, now he skillfully threw himself into the field of law like the most experienced attorney. He began the task of refuting the charges and accusations. Everything was a scheme to do harm to Professor García Bárcena and his compañeros, he said. Abejón "had fled from the courtroom" to avoid submitting to his questioning, which was designed to prove that the arrests at the house of Eva Jiménez Ruiz were the result of a passing suspicion and not the product of vigilance, of having previously received confidential information.

"April 5," Armando Hart declared, "was allegedly the day chosen for the uprising to take Columbia by force of arms. And yet on this very Sunday the de facto president, the head of the army, and his high officials were on a summer trip to the Isle of Pines. . . .

"Were they abandoning their men in a grave hour of danger? Or is it simply false that the defendants were conspiring?"

With a broad gesture, he concluded:

"Let the prosecution choose which it is!"

Chapter 3

July 26, 1953

On July 26, 1953, the country was shaken by news of the heroic events at the Moncada garrison. We learned the news during the morning of that historic Sunday. My brother Enrique and I began making inquiries everywhere to find out what had happened. The initial reports talked about army units rebelling against Batista. At 2:00 or 3:00 p.m., however, a leader of the Orthodox Youth called to tell me that Fidel was the one who had led the assault. In the evening, details and an official communiqué on the event appeared in the press. In the following days we received more information.

These actions aimed to capture by surprise attack the Santiago de Cuba and Bayamo garrisons, as well as the Provincial Court and the Civilian Hospital, in order to then summon the entire country to a general strike. The final speech of Eduardo Chibás was to be rebroadcast to the Cuban people. If the attack was defeated, the plan was to try and continue the struggle in the mountains. And that was the alternative Fidel put in practice when the attack failed. He was arrested, however, by a military patrol under the command of Lieutenant Pedro Sarría, who acted with a dignity highly unusual in that army and took Fidel to the municipal jail to face trial, rather than handing him over to Chaviano, the commander of the Moncada garrison. Fate worked this time in favor of the revolution.

Marta Rojas, a journalist who happened to be in Santiago de Cuba at the time, described the dramatic events in three articles that have become documents of great historical value.

Fidel denounced the criminals in his courtroom testimony. In his historic defense speech, *History Will Absolve Me*, he explained the organizational preparations, the program, and political platform of that endeavor.

In memory of the martyrs and heroes, we reproduce here a few paragraphs:

> The plan was drawn up by a group of young people, none of whom had any military experience at all. . . . Half of them are dead, and in tribute to their memory I can say that although they were not military experts they had enough patriotism to have given, had we not been at such a great disadvantage, a good beating to that entire lot of March 10 generals together who are neither soldiers nor patriots. . . .
>
> With them was Abel Santamaría, the most generous, beloved, and intrepid of our young men, whose glorious resistance immortalizes him in Cuban history. We shall see the fate they met and how Batista sought to punish the rebelliousness and heroism of our youth. . . .
>
> In the annals of crime, Sergeant Eulalio González—better known as "The Tiger" of the Moncada garrison—deserves special mention. Later this man did not have the slightest qualms in bragging about his unspeakable deeds. It was he who with his own hands murdered our comrade Abel Santamaría. But that did not satisfy him. One day as he was coming back from the Boniato jail, where he raises fighting cocks in the back courtyard, he got on a bus on which Abel's mother was also traveling. When this monster realized who she was, he began to brag

about his grisly deeds, and—in a loud voice, so that the woman dressed in mourning could hear him—he said: "Yes, I have gouged many eyes out and I expect to continue gouging them out." The unprecedented moral degradation our nation is suffering is expressed beyond the power of words in that mother's sobs of grief in face of the cowardly insolence of the very man who murdered her son. When these mothers went to the Moncada garrison to ask about their sons, it was with incredible cynicism and sadism that they were told: "Surely madam, you may see him at the Santa Ifigenia Hotel[1] where we have put him up for you." Either Cuba is not Cuba, or the men responsible for these acts will have to face a terrible reckoning!

Before March 10, 1952, Fidel had already been a widely known figure among youth and students. Although I had not had any contact with him personally, I knew him from the university and from political struggles inside the Orthodox Party. After the coup, he became one of the outstanding revolutionary leaders of Cuban youth.

I first felt the force of his personality in the period between March 10 and Moncada, at a meeting in the Orthodox Party headquarters, located at 109 Prado. A group of us young people were discussing what type of figure would assume the leadership of the revolution. On that occasion Fidel put forward the view that totally new and different leaders would arise. There was a hot debate in the old Prado building, during which I was among those in full agreement with Fidel.

I left together with him. We strolled along several blocks. With his arm on my shoulder, he pursued the topic further. I was surprised when he showed interest in the fact that I was going to the FEU offices with a group of compañeros to learn the use of weapons. After the Moncada assault, I learned that Pedro Miret—the student responsible for training young people there—was among the participants in that heroic event. I then

1. Santa Ifigenia is Santiago de Cuba's main cemetery.

realized that it was through him that Fidel knew about those of us who were going to the FEU offices with insurrectional aims.

In January 1954 the University of Oriente invited me to give a lecture on Martí. The event would inevitably have taken on a political coloration, one of struggle against the tyranny. The university authorities, although firmly opposed to the regime, eventually decided to call it off. I used my stay in Santiago to win new converts, and also sought news of Abelardo Crespo, one of the Moncada attackers who had been wounded and taken prisoner and was now hospitalized.

What I learned about the heroic events gave me a clearer image than I had been able to form in Havana. The events of July 26, 1953, had an impact on the country as a whole, but while I was in Oriente—that indomitable province—I learned details of particular interest to me.

I visited Cayita Araújo, whom I met at that time. She told me magnificent stories about the Moncada events. Interested as always in the ideological and moral aspects of revolutionary struggle, I was greatly impressed when Professor Max Figueroa Araújo, Cayita's son, told me that Fidel and his compañeros had read and studied Martí. This was very important to me. They gave me Fidel's first manifesto, in which he described the Moncada events and denounced the crimes committed there. This document had a big impact on me.[2]

I realized that a movement of great ethical and political importance had arisen. In Havana I had admired the deed, but in Santiago I came to understand that these heroes and martyrs were giving us a profound message that would leave a permanent mark on Cuba's history.

July 26 expressed the synthesis of José Martí's ideas and program with the realities and demands of Cuban society in the 1950s. Both its principles and its form and style of action corresponded fully to our revolutionary tradition.

As I have said, in the 1950s there was an ethical void in the

---

2. See page 78, "Message to Suffering Cuba."

political landscape of Cuban society. As a result of the July 26 Movement's action, we now saw rising a moral and cultural force with broad social reach. Reality is found not merely in phenomena evident at first glance, but also in the imperatives that lie beneath the surface and at the core of social life. To grasp them, assimilate them, and discover practical methods of satisfying them—such is the distinguishing mark of those who shape history.

The assault on the country's second most important military fortress was the necessary response to the coup's implications. The combatants' heroism and audacity decisively changed the political and social situation.

Moncada forms part of the birth of the Cuban Revolution, which proclaimed its socialist character in 1961. Although a socialist content was not clearly visible in that action, it was nevertheless inherent in the economic, social, and moral demands that, much later—between 1959 and 1961—provided the preconditions for a socialist program.

A revolution of the kind Cuba needed was possible only through the kind of strategy advanced by Fidel Castro, who had a radical Cuban spirit and a global socialist vision.

The definition of "the people" expressed in *History Will Absolve Me* is based on a social and class characterization that corresponded completely to our social and economic reality. When I studied the ideas of socialism more deeply, I was greatly surprised by the fact that almost no one had then noticed this revolutionary content. Fidel distanced himself from the traditional forms of analysis that the political literature of the time was accustomed to using to describe such phenomena. His analysis displayed a deep philosophical and cultural understanding, achieved through exceptional oratory presenting legal, political, social, and historical arguments. On an intellectual level, *History Will Absolve Me* stands as the highest achievement of Cuban thought in the 1950s.

What was the content of the July 26 Movement's program and goals, a content that runs throughout the revolution's entire forty-five-year history? It can be found in the fusion or the best ethical traditions of Cuban society with the economic and social measures necessary for emancipation.

In that founding document, Fidel described with magnificent prose events whose very essence was an ethical conception of life and a program of human and social redemption. Political action poses the need to reach a broad public. To do so, literature is needed that is consistent with one's proposed aims, and that requires intellectual rigor.

The Centennial Generation found this type of thinking and feeling—closely linked to the need to open the road to political action—in the patriotic, literary, and moral tradition transmitted, despite great obstacles, by Cuba's schools. That is what made us become revolutionaries.

Already in Cuba's formative period, these ideas and sentiments acquired a moral tradition when in the early nineteenth century the priest Félix Varela, in the school he had founded, called for the abolition of slavery and national independence. The content of our ethical tradition was characterized by Luz y Caballero, who in the middle of that century called justice "the sun of our moral world." This tradition achieved universal scope when in 1891 José Martí proclaimed, "I wish to cast my fate with the poor of the earth."

Ethical and patriotic commitment, the heroic meaning of Moncada, the demand for equality and social justice—all are contained in *History Will Absolve Me* and are at the very center of it. This linkage continues up to the present day and carries forward into the future. Ethics and social justice are today what is most urgently needed in Cuba, in the Americas, and in the entire world. That is why Moncada was and will continue to be an event that history has recognized, not just by absolving the combatants, but also by awarding them the eternal gratitude of posterity.

Message to suffering Cuba: Manifesto to the nation

Fidel Castro
December 12, 1953

The following manifesto was written from prison on the Isle of Pines and circulated clandestinely.

I am writing this document with the blood of my dead brothers. They are the only motivation for it. More than liberty and life itself for us, we demand justice for them. The justice we call for at this moment is not the building of a monument to the heroes and martyrs who fell in combat or were murdered after the battle. Nor is it the creation of a tomb to allow the remains that lie spread over the fields of Oriente—in places that are often known only to their murderers—to rest together in peace. One cannot even speak of peace for the dead in this oppressed land. Posterity, which is always more generous to the righteous, will erect symbols to their memory, and the generations of tomorrow will, at the appropriate time, render due tribute to those who saved the honor of the homeland in this hour of infinite shame.

Why has there been no courageous denunciation of the atrocious tortures and the mass, barbaric, and insane murders that snuffed out the lives of seventy young prisoners on July 26–29,

1953? That is an unavoidable duty for those living today; not to fulfill that duty is a stain that will never be erased. The history of Cuba knows of no similar massacre—either during the colonial period or the republic. I understand that terror may have paralyzed hearts for a long time. But it is no longer possible to put up with the total shroud of silence that cowardice has cast over these frightful crimes. Crimes of such low and brutal hatred are the response of an unspeakable tyranny that has gorged its vengeance against the natural and rebellious act by the enslaved sons of Cuba's heroic people, against its purest, most generous and idealistic. To keep enduring this would be shameful complicity, as revolting as the crime itself. The tyrant is probably licking his chops in satisfaction at the ferocity of the henchmen who defend him, and at the terror they inspire among the enemies who fight them.

The truth is known. All Cuba knows it. All Oriente knows it. All the people speak of it in low voices. On the other hand, the people also know that the despicable charges made against us of having treated the soldiers inhumanely are completely false. During the trial the government could not back up a single one of its assertions. The twenty soldiers who were taken prisoner at the beginning, and the thirty wounded during the battle—to whom we did not direct even a single offensive word—went there to give testimony. The forensic surgeons, legal experts, and even the witnesses for the prosecution did the job of demolishing the government's account. Some gave testimony with remarkable honesty. *Evidence was given that our weapons had been acquired in Cuba, that we had no connection to old-time politicians, that we had not stabbed anyone, and that there had been only one victim at the Military Hospital, a patient who was wounded while looking out a window.* In an unheard-of admission, the prosecutor himself was forced to recognize, in his closing statement, "the honorable and humane conduct of the assailants."

On the other side, where were our wounded? There were only five. Ninety dead and five wounded? Can one conceive of such a proportion in any war? What became of the rest? Where are the combatants who were arrested on July 26, 27, 28, and 29? Santiago de Cuba knows the answer very well. The wounded were dragged away from private hospitals, even from the operating tables, and finished off instantly, at times even before leaving the hospital. Two wounded prisoners entered an elevator alive with their guards and came out dead. Those at the Military Hospital were injected with air and camphor in their veins. One of them, the engineering student Pedro Miret, survived this deadly procedure and told everything. Only five—I repeat five—were left alive! . . .

As to the prisoners, the entrance to the Moncada garrison might well have displayed the inscription appearing on the threshold of Dante's inferno: "Abandon all hope, ye who enter here." Thirty were murdered the first night. The order arrived at 3:00 p.m. with Gen. Martín Díaz Tamayo, who said "it was shameful for the army to have had three times as many losses as the assailants in the battle, and that ten dead were required for every soldier killed." This order came out of a meeting of Batista with [Francisco] Tabernilla, [Manuel] Ugalde Carrillo, and other military leaders. To smooth away legal difficulties, the Council of Ministers that very Sunday evening suspended a number of provisions, including Article 26 of the Statutes, which establish a guard's responsibility for the life of an arrested person. The order was carried out with horrible cruelty. When the dead were buried they lacked eyes, teeth, testicles, and their killers deprived them even of their clothes, which they later showed without any shame. Scenes of indescribable courage took place among the tortured. . . .

In the outskirts of Santiago de Cuba, forces led by Major Pérez Chaumont murdered twenty-one combatants who were unarmed and scattered. Many of them were compelled to dig their own graves. . . .

I hope that one day, in a Free Homeland, the heroic bones of our comrades will be brought together from the fields of indomitable Oriente and buried together as martyrs of the Centennial in one great tomb beside that of the Apostle. Their epitaph will be a phrase by Martí: "No martyr dies in vain, no idea is lost in the blowing of the wind. It is moved farther or brought closer, but its passage always remains in one's memory." . . .

We are twenty-seven Cubans suffering imprisonment on the Isle of Pines, but our banner flies high because we still have strength to die, and we still have fists to fight with.

Forward, to the conquest of freedom!

Dr. Fidel Castro Ruz
ISLE OF PINES,
DECEMBER 12, 1953

Chapter 4

I become a Fidelista

We gradually came together in a tightly knit group within the MNR. Faustino Pérez, Pepe Prieto, Mario and Alonso "Bebo" Hidalgo, Enrique Hart, and I began to establish ties with young people in the various provinces. We tried to win people over to the cause of liberty, with the goal of building an insurrectional organization across the entire country.

I visited Santiago de Cuba with compañero Allan Rosell, an MNR leader in Las Villas, to make contacts and organize cells. During this trip I received word that a strong youth organization that favored armed struggle existed in several municipalities of Oriente province. That was how I met Frank País García—at a meeting at the University of Oriente. He was twenty years old in 1954, and he had a strong movement behind him in that province, particularly in Santiago. Subsequently, Frank and I visited various regions of the province to carry out work for our cause.

García Bárcena was still in jail at the time. I went to the Isle of Pines prison on the pretext of being his lawyer, but in reality to discuss political issues with him. García Bárcena, however, knew little or nothing about the work some MNR members were doing to organize the movement in the rest of the country. He was not interested in such matters, since he thought change would occur through a military conspiracy against Batista. He knew we were doing propaganda work and winning recruits, but he did not give much importance to such activity.

I met Fidel Castro on that occasion. It was at the prison's main gate; they were taking him in an army jeep under heavy escort from Nueva Gerona, the main city on the Isle of Pines, to the prison. I greeted him, and he told me he had heard that when he was taken to the courthouse in Havana, I had gone there to make inquiries on his behalf.

I approached the prison administration and asked to speak with the Moncadistas. I was allowed to see a group of them. I think they were surprised I had been able to reach their cellblock.

During those months there was a great deal of protest activity in Cuban universities condemning the U.S. imperialist intervention in Guatemala that ended in the overthrow of the Jacobo Arbenz government. According to the propaganda, Arbenz was a communist.

Although I had already graduated, I took part in these activities. Tyrants like Somoza in Nicaragua, Trujillo in Santo Domingo, and Pérez Jiménez in Venezuela were symbols of oppression and sworn enemies of Cuban youth. We learned from José Martí to love Latin America, our great homeland. For our students, the fight for democratic principles did not end in Cuba; everywhere in the world, that fight was a duty for revolutionaries.

In June 1954 García Bárcena was amnestied. I traveled again to the Isle of Pines, where I took part in a long interview, later published by *Bohemia* under the title, "Without Morals You Cannot Talk of Revolution or Counterrevolution." The professor demanded that Fidel and the Moncadistas be freed. I returned to Havana, where we prepared a welcome for him at Rancho

Boyeros Airport, with representatives from the students and popular sectors.

Our group asked the professor to meet and discuss the need to organize the MNR nationally and prepare conditions for the future development of an armed insurrection and a general strike. He agreed to meet with us.

The day of our meeting coincided with a visit to García Bárcena by Melba Hernández and Haydée Santamaría. They had served out their prison terms for participation in the Moncada action and had been released in February 1954. They brought the professor a message from Fidel.

Melba and Haydée were talking to García Bárcena when I arrived at his home. When their discussion ended, the professor and I went to the town of Calabazar in Havana province, where we met in the small house of my brother Enrique. For several hours compañeros laid out to García Bárcena the need to do work across the country to prepare for a great armed movement and general strike against the regime. After a long discussion, our belief was confirmed that the professor, although an honest revolutionary, was incapable of leading a real revolution.

He was again subjected to persecution and had to move abroad. He returned only a year later, in May 1955, after the general amnesty that included Fidel and the Moncadistas.

Meanwhile, Batista was preparing the general elections of November 1954, which fraudulently tried to make his illegitimate regime appear legal. Honest political people and, more broadly, those who aimed to win popular support rallied to the insurrectional line. Others did so in a hypocritical way, using this idea as a tool for their irresponsible game. The stance taken by the majority of the country's political forces reflected the rejection by the people—and above all the youth—of any electoral conciliation.

Batista was determined to remain in power, and that stance excluded any peaceful solution. The tyrant's stubbornness contributed to the ongoing radicalization. In fact, when reactionaries refuse to resolve the institutional problems they create, they "serve" the revolution, and their obstinacy only accelerates change. By his arrogance, Fulgencio Batista "helped" precipitate events.

My brother Enrique, who detested the prevailing petty politicking, once told me, "Batista, with his coup d'état, gave the country a chance at a radical revolution." In the same spirit, young people at that time believed that the breakdown of constitutional rule was not the cause but the result of the general crisis of the republic.

❋

On October 10, 1954, a group of compañeros, including Mario and Bebo Hidalgo, Faustino Pérez, Eloy Abella, Pepe Prieto, Enrique Hart, and I, were meeting in the Havana Teachers College at 411 Malecón. We were discussing how to respond to the November electoral farce and what contacts to make in other provinces through the young people we had political relations with. At about noon, the police broke in and arrested us all.

We were taken to the Bureau of Investigation located in a sinister building on 23rd Street, which was destroyed after the triumph of the revolution. Every time I pass by that location, I recall the interrogations, the beatings, and the compañeros who suffered repression there.

They searched our homes, and at 222 Salud, where Faustino Pérez worked, they found a good number of hand grenades. We were intending to use these to carry out sabotage and other actions against the elections. Some weeks earlier, Frank País had arrived in Havana to make contact with us and coordinate similar activities in Santiago de Cuba.

We were transferred to the holding cells at the Havana city jail, which was packed with oppositionists of every type. The tyranny had carried out a large-scale roundup to ensure that the electoral farce did not take place amid acts of violence.

And indeed in November 1954, two and a half years after

the coup, Batista was "elected"—with the prisons full and with the great majority of the opposition rejecting his fake election.

Haydée came to visit us and inquired about Faustino and me. She and Melba, desiring to establish relations with revolutionary groups of every type, were working to win support for an amnesty. They were busy distributing Fidel's main documents, particularly *History Will Absolve Me*, which had begun to circulate in October.

After the elections, a number of us were set free. The main charges were filed against Faustino Pérez, because of the grenades they had found. He did not get out of prison until the general amnesty proclaimed in May 1955.

At the time I was released, there was great concern about a plan of Batista and the imperialists to cut a canal through the island—the "Via-Cuba Canal"—which would give the Yankees jurisdiction over a wide swath of national territory, from north to south through what was then the provinces of Matanzas and Las Villas. We called it the "Break-Cuba-Apart Canal," and our propaganda against it was developing vigorously.

As soon as I got out of prison, I contacted Melba and Haydée. They talked to me about what Moncada represented and told me of the work carried out by Abel Santamaría and the group of compañeros who together with Fidel had prepared the action. They also explained Fidel's ideas and program to me, as well as this revolutionary leader's fundamental opposition to the traditional parties. I came to the conclusion that, if united, the supporters of García Bárcena, the students, and the Moncadistas could provide a solid foundation for the development of the revolution we aspired to.

At that time, all the political and social organizations of the opposition began to mobilize broadly in support of an amnesty for Fidel and the Moncadistas; it in fact became a demand of the nation. The regime was forced to decree the amnesty in May 1955.

The people were waiting for the brave freedom fighters to be released from their cells. Everyone knew of the spirit that had inspired the Moncada and Bayamo combatants and had governed their actions. These fighters had confronted the tyranny, and for that they had been sent to prison or had fallen courageously.

The sorrow then prevailing across the entire country was interrupted by the joyful welcome given to the young people who had so fearlessly fulfilled their duty. During that moment of euphoria, there was also a heartfelt remembrance of those who could not return.

Cubans were duty-bound to take a stand for rebellion because peace and social tranquility would not be attained by the tyranny's bayonets. They would flow from a true equilibrium that could be achieved only through revolution.

The government tried to use the amnesty to present itself as the "dove of peace," but its actions revealed this claim to be a total farce. The amnesty did not represent so much as a single step to restore tranquility to the country. Hunger was growing, unemployment still stalked the land, dissatisfaction was increasing, and we could not put up with any more deceit. Batista compelled us to go to war. The government was the first and most obvious obstacle to genuine harmony.

On May 16, 1955, swallowed up in the crowd that overflowed Havana's central railway station, I awaited Fidel and other Moncada combatants. They had traveled from Nueva Gerona to Batabanó in the vessel *El Pinero*, and were continuing on by train to the capital. Anyone with an ounce of sensitivity toward the people could not fail to be deeply affected watching the crowd that greeted the leader of the Moncada action. Many people commented on the fact that, during their journey, local residents along the route had acclaimed Fidel and his compañeros as heroes.

For the most dynamic social layers of the population, Fidel had become the center of attraction and the most important political figure. He was already the natural leader of the new generations of young revolutionaries, as well as of broad sectors of the population. This was because young people politically supported the insurrectional line and valued the Moncadistas' heroic conduct and determination to do battle. Moreover, the Moncada group was not tied in with the traditional parties, but represented their very negation. In the leader of the July 26 action we found what we had been looking for since March 10 and even before: a political and revolutionary leader, with deep popular and democratic roots, with no ties to the existing system, and, at the same time, capable of organizing the masses to action.

I joined the July 26 Movement as the result of a natural process. The Moncada program concretized for me the ethical sentiments that were deeply rooted in the Cuban patriotic tradition.

A powerful wave of rebellious people gathered around Fidel. As the struggle developed, this unstoppable whirlwind was transformed, over the course of months and years, into a true revolutionary hurricane. From that moment on I understood that anyone who did not join this movement could well be left behind, unable to contribute to the people's cause and to the historical progress of our country.

Fidel began to live at his sister Lidia's apartment, in the building at Le Printemps Gardens, at the corner of 23rd and 18th Streets. The apartment was a beehive with people coming and going. There I ran into many leaders of the Orthodox Youth, as well as of the FEU and various opposition groups.

Fidel set out to win people over, eager to add new forces and close ranks. The objective was to unite all honest men in the country in the insurrectional struggle against Batista. He had become the principal leader of those opposed to the regime.

✻

After the amnesty, García Bárcena was able to return to Cuba. We went with Fidel, the leader of the Moncada attack, to Rancho Boyeros Airport to welcome him, and then we all went to the house of a relative of his who lived in the Vedado neighborhood.

I thought we would talk about the fight against the tyranny and the strategy to follow, but instead we talked about various aspects of the professor's family life.

Political discussions began a few days later. We suggested it would be useful for Fidel and García Bárcena to meet with each other. It seemed to me that if they came to agreement, this would draw in the student movement and other forces, and thus be the beginning of unity of the revolutionary forces.

The meeting took place at the professor's home, in the La Sierra neighborhood of Marianao. Faustino and I were there. García Bárcena said he would work toward a military conspiracy, and Fidel stressed that the July 26 Movement would organize the people for insurrection. Clearly there were two different plans as to how to vanquish the tyranny.

Fidel, Faustino, and I left the professor's home by car and headed toward downtown Havana. Fidel told us, "You can be with us, and if García Bárcena brings about a coup d'état, then you can give him your support." What he was saying, in effect, was that if the coup was military in character, there was nothing for us to do during its preparation. If, on the other hand, the task was to organize the people, then we could work for the revolution.

In fact, from the moment we left the professor's house, we were already a part of the movement led by Fidel.[1] Faustino and I assured Fidel that we were immediately joining him and his compañeros.

---

1. García Bárcena maintained a position of dignity against the tyranny, but he ceased to exercise leadership. In the initial years after the triumph of the revolution he was Cuba's ambassador to Brazil. He died in 1961. I was assigned to deliver his eulogy. [AH]

Chapter 5

'We will be free
or we will be martyrs'

Ever since March 10 we had maintained that the dictatorship could be overthrown only by a popular revolution. Fidel's tactical orientation, however, was not to immediately raise the question of armed struggle, since responsibility for such a course should fall upon the tyranny, not the revolutionaries. The Moncada combatants had just been amnestied, so it made no sense to raise the slogan of insurrection.

Despite the obstacles, Fidel tried to find peaceful and political solutions. But the government slammed all doors. It blocked the convening of a large rally on the university steps called for May 20, 1955. There was also discussion about having Fidel appear on a well-known political television program called "Meet the Press" and on the radio show "The Orthodox Hour," but these were not allowed either.

Then we began to wage the most important political battle—denouncing the crimes committed by the regime on July 26, 1953, and the days that followed. Even though the accusations were not a call to revolution, they damaged Batista more than raising insurrection would have. Without calling for a war, Fidel demoralized the enemy to such an extent that an official—Waldo Pérez Almaguer, who had been governor of Oriente province at the time—decided he did not want to take responsibility for the horrible crimes of July 26–29, 1953. Spurred on by Fidel's public appeal, Pérez Almaguer set about confirming the charges.

It was not easy to find a newspaper in Havana able to print these revelations. But the daily *La Calle* [The street], a tribune of the people run by Luis Orlando Rodríguez, did so on June 3. I went with Fidel to the newspaper's offices to see the pages being prepared.

Fidel's article "You Lie, Chaviano!" became the most important accusation against the tyranny. Soon afterwards, the government ordered publication of *La Calle* suspended.

✳

During the days when people awaited the combatants' release from jail, the Orthodox Party launched the radio program, "The Voice of the Groups Supporting the Doctrines of the Revolution." I participated several times in that program. This is how I analyzed the situation in Cuba in June 1955:

> The events of recent days reconfirm the regime's violent course. On a national level, what has happened the last two weeks proves that the government continues on the road to insecurity and disorder, the road of abuse of power. Consistent with their origins, those who govern today are extinguishing the hopes for peace that some sectors of the public cherished after the political amnesty.
>
> The regime's first steps were Río Chaviano's provocation directed at the Moncada combatants and the government media's insulting reply to Fidel Castro's rejoinder. Batista's announcement that "the tough guys in Yateras are gone"[1] showed

---

1. A refrain from an old Cuban song, signifying that the troublemakers have been put in their place. Yateras is a village in southeast Cuba.

the government's hysterical reaction to its rejection by the people. The death of Jorge Agostini struck a somber and dramatic note in this process. And lastly, the culminating point of the arbitrary acts committed during these days was the illegal suspension of the courageous newspaper, *La Calle*.

The portrait of life in Cuba cannot be any more dramatic at this moment. The regime found itself at a crossroads where it had to choose between giving in to the popular clamor or officially proclaiming a dictatorship. As many of us expected, it decided that the latter would better defend its interests. . . . The police report to the Urgency Court and the latter's arrest warrants against numerous citizens heighten the atmosphere of uncertainty and are the seeds of insecurity that this government has been planting.

But all this police repression is nothing but the external manifestation of a weakening government. The more it must resort to force, the less force it has. The fact is that in the end, the very serious problems in Cuba—the growing economic crisis, labor conflicts, the nation's universal discontent with the government's measures and arbitrary acts—make the men who usurped power disconcerted, indecisive, and even terrified. Meanwhile, they will try to use soldiers to keep themselves in power. . . .

There has been no regime as reactionary or more opposed to the Rights of Man than that of Fulgencio Batista. . . . In these three years it has done nothing but dramatize the gravity of the Cuban situation. . . . Popular discontent will lead to a government that comes out of a revolution, one that truly confronts national problems, as ordered by Martí, "with sleeves rolled up." This crisis that the government aggravates day by day with its mistakes and errors demands very careful attention from all sectors of the population and the greatest sacrifice from every one of us. The effects of the dictatorship sooner or later will touch every Cuban directly. Yesterday it was Mario Fortuny, today Jorge Agostini; tomorrow there may be new names on the already long list of martyrs of the March coup. Now the economic

Revelaciones de Waldo Pérez Almaguer sobre los sucesos del Moncada

YO VI FUSILAR A MAS DE 30 REVOLUCIONARIOS

AL LLEGAR CHAVIANO COMENZO LA MASACRE

A mi lado fue asesinado el doctor Muñoz

El Diario de la Revolución Cubana   5 Centavos

La Calle

Cierre 7. P.M.   Director: Luis Orlando Rodríguez

AÑO I   LA HABANA, VIERNES, 3 DE JUNIO 1955   NUM. 43

FIDEL CASTRO, el jefe de los combatientes del Moncada, cuya apelación pública al ex gobernador de Oriente en la época en que ocurrieron los sangrientos hechos, Waldo Pérez Almaguer, hoy Representante a la Cámara, ha tenido cumplida y sensacional respuesta por parte de éste al relatar cívica y valientemente lo que vió y lo que nadie podrá desmentirle. Quisiéramos ver la cara de los falderillos aullantes del régimen que han llenado de improperios y de protestas y calumnias, las columnas de los periódicos gubernamentales y atronado los espacios radiales que pagan, para desmentir la digna respuesta de Fidel Castro a Chaviano titulara. "Mientes Chaviano". Sólo cabe esperar ahora de nuestros Tribunales de Justicia el procesamiento de oficio del CHACAL DE ORIENTE como muy bien llama a Chaviano, Waldo Pérez Almaguer ? Será capaz el régimen marcista que encabeza el general Batista de dar esta prueba de justicia ?. La nación espera...

Holguin, junio 1 de 1955
Sr. Luis Orlando Rodríguez
San José Número 458
Habana

Distinguido amigo:
     Un saludo afectuoso. Necesito un periódico tan valiente como lo es LA CALLE, diario de la Revolución cubana, para que le brinde benévola acogida a las declaraciones que adjunto, y que éstas respondan al emplazamiento que me hiciera el gran líder de la Juventud cubana doctor Fidel Castro, para que, abundose en detalles inéditos sobre el asalto y sucesos ocurridos en el Cuartel "Moncada" de Santiago de Cuba, el 26 de julio de 1953.
     Un periódico valiente como LA CALLE, espero que habrá de publicar mis declaraciones, de las cuales me hago único responsable. en la redacción de las mismas. Hay necesidad de decir la verdad en estos momentos en un régimen de "fuerza y mentira", y esa verdad la expresa el que suscribe en cuanto a los espeluznantes y tétricos sucesos que siguieron al asalto y rendición de los gallardos muchachos revolucionarios que combatieron en el Cuartel "Moncada", por el ideal de una Cuba más democrática y más pura.
     Aprovecho esta oportunidad para reiterarle mi afecto y consideración.
                 Atentamente
                 Waldo Pérez Almaguer
                 Representante a la Cámara
                 Ex Gobernador de Oriente.

On June 3, 1955, *La Calle* published the revelations of Waldo Pérez Almaguer on the massacre that took place after the Moncada attack. The headline reads: "I saw more than 30 revolutionaries shot." The photos are of Maj. Alberto del Río Chaviano (left) and Fidel Castro.

crisis hurts the neediest social classes, but tomorrow it will affect the entire people. . . . The sinister effects of official policy will reach everyone, because one cannot govern a country against the will of the entire people without hurting the rights and guarantees of all citizens. Cuba was never in greater danger. . . .

More than ever the people must be united, because each governmental act must be answered powerfully by the citizenry. . . . Forward, Cubans; the future is ours! Forward! The national revolution shall overcome all these evils!

Fidel had come up with revolutionary plans. During those months he talked to us about the expedition and the general strike. He said we had to create a leadership to support these efforts, explaining that such a leadership should be made up of compañeros of different tendencies who had accepted the plan. He informed us that Faustino Pérez and I would be part of it. He also mentioned the names of other compañeros whom I will refer to later.

One night, several weeks before his departure for Mexico, there was a meeting at a house on Factoría Street. There I learned for the first time, from remarks by Fidel, that the organization was to be called the July 26 Movement. The leadership of the Movement in Cuba was established at that meeting. It consisted of Pedro Miret, Jesús Montané, Faustino Pérez, Haydée Santamaría, Melba Hernández, José Suárez Blanco, Pedro Aguilera, Luis Bonito, Antonio "Ñico" López, and myself. Fidel also pointed out that in Santiago we possessed a compañero with outstanding qualities. I remember that before he finished his sentence I said to him, "That's Frank." In point of fact, a compañero of such extraordinary abilities could be none other than Frank País García.

The process of putting together the Movement's leadership was marked by unity. We had come from another organization, yet were received with a broad spirit of collaboration. From the beginning, Faustino and I were able to work very closely with

Pedro Miret, Ñico López, Jesús Montané, Haydée Santamaría, Melba Hernández, and many other compañeros.

The Movement's leadership committee, constituted in 1955, as well as the most important leaders grouped around it in the underground work came mainly from two branches of the Orthodox Party: First, those who had been part of Moncada under Fidel's leadership or who had been under his political influence within the Cuban People's Party. Second, those of us who came from the MNR, which by that time had practically ceased to exist, and whose principal banner-holder had been Rafael García Bárcena. Both these political currents had their origin in the broad mass movement created in the country by Eduardo Chibás. All the compañeros in the leadership committee established in Cuba at that time remained loyal to the revolution.

María Antonia Figueroa, from Oriente province, acted as treasurer. In that province the center of the whole movement was Frank País, who, as already explained, had a vast underground network in almost the entire region. Working with Frank were Vilma Espín, Julio Camacho Aguilera, Léster Rodríguez, Taras Domitro, Pepito Tey, Tony Alomá, Otto Parellada, Arturo Duque de Estrada, Enzo Infante, Agustín Navarrete, Carlos Iglesias and dozens of other cadres. That province was where the organization had advanced the most.

In Havana the most important meetings and points of contact were at 107 Jovellar Street, third floor. This was the home of Melba Hernández and her parents, both of whom worked with us in an intense and determined way. This house was connected at the rear with the apartment where Pedro Miret and his wife lived.

Cayita Araújo and María Antonia Figueroa had visited Melba at her home. They had a meeting there with Fidel and a group of us, discussing the history of Cuba, Martí, Maceo, our forefathers, the struggles for independence. It was a beautiful day, full of patriotic remembrances. During this session Fidel sketched out the revolutionary plan he had conceived. María Antonia

Figueroa referred to that meeting in an interview published twenty years later by the magazine *Santiago:*

> At the apartment at 107 Jovellar Street (the home of compañera Melba Hernández) I met with Fidel, Haydée Santamaría, Armando Hart, Jesús Montané and others—that is, the compañeros who from that moment on made up the incipient leadership of the July 26 Revolutionary Movement.
>
> At this meeting, which lasted seven to ten hours, Fidel laid out for us the Movement's guiding principles. He read us his farewell letter to the people of Cuba, since he was already about to leave for exile in Mexico to prepare the armed insurrection. He also informed us of the trip to the United States he was thinking of making, following the same route taken by José Martí in the last century.[2]

Another place that was frequented in those days was the office of the Cuban People's Party at 109 Prado Street. All of us went there, including Faustino, Ñico, Pedro, Haydée, Montané, Melba, and other compañeros. We organized meetings, carried out recruitment work for our cause, and left discussing our ideas along the Malecón until we reached Jovellar Street.

❋

I would like to record here my boundless admiration for Ñico López, a rank-and-file member of the Orthodox Party. In my eyes he represented the purest of its combative masses. He was one of the most valuable cadres the country lost in the struggle for its freedom. He was from a very poor background, extremely tall and thin, with clear eyes, a wide smile, and an extended hand. His father worked—when he could find employment—at Havana's Central Market. Che Guevara once said that Camilo Cienfuegos was the image of the people. The

2. *Santiago,* June–September 1975.

same could be said of Ñico.

Self-educated, Antonio López analyzed and discussed political questions with a passion. He possessed a clear intelligence and an extremely keen popular instinct. He had a special gift of relating to others and mobilizing them. He was a magnificent speaker. At that time, I thought Ñico López had been influenced by the Popular Socialist Party. Almost two decades later, on the twentieth anniversary of the Moncada assault, I commented to Fidel that Ñico was already a communist in 1955. René Rodríguez was present at the time, and he told me that Ñico had gotten those ideas from Fidel himself.

I am proud that this young man from Havana had a powerful influence on me and taught me what a popular revolution is. He seemed like a figure drawn from the Jacobins, from the Paris Communards, from the Russian Bolsheviks. He was truly a party man, one who knew how to win the sympathy of others and the support of the masses. In every activity or public demonstration that the revolution organizes, this magnificent son of the people comes to my mind.

From Ñico López I found out that in Guatemala there had been an Argentine doctor with communist ideas, who Ñico wanted to introduce to Fidel. It was none other than Ernesto Guevara. To me Ñico's memory is closely linked with the figure of Che.

A few weeks before the *Granma* landing, in the apartment in Vedado where Pedro Miret, his wife Melba Ortega, Haydée, and I lived, we bade Ñico farewell for the last time. I'll never forget him with his white guayabera, his long legs, his faith in Fidel, and his extraordinary capacity as a mass agitator.

✳

The second meeting of the leadership took place, with Fidel present, at a new office of the Orthodox Party, at 24 Consulado Street, which many people frequented. At midnight the police arrived in the neighborhood. Just when we were about to end our meeting, they approached with the apparent purpose of making some arrests. I was impressed by the way Fidel talked to Batista's cops. "There's no problem," he said to them. "We've already finished and are on our way home." Amid the hubbub, he acted completely naturally, like someone leaving a legal activity. By his demeanor, he dominated the situation totally.

Batista had no way out other than to unleash more violent repression against the Fidelistas, and that was what he did. We were running the risk they would murder Fidel, Raúl, and other Moncadistas, since there were hints that such plans were already in the works. Taking the road of exile in order to organize an armed expedition was advisable. Raúl sought asylum at the Mexican embassy—he was going to the Aztec capital to prepare the continuation of the struggle. Fidel left for the same destination by way of Rancho Boyeros Airport on Friday, July 7, 1955.

As I have already pointed out, the idea—publicly advanced— of a peaceful way out did not last very long. Through the persecution of Fidel and his compañeros, Batista showed that the only road possible was that of insurrection. It took only two months for the commander of the revolution to formulate once again plans for armed struggle. "In this journey," Fidel stressed when he left Havana, "either we won't return alive, or we'll return with the tyranny beheaded at our feet."

The way those of us remaining in Cuba saw it at the time, our tasks consisted of helping to send a group of combatants to Mexico who would participate in the expedition, organizing support for that action all over the country, building the July 26 Movement in the provinces, working to raise funds, and carrying out propaganda and agitation.

In those days, Pedro Miret, Faustino Pérez, and Pepe Suárez were in charge of everything related to weapons. Ñico and I concentrated on propaganda, and we all worked on recruiting compañeros, raising funds, and making contacts in the rest of the country.

After Moncada, Haydée worked in an office of the Property Registry. She had gotten this job through a friend in the Orthodox Party—the old leader José Manuel Gutiérrez, who was to die abroad, where he moved after the triumph of the revolution. All those who were leaving for Mexico had to go through that office. Haydée made the necessary arrangements with the help of several employees.

On October 10, 1955, Melba Hernández left for Mexico to work with Fidel, and we went with her to the airport. Montané had already left. Melba returned to Havana several times, before staying in Mexico to work alongside Fidel. During that period, her activity was closely related to what we were doing in Cuba.

In a public event held abroad, as reported by *Bohemia*, Fidel mentioned an old-time politician who had made millions in governments prior to Batista, yet nevertheless presented himself as an honest man. Part of his political base was located in the area of Encrucijada, Las Villas, the hometown of Abel and Haydée Santamaría. This phony, apparently convinced nobody would answer him in the manner he deserved, denied Fidel's statement, demanding that Fidel ask "his friends from Encrucijada" about the man's "honest attitude." I don't know what this senator and minister of the vassal republic could have been thinking. Haydée and I agreed it was necessary to write him a fitting reply. Simultaneously we received instructions from Mexico that Haydée, as a friend of Fidel, should respond. For that reason I went to Encrucijada to look for facts at the Property Registry to prove that this man had become a millionaire in just a few years.

On December 25, 1955, *Bohemia* published an article by Yeyé [Haydée] against the above-mentioned politician entitled, "A Reply to Dr. Andreu." In this piece he was used as an example of everything that signified corruption in Cuban society. The text of the reply shows how we thought in the mid-1950s.

Andreu did not answer. "He couldn't answer," someone said to me. "It was as if an angel had crossed his path, holding a sword on high in the form of a crucifix!"

For me, everything was related to, everything was an integral part of the great revolutionary and historical task we had ahead of us. Nothing in my life was alien to this, I felt. In the second half of 1955 my personal relations with Haydée became closer. They reached so deep that for me it is very difficult to describe the exquisite and marvelous woman that I knew.

In this account I am describing the personal characteristics of various compañeros, and Haydée holds an outstanding place in this history. She pervades my personal memories of that period and, of course, of the following ones. But it would require great talent to depict in words the image of her engraved in my memory. The personal and the historical aspects of these recollections mix so intimately that it is not easy to make the necessary demarcation. I hope I will receive indulgence for these unavoidable limitations. We were practically the same person, and we worked together without a single political or revolutionary difference or disagreement. As they say, she was half of me and I was half of her. I carry this with me with honor and an everlasting memory.

✳

In those days, CMQ radio organized a televised round table on the country's situation, in which the different political tendencies took part. I participated, technically representing those belonging to "no party." I took a radical approach, denouncing the old society and its leaders. The political and social map was sure to change substantially in Cuba, I explained. Haydée and other compañeros told me I had gotten too worked up—I certainly should have responded more calmly and been less vehement in my formulations. But the fact is that I asserted truths that were confirmed by history.

✳

A third meeting of the Movement's leadership was held at 24 Consulado Street, this time without Fidel. We discussed the distribution of tasks among us and analyzed the actions in support of the landing and those to promote the general strike. We also discussed a point on the elections that were about to be held inside the Orthodox Youth.

Because of its mass strength, we were interested in having a cadre of the July 26 Movement at the head of the Orthodox Youth. The esteem earned by Ñico López suggested that he be proposed for this responsibility. It was a rather lively discussion. Proposing Ñico seemed to be the appropriate step at the time. Fidel pointed out to us, however, that the correct thing politically was to demand from the leaders of the Orthodox Youth that they support the insurrectional line, and that they should be allowed to choose their traditional leaders, if that's what they in fact wanted.

Given the strength of our movement, we did not consider this the best course, but we were mistaken. There was no point politically in getting mixed up in what could look like an attempt to insert the July 26 Movement into the Orthodox leadership. That's what was finally decided. In fact, we would have gained nothing by taking over the leadership of the Orthodox Youth, since the strength of the July 26 Movement was already such that we did not need it.

Looking at Fidel's tactics, one can appreciate his rejection of factionalism and how he put himself above momentary concerns. He tried to keep the July 26 Movement out of the internal quarrels of the Orthodox Youth. The bulk of that organization was with us; in fact, they were joining the Movement.

These were months of intense activity. Fidel had proclaimed that in 1956 we would be free or we would be martyrs. Meanwhile, the traditional opposition parties kept trying to reach a peaceful arrangement with Batista.

Melba, Haydée, Faustino, and I maintained contacts on behalf of the Movement with the Martí Civic Front of Women, an organization that had been born in November 1952 to bring together Cuban women in the fight against the tyranny.

Shortly after Fidel left for Mexico, we received Manifesto no. 1, which he had drawn up and signed. In this document, the

Moncada leader reiterated the road of insurrection and emphasized the measures that in essence had been presented in *History Will Absolve Me*. In a fifteen-point program he set forth
the first measures that a revolutionary government would
implement, and this was the program he carried out in the first
months of 1959. We worked intensively to publish the Manifesto and distribute it clandestinely. It became the vehicle for
organizing cells of the July 26 Movement, and it was distributed from one end of the country to the other.

Sometime later, in December 1955, Fidel issued Manifesto
no. 2. These materials were a political call with a very clear revolutionary content. Together with *History Will Absolve Me*, they
would become the guide for immediate action and the program
of the Cuban Revolution.

✳

Throughout these months, the expedition was being prepared
in Mexico, and in Cuba organizational work was being carried
out in support of the landing. We directed all the organization's
tasks to these ends.

The Movement was also involved in other events during
this period, of which I'll mention the most significant.

A meeting was held of representatives of the membership of
the Cuban People's Party to debate the political line to be followed
in those times of revolutionary ferment. Given the significance
of that meeting, the main party leaders attended. Among those
representing the party organization were political bigwigs serving only their own venal interests. In addition, there were honest men like Manuel Bisbé, and progressives like Leonardo Fernández Sánchez. The latter two supported Fidel's positions.

Ñico López, Faustino Pérez, Pedro Miret, and I also attended,
with the task of asking the Orthodox Party to formally approve
the insurrectional line. The heart of the matter was that a large
number of party members were putting pressure on it to decide on revolutionary action. With the support of honest lead-

ers, they were demanding that the Orthodox Party formally approve the July 26 line, that is, for revolution.

The atmosphere was hot. The Orthodox Youth, our main ally within the organization, was becoming stronger every day. Fidel's prestige among the youth and the party ranks was growing, to such a degree that in the minds of many leaders and members he was filling the space left by Eddy Chibás.

In the midst of a large group of delegates, Faustino read out the July 26 Movement's proposal, calling for the Orthodox Party to proclaim the insurrectional line.

The general atmosphere in the country, the popular roots of the Orthodox Party, Fidel's prestige, and the action of a vanguard—all this resulted in the positions of the July 26 Movement being approved by that meeting. This was the last time all the elements that made up the Orthodox Party came together. The rank and file of the party and its youth had surpassed their traditional leaders.

Anyone who opposed the proposal of the July 26 Movement would have been rejected. The petty politicians were morally very weak, and they turned out to be the only real enemies at the meeting. They acted demagogically, and to their surprise they found themselves in a position they had not anticipated. Since they claimed to support the insurrectional line, and since this line was being put forward for official vote, they had no alternative but to accept it formally. For the big-shot politicians of the Orthodox Party there was no alternative: either they united with Batista or they joined the revolution. A leadership had emerged in Cuba capable of transforming and developing the purest ideas of the Orthodox Party.

Fidel used to point out that the July 26 Movement was the revolutionary instrument of the Orthodox Party. But he knew that neither the Cuban People's Party nor its youth organization would be adequate to carry out the insurrectional line, since they were incapable of moving the revolution forward.

The best of the rank and file of the Orthodox Party had joined the July 26 Movement, which was already at the head of the popular movement. Thus Ñico, Faustino, Pedro, and I, on behalf of the July 26 Movement, witnessed the party's death. The Orthodox Party's youth and its best rank-and-file cadres were to make up the basic structure of the July 26 Movement. Although the party ceased to exist, it should be emphasized, we never abandoned its ideals.

Juan Manuel Márquez, the most outstanding revolutionary leader of the Orthodox Party, built up a close relationship with Fidel and became one of his closest collaborators. He worked with Fidel in Mexico and the United States, came on the *Granma*, and died heroically after the landing.

Other members of the Orthodox Party leadership closely identified with us at that time included Luis Orlando Rodríguez, Conchita Fernández, Vicentina Antuña, Manuel Bisbé, and Leonardo Fernández Sánchez.

✳

On September 1, 1955, several bank strikes erupted. This was a very sensitive matter for the ruling class, since the strikes threatened to develop an openly political character. The strike's organizers were opponents of the regime. My brother Enrique, who worked in the bank at Línea and Paseo, was one of the most outstanding promoters of the strike. He did it with a very clear understanding that he was contributing to the fight against the tyranny. He did not have the slightest uncertainty in this regard.

Enrique was arrested. Taking advantage of being a lawyer, I inquired into his case at the Urgency Court. They had ordered others arrested to be set free, but they did not want to let Enrique out since they regarded his case as a political one, not solely a labor matter. The judge who functioned in this repressive body refused to hand over the file to me. A big uproar took place at the courthouse that could have ended in an altercation. In order not to be arrested, I left and went into hiding at the home of some relatives who lived in the Víbora neighborhood.

A few days later the strikes ended and the court had no alternative but to let Enrique go. He was released along with all the others detained, since from a strictly legal point of view they were all equally involved.

✻

The traditional opposition parties were still strong enough to convene a great outdoor public meeting November 19, 1955, which we all attended because the people were there. That was the famous rally at the Plaza of the Forsaken at Muelle de Luz pier, organized under the leadership of Don Cosme de la Torriente, a veteran of the Independence War and by then an octogenarian, who had become a political figure for the traditional opposition parties.

In order to discuss what we should do at that meeting, as well as to evaluate other political questions, I traveled to the United States to meet with the head of the movement. Fidel was there touring different cities and carrying out recruitment work among exiles and immigrants.

I witnessed his tireless activity. It seemed to me as if we were in times like those of the War of Independence or the struggles of the 1930s against the Machado tyranny. Today I feel as much pride in that visit as would any nineteenth century Cuban who traveled to Key West to visit Martí. In Miami Fidel spoke to me about economic questions and programmatic measures that were reflected in the documents mentioned earlier.

I raised with him the situation with regard to unity of the opposition and the efforts that Cosme de la Torriente, José Miró Cardona, and other leaders were making. Fidel recommended that I speak to Don Cosme and ask him to play a recorded speech by Fidel during the rally at Muelle de Luz, which was supposed to be an act of unity.[3]

Upon my return, Haydée and I met with Don Cosme at his office in Old Havana. The meeting was arranged by Miró Car-

3. See page 118, "Letter to Cosme de la Torriente."

dona. Pelayo Cuervo Navarro also participated in it.[4] It was an unpleasant situation. Don Cosme began speaking and would not let us get a word in. In an attempt to say something and not "interrupt him disrespectfully," I began my arguments with the words, "Venerable patriot." But the abyss separating us prevented any dialogue. He even said Fidel should organize his own meeting, since the one at Muelle de Luz had different objectives from those being pursued by the head of the July 26 Movement. Don Cosme was right about that. But what he didn't know was that Fidel Castro, just a few years later, was to organize the largest political rallies in the history of Cuba and the Americas.

When the rally at Muelle de Luz took place on November 19, 1955, it ended, as the Cuban saying goes, like the "Guatao party"—that is, by almost coming to blows. Groups of Authentic Party supporters physically attacked the revolutionary militants as we chanted, "Revolution!" That effectively dispersed us. I left with Haydée and other compañeros to meet at Melba's house to discuss the events.

The popular rally, according to its main organizer, had the goal of compelling Batista to agree to a solution acceptable to all the traditional oppositional parties. Although an immense crowd of tens of thousands was brought together, the rally also completely revealed the opposition's weaknesses and ended up breaking apart. "The opposition is divided," the tyrant said. We thought—and history confirmed—that it was necessary to "change the platform," that is, the leaders. And in fact that's what happened, but at the cost of struggle and blood.

As expected, Batista did not accede to the pressure and summoned Don Cosme to the palace to meet. The latter presented himself to the dictator with the intention of laying down his demands, but he was unable to speak. The big chief of March 10 seduced him with words and treated him "deferentially." After leaving the presidential mansion, Don Cosme and what he rep-

4. Pelayo Cuervo Navarro was brutally murdered by the tyranny's henchmen on March 13, 1957. [AH]

resented were totally finished. José Miró Cardona, who was present at the meeting, told me that the situation was rather embarrassing. Miró Cardona left the meeting ashamed by the way Batista had manipulated the veteran.

What had happened was simply that Don Cosme de la Torriente was representing the bourgeoisie, which could not lead any type of a revolution in Cuba, because it lacked real strength.

After that, no one else was capable of uniting all the traditional opposition parties in a public rally that could confront the Batista government. That event, at which Don Cosme de la Torriente did not want us to play Fidel's speech, was the swan song of traditional Cuban politics.

There were other political meetings later on, of course, even in the midst of generalized insurrection throughout the country. But they were so servile and submissive to the tyranny that they cannot be properly regarded as opposition.

At Muelle de Luz, the epitaph of the traditional parties was written. Perhaps a commemorative plaque should be erected there to the country's impotent, mediocre, and subservient bourgeoisie. I have called it "the bourgeoisie that did not exist," because the United States prevented an independent development of capitalism in Cuba.

From that moment on, the opposition to Batista broke apart forever and remained dependent upon the dictates of the tyranny or the outcome of a true revolution.

※

Days later I traveled to Camagüey to participate, together with other speakers, in an important social event that had been organized by the High School Students Association of that city, whose president was Jesús Suárez Gayol.[5] At that event we com-

5. An outstanding combatant of the July 26 Movement who participated in the revolutionary struggle. He died heroically in Bolivia alongside Commander Ernesto Che Guevara. [AH]

memorated November 27, 1871, and unveiled a portrait of Abel Santamaría.

That same day I spoke on a radio program that was broadcast at 7:00 p.m. It was conducted by Jorge Enrique Mendoza. Together with the best of Camagüey's youth, originating in the ranks of the Orthodox Party, Mendoza had also joined the July 26 Revolutionary Movement.

Mendoza had the capacity and the vocation for political agitation, propaganda, and the dissemination of ideas. He was active, educated, enthusiastic, communicative, and a follower of Martí and of Fidel. His integrity, honesty, and generosity of character were also outstanding. Loyalty to his people and an ethical sense of life always inspired his conduct as a revolutionary.

He worked intensely in the underground movement of his native city in the days prior to November 30 and the *Granma* landing. When the time came to reorganize the Movement, he had already become one of the essential links of the new revolutionary stage in Camagüey province. Among other tasks, he was responsible for transferring weapons and explosives, and also for broadcasting from an underground radio station during the strikes of August 1957 and April 1958. Later he joined the fight in the Sierra Maestra and was one of the founders of Radio Rebelde.

On January 1, 1959, when all the radio transmitters in the country hooked up to broadcast the call for a general strike in support of the revolution, Mendoza's voice was heard. His words were a genuine expression of all that is Cuban.

Under Fidel's encouragement and leadership, the whirlwind of great events that were gestating throughout the 1950s left an imprint forever on Mendoza's life and conduct. He was not one to do things part time; for him it was always.

Cándido González, also an organizer of that event, was of a similar stripe. Enthusiastic, intelligent, a tireless organizer, he exerted great influence upon the youth in Camagüey. He was the most important combatant of the Movement coming from the Orthodox Youth in the provinces who signed on to "be free or be martyrs" in 1956. He was a genuine representative of the Centennial Generation. He traveled to Mexico, where he became an extraordinarily valuable assistant to Fidel. He was killed following the *Granma* landing. He could have been one of the most important political leaders of the revolution.

Jesús Suárez Gayol, Jorge Enrique Mendoza, and Cándido González remain engraved in my memory as the purest of the youth from the province of Agramonte in the days prior to the landing on December 2, 1956.

✳

From Camagüey I returned to Havana with Haydée. On the way we stopped off in Las Villas to visit her parents' house in Encrucijada. Before that, we stopped off at the town of Florida, where we held a clandestine meeting organized by the Movement with a large number of peasants. We spoke of Cuba's future, of generalized insurrection, of the misery in the Cuban countryside, of agrarian reform, of Latin America, of the role of Cuba in the world, and many other dreams. These meetings served to make propaganda and develop contacts.

✳

Late in December 1955, strikes among sugar workers broke out and a movement of "dead cities" spread.[6] The objective was to win labor demands that were intertwined with the interests of various layers of the population in the provinces. As a result, a powerful mass movement was born. The FEU sent cadres to the different provinces. The strikes, together with the "dead cit-

6. In December 1955 a strike by over 200,000 sugar workers took place, centered in Las Villas province, to protest a government move that would have reduced workers' wages. A number of towns were basically taken over by strikers and supporters. Virtually all economic activity in these towns was paralyzed, leading them to be termed "dead cities."

ies," inevitably took on a political character in opposition to the government. It seemed we were on the eve of an outbreak of generalized strikes, but the storm dissipated and we continued working on preparations for what would become the *Granma* landing and November 30. We were confident that in 1956 we would start the armed struggle.

✳

In those days an intense political and publicity campaign was being carried out through an organization known as the Society of Friends of the Republic (SAR), composed of representatives of the bourgeois opposition to the tyranny. On March 5, 1956, a meeting was held at the Pan-American Colombian Society, where Casa de las Américas is today. It was a meeting of representatives of all the traditional parties, both those in the government and those from the opposition. As the participants saw it, "the entire nation" was sitting in debate.

The country's bourgeois representatives, without a destiny and without a future, remained alone and isolated in those talks. The meeting was a farce; it accomplished absolutely nothing. It was the old Cuban politics, discredited and corrupt to its very core, that met at that masquerade, doomed to utter historical failure. At the time, nevertheless, it was considered a "great political event."

✳

The radio and other means of communication and information had great influence. From Mexico, Fidel followed events in the country closely and responded to every one of them. The systematic publication of his writings had an incalculable impact and made it possible to spread his ideas and program widely.

Only *Bohemia* published Fidel's articles in 1956. It ran several, including "Against Everyone" (a reply to the article "Cuba

Is Not Fidel"), "The Condemnation Requested of Us," "The July 26 Movement," and "Enough Lies."[7]

※

Around that time the tyrant Trujillo, from Santo Domingo, clashed with his friend Batista. There was talk of a conspiracy against Batista by Trujillo supported by military groups called the *tanquistas.* These were some of the worst elements within the Batista military clique.[8]

Bohemia conducted a survey to find out the opinions of different sectors of public opinion with regard to the Trujillo conspiracy. I was asked for a statement on behalf of the July 26 Movement, which was published in the issue of March 25, 1956:

> The Cuban people, who love liberty deeply, have always wanted to cooperate with ousting dictatorships on the continent.
>
> Today, when all rights have been taken from Cubans in their own land, they are willing to give a new example of how to exercise their sovereign power.
>
> Tomorrow, when Cuba enjoys full democracy, it will become the strongest enemy of the consortium of Latin American tyrannies. The neighboring dictatorships know this perfectly well and, consequently, are trying to prevent a revolutionary triumph in Cuba. Herein lies the main reason for the Trujillo conspiracy, which *Bohemia* foresaw and denounced.
>
> The most dangerous aspect of the international incident caused by Trujillo lies in the relations he may have with some of the worst elements in the army. Already prior to March 10, one could see a shameful identification by certain Cuban military elements with reactionary regimes on the continent. This identification becomes more acute whenever a revolutionary

7. These articles appeared in the issues of Jan. 8, March 11, April 1, and July 15, 1956, respectively. [AH]
8. See glossary.

movement has a chance of coming to power, since in those circumstances an elementary instinct of self-preservation makes certain military sectors look for support, or at least encouragement, from those governments that resemble themselves, such as the ones in Santo Domingo, Venezuela, Nicaragua, etc.

That was the origin and significance of the March 10 military coup. From reliable reports one may assert that the tyranny that oppresses Venezuela inspired and encouraged the mutinous group. A reactionary coup was the preemptive reply to imminent elections that would have consolidated Cuban democracy and certainly resulted in an electoral triumph for the most progressive forces. . . .

Particular attention should be paid to the fact that well-known collaborators of Trujillo had also previously been collaborating with the present regime. The military danger of a Trujillo conspiracy is thus reduced to the influence it may exert over the *tanquista* group and to the strength that the latter may develop. Four years ago, that same *tanquista* group destroyed the discipline of our army under the pretext of eliminating gangsterism. Today, it utilizes gangsters, and lets Trujillo arm and train them, because these gangsters are meant to fight against the popular revolution and try to create chaos, anarchy, and confusion.

It was not possible to repel the March 10 coup due to the lack of a revolutionary organization. This will not happen again because the Cuban democratic forces, awakened to their own liberation at home, are ready to combat all their enemies. The Cuban democratic forces know who and where their enemies are. They will not allow anyone to confuse them because their maturing revolutionary consciousness is enabling them to march down the road to true freedom.

＊

It was necessary to project the publication of a newspaper that would be capable of disseminating information, provide an orientation, and present our program. Under the name *Alda-*

bonazo, the official organ of the Movement was born.

But every political meeting called by the opposition to Batista was attended by the Movement's militants, particularly its youngest forces, the Youth Brigades led by Ñico López. They went there to shout out the slogan born at Muelle de Luz: "Revolution! Revolution! Revolution!" We were already publicly identified with this word, so we decided to change the name of our newspaper to *Revolución*.

❋

In April 1956 a group of commissioned officers, full of democratic ideas, organized a conspiracy against the tyranny. An editorial in *Aldabonazo* tells the story.[9] This conspiracy was aborted on Tuesday, April 3, and arrests began. Col. Ramón Barquín López, who was the military attaché in Washington, headed the long list of those arrested, which included, among others, Lt. Col. Manuel Varela Castro, Maj. Enrique Borbonet Gómez, several captains, and José Ramón Fernández, then a lieutenant.

The conspirators put Barquín up front, because he was the highest-ranking military officer among them. But the motor force behind the conspiracy was not him but rather the army's junior officers. The real organizer was Enrique Borbonet.

When analyzing this movement, one must bear in mind the background of Batista's army. For several years the tyrant had selected and promoted those most loyal to him, with no academic training. Many officers, however, had been educated but could not rise in spite of their academic merits or professional competence. They felt relegated to the sidelines by officers who were not qualified to hold positions of responsibility in the army.

The officers implicated in this conspiracy enjoyed great

9. See page 124, "Revolution: the Only Way Out." See also page 123, "Circular of the Civic Resistance Movement."

prestige within the military institutes, since it was the cultural factor that moved them to act. They intended to bring about not merely a military change but the institutional reorganization of the nation based on the principles of the 1940 constitution.

The conspiracy of "Los Puros" [the pure ones], as they came to be known, had an enormous impact on the population.

✳

On April 29, 1956, the assault on the Goicuría garrison in Matanzas took place.[10] It ended in tragedy since the regime knew of the plans ahead of time. On behalf of the leadership of the July 26 Movement, Pedro Miret, Faustino Pérez, and I shared the opinion that we had to try to convince the compañeros not to go ahead with the action. Faustino went to Matanzas to discuss the matter with them, but did not find them. They wrote another heroic page in our history.

Since we knew what was going to happen, a group of us went completely underground. Faustino, Aldo Santamaría, Mario and Bebo Hidalgo, Haydée and myself, among others, were at a friend's home when, to our surprise, José Antonio Echeverría showed up to also find refuge. The owners of the house were friends of both the July 26 Movement's members and the compañeros from the Revolutionary Directorate.

✳

Those were days of revolutionary upswing. As our work became more intense, we established relations with a larger and larger number of persons, and the risk of being arrested increased. Discretion became imperative, as did the necessity of

10. On April 29, 1956, a group of young people of different political affiliations attacked the Goicuría garrison in Matanzas province. Six were killed in the unsuccessful battle. Nine were taken prisoner and murdered.

sleeping somewhere other than our homes. We felt a growing support from the people—we were slowly going underground. A government that forces underground those who are winning the support of the population is in trouble.

Ever since my courtroom arguments on behalf of Rafael García Bárcena, I had become increasingly well known and had been jailed on several occasions. Faustino too had been arrested many times. We had achieved notoriety with the police, particularly after the seizure of the grenades at 222 Salud Street.

The compañeros who had participated in the Moncada assault were being harassed severely; the repressive organs focused special attention on them. Nevertheless, the regime apparently still did not consider the July 26 Movement to be its most dangerous enemy. It underestimated us at the time, and did so until much later. It did not take sufficiently into account the commitment we had made, or else they believed we could not attain our goals. Perhaps the enemy thought it was a matter of a few idealistic youth, with no chance of accomplishing anything that would threaten the government's stability. Imperialism might also have believed that we were a group of demagogues and opportunists who, at the appropriate moment, would subordinate ourselves to their interests.

The Batista government was starting to move against Fidel, however. Months before the *Granma* set sail, as preparations for the expedition were advancing, the Mexican authorities arrested the leader of the Movement and several other compañeros. Then the hospitality in that country made itself felt. Lázaro Cárdenas took an interest in the situation of Fidel and his compañeros and helped them in that complex situation. Later they were released.[11]

A group working to support Fidel's insurrectional plans could do little from Cuba about the arrests, but our character and tem-

---

11. Fidel Castro and twenty-seven other future expeditionaries and collaborators were arrested by Mexican police between June 24 and July 3, 1956. Castro was released July 24; the last expeditionaries were freed a week later.

perament did not permit us to do nothing. Therefore, we in the leadership of the Movement prepared a letter addressed to the president of Mexico, explaining the position that the combatants took with regard to the arrest of Fidel and his compañeros.[12]

*

During those months other political events of great significance also took place. On August 31, 1956, the Mexico Letter was signed by Fidel and José Antonio Echeverría.[13] This was extraordinary news to us. I recall reading in big headlines in the old newspaper *El Mundo* on September 2, 1956: "FEU Pact with Fidel Castro Revealed. Signed in Mexico. Advocate Insurrection against Government Supported by General Strike."

We felt that something totally new was being born, that the world of the petty politicians and the traditional parties was tumbling down. We were confident about the future.

*

All over the country, the organization of the Movement continued to advance. In the weeks preceding the *Granma* there was no municipality or corner of the island without its underground leadership and cell. The existence of a solid structure prior to the landing was an element that would later acquire great importance. It became crucial in 1957 and 1958, when the main task of the July 26 Movement in the cities became sabotage actions, plus the Civic Resistance and support to the guerrilla effort. There was no province that our main leaders did not visit. I personally visited almost all of them during those months. We organized cells, carried out propaganda, raised money, and

12. The letter (see page 131) could not be delivered since we could not evade the guards at the ambassador's residence. [AH]

13. In this document, the July 26 Movement and Revolutionary Directorate pledged to coordinate armed action to oust Batista.

established contacts who created action groups.

I worked intensively in the countryside surrounding Havana and in Camagüey province. Several times I toured that region with Cándido González. Raúl García Peláez and Calixto Morales were our main contacts there.

On various occasions I visited Matanzas province with Aldo Santamaría, who worked as coordinator of the Movement in that region. He worked at the rayon plant and from there maintained links with the towns. Manuel Piñeiro and Ricardo González *(Teacher)*, among others, worked in that province. During that time I also traveled to Santa Clara, where I was in touch with Quintín Pino Machado, Margot Machado, Allan Rosell, Guillermo Rodríguez, Santiago Riera, Osvaldo Rodríguez, and Enrique Oltuski. The Pino Machado family became an important center of conspiracy, through which the Movement established contact with all towns in Villa Clara.

In the countryside of Havana, Héctor Ravelo put me in contact with the towns. In Pinar del Río our closest contacts at the time included Pancho González, José *(Pitute)* Arteaga, Juan Palacios, Luisín Fernández Rueda.

These trips took place daily in the different provinces. In this way I met hundreds of men and women from among the people; many of them later held leading positions in the insurrectional struggle. Young people constituted the major source of recruitment. Moved by ideas of freedom, progress, and social justice, they felt the need for deep revolutionary change. There were also numerous trips by different compañeros to Mexico and meetings of the National Directorate.

Prior to the *Granma* landing and the November 30 uprising, I prepared a document that was published in the clandestine newspapers of the Movement. After the triumph, this document was reproduced in the weekly magazine *Lunes de Revolución* under the title "Defense of the Revolution and Strategy against the Dictatorship." That was our platform of ideas.

With that spirit, Haydée and I traveled to the eastern region of the country in November 1956.

Letter to Cosme de la Torriente

Fidel Castro
November 1955

The following letter was written from exile, where Fidel Castro and other central leaders of the July 26 Movement were preparing to relaunch the revolutionary war against the Batista dictatorship. The letter refers to the mass rally being organized by the bourgeois opposition forces, led by Cosme de la Torriente, at Havana's Muelle de Luz pier on November 19, 1955.

Señor Don Cosme de la Torriente
President of the Society of Friends of the Republic
Havana

Illustrious compatriot:

I will not be at your side when you receive this letter, as I have been forced to leave my homeland by a campaign of hatred, cowardly provocation, and tenacious persecution. This campaign was unleashed against the political prisoners as soon as we left the cells where they had kept us in solitary confinement for two years. It ended up by depriving us completely of the right to appear in any type of public event, radio or television program, or to express our thoughts orally or in writing. Finally, they closed down the last newspaper that gave space to our opinions, solely because we spoke the truth without deception and wanted what our people most deserve. When I left Cuba, I said to my fellow countrymen—and swore to myself—that either we would not return from a trip as bitter as that I was about to embark on, or else we would do so with the tyranny beheaded at our feet.

I nevertheless consider it necessary and useful to send you this letter on behalf of my comrades in struggle and ideas. Today's meeting would not be a symbol of the unity of all Cubans who oppose the regime if it did not include the rebel group that from day one stood up to the tyranny in a fight to the death. A group that has given the homeland eighty martyrs, a legion of prisoners and exiles, and that will be the last to lay down its arms so long as the solution being sought is not one truly worthy of Cuba.

Will anyone seek to deny us that right? If so, if the group of Cuban rebels are denied that right at the very moment we all come together to demand rights from the group in power that tyrannizes us, then today's meeting would be nothing but a gathering of loudmouths from which the most self-sacrificing Cubans have been banned in advance out of fear or jealousy. If I thought that was a possibility, you can be sure I would not be addressing these lines to you.

What we wish is to set forth our views, not force them on anyone. They are the views of thousands of Cuban emigrés who have had to abandon their homeland due to oppression and hunger. They are the views of a hundred thousand fighters who today group themselves under the banners of the July 26 Revolutionary Movement. Let our point of view be heard. Let the people hear it. Let the people decide.

None of the passion I am putting in this letter would be present were I not deeply convinced that the dictatorship, and the dictator himself, are going through the most critical moment of their existence. So critical that even a limited amount of vision, energy, and firmness would suffice to bring down the oppressors without a drop of blood. A single minute of vacillation could ruin a people if that minute coincides with this moment of opportunity.

Barely two months ago, when the Society of Friends of the Republic put forward a document laying out the opposition's demands, the dictator Batista, with unheard-of contempt and arrogance bordering on madness, replied that he had no time to read it. Despite that humiliating response, barely one week ago you gathered around yourself—as an illustrious founder, worthy of all due respect for that reason—the greatest degree of public support the people have given anyone in recent years, and you requested a meeting with the dictator to find an honorable and bloodless way out of the shameful Cuban situation. Yet he responded to you with the same arrogant and odious tone, saying you were just another oppositionist, and he would receive you only to discuss the conditions in which limited elections would take place in 1956 and general elections in 1958, i.e., under his own onerous conditions.

This senseless answer was the latest link in a chain of humiliations the people have been suffering for four years. The cup of political patience overflowed, producing the miracle of the mass rally that is being witnessed tonight with the participation of all sectors in Cuba, including our underground revolutionary organization.

This fact changes completely the national picture.

It is now the people—who at bottom have felt tremendous humiliation as a result of this situation—who have the floor.

It is now the people who must set the terms. And once the people have had to go into the streets, Señor Don Cosme, they can no longer be satisfied with a simple promise of general elections presided over by Batista himself. Exercising a usurped power, he offers guarantees to no one. Perhaps the people would have accepted such a promise two months ago when they were divided and disoriented, when it was so senselessly denied them by the dictator. Now it is too late. Now the people are united. Now all advantages are on their side, and they will not resign themselves to so little. The giant that has stood up does not want only crumbs; he demands all the rights that have been snatched from him.

What the giant wants is punishment for those who murdered

our comrades at Moncada, as well as Jorge Agostini, Mario Fortuny, Mario Aróstegui, Gonzalo Miranda, Rubén Batista, Vitico Muñoz, Narciso Martínez (the most recent one), and many other valiant Cubans.

Punishment for those who have ruined the republic!

Punishment for the traitors of March 10!

No guilty ones should go unpunished!

The giant is hungry for liberty, justice, and bread.

I am one of those Cubans, Señor Don Cosme, who cannot put out of their mind the infamous, unforeseen, and treacherous way in which Batista snatched from the republic its democratic institutions in the dark, wee hours of the morning on March 10. I am one of those Cubans seriously concerned about what guarantees the country has that similar actions will not happen again in the future. I am one of those Cubans who ask themselves if those crimes that wound the homeland will go unpunished. I am one of those Cubans who ask themselves whether a disastrous precedent is at stake for the future of the Cuban nation: the very idea that a group of ambitious men could engage in plots during an hour of misfortune for the homeland, conspire in the shadows against it, stab the republic in the back with the very saber the republic placed in their hands to guard it, govern it afterwards at their whim, dispose capriciously of the nation's honor, of the lives of its citizens, and of the public wealth—and that in the final hour, when the time comes to settle accounts, it's not even demanded that they resign their posts, not to mention returning everything they have stolen and receive punishment for their crimes.

The nation's honor demands that we start by demanding Batista resign. One has to be blind not to see that the opportunity has arrived to call for this. Batista's resignation and the transfer of power to an illustrious veteran of the War of Independence who has served his country with patriotism for sixty years inside and outside Cuba, would be accepted without resistance by the armed forces. They would moreover see in it the opportunity to free themselves from the disaster.

And if Batista refuses to resign, placing himself in opposition to the interests and tranquility of six million Cubans, it would suffice for the Society of Friends of the Republic—with the enormous prestige it has acquired and the unanimous support of the entire country evidenced in today's rally—to declare civic resistance and the nonpayment of taxes, causing the regime to collapse in a week, because it would not even have enough to pay the forces supporting it. The Society of Friends of the Republic should not renounce the glory it deserves at this hour. The Society of Friends of the Republic should be firm.

To accept any other formula, with general elections presided over by Batista, would not be a solution, because the people would not believe in it. The people cannot believe in it after the barracks coup of March 10, just eighty days before general elections, or following the shameful intimidation of November 1.[1] Batista respects and fears a people united. But if the people are divided again into electoral groups, Batista would not have the slightest scruple in betraying them once again.

That is our opinion, Señor Don Cosme.

The only thing left to say is that we trust in you, in your tireless patriotism, your irreproachable austerity, and your unshakable firmness.

Respectfully,
Dr. Fidel Castro

1. On November 1, 1954, the Batista regime held fraudulent elections in which he was "elected" president.

Circular letter of the Civic Resistance Movement

The following circular was distributed to members of the Civic Resistance Movement in the wake of the military conspiracy of "Los Puros" (the pure ones).

Citizen:

On April 4, 1956, an important sector of the army, under the command of Colonel Barquín, Major Borbonet, and others, was about to carry out a revolutionary coup against the dictatorship. Interpreting the feeling of the majority of their comrades-in-arms, they planned to return the people's rights and liberties.

They were aspiring only to general elections with real guarantees, to the imposition of legality, and to constitutional normalcy.

They wanted civilians such as us to know that the majority of the military is not responsible for the fact that a group of murderers is enjoying power. They wanted brotherhood between civilian and soldier, genuine harmony among Cubans. Men who had become officers through merit and personal effort risked their lives and military careers for these ideals. For these principles, those who truly represent the Cuban military today endure prison on the Isle of Pines.

The Civic Resistance Movement agrees on the following to commemorate this date:

1. To declare April 4 as the Day of National Brotherhood.

2. To request that each citizen send a friend of his in the military a letter signed "A friend." A sample letter will be distributed by our organization.

3. That we all put up signs on city walls reading, "Long live free Cuba!"

4. That the Civic Resistance Movement address a letter to soldiers.

5. To strongly urge every civilian to fraternize with military friends and make known to them that we do not fight against them, but against those who rely on the soldiers and military discipline to maintain the abnormal situation and the dictatorship.

Citizens:

Act in harmony with this slogan:

"April 4—Day of National Brotherhood!"

Civic Resistance Movement

Revolution: the only way out

May 15, 1956

The following editorial was published in issue number 1 of *Aldabonazo*, clandestine newspaper of the July 26 Movement.

By an imperative, collective necessity, a new generation has arisen to confront the revolutionary frustration that led us to the disaster of March 10, 1952. On that date a gang of common criminals seized power and destroyed the public order of the republic. The July 26 Movement, which spoke the language of facts, is a categorical response to the March coup. The Movement's origin and aims, which we will present in these pages, reveal to us how Cuban youth have become unwilling to put up with the status quo that made possible the resounding collapse of our hollow political democracy. For this reason our aim is to become the revolutionary instrument of this new generation.

For the July 26 Movement, only those who aim at something more than simply toppling the dictatorship are capable of really eliminat-

¡REVOLUCIÓN!

TAMBALEANTE LA DICTADURA

ALDABONAZO

ÓRGANO DEL MOVIMIENTO REVOLUCIONARIO 26 DE JULIO
Impreso en algún lugar de Cuba · Mayo 15, 1956   No1

REVOLUCIÓN: ÚNICA SALIDA

Por imperiosa necesidad colectiva ha surgido una nueva generación para enfrentarse a la frustración revolucionaria que nos condujo al desastre del 10 de marzo de 1952, cuando una pandilla de delincuentes comunes asaltó el poder y destruyó el orden público de la República. El Movimiento 26 de Julio, que habló el lenguaje de los hechos, es una respuesta categórica al golpe marcista. Sin embargo, su origen y proyección, que en estas páginas iremos exponiendo, nos revelan cómo nace la inconformidad sustancial de la juventud cubana contra el estado de cosas que hizo posible el derrumbe estrepitoso de nuestra vacía democracia política. Por esta razón aspiramos a convertirnos en el instrumento revolucionario de esta nueva generación.

Para el 26 de Julio sólo podrán liquidar la dictadura quienes se propongan algo más que su simple derrocamiento, porque sólo así se puede aglutinar las fuerzas morales del país. Aquellos que simplemente pretendan «tumbar al dictador» ni siquiera eso lograrán porque carecen de razones seri   apoyo ocial para oponérsele   y   r   lo

dictatorial, corrompido y mediocre que padecemos si no se propusiera la transformación revolucionaria de la serie de causas morales, políticas, económicas y sociales que hicieron posible la acción criminal del grupo sedicioso. He ahí el porqué de nuestra independencia revolucionaria y la razón de ser de nuestra fuerza creciente.

El problema cubano es tan grave que llega a ser de carácter moral. El germen de la destrucción ha penetrado tanto en las minorías dirigentes, que hay quienes afirman que la moral no tiene que ver con la política, como si no fuera un presupuesto indispensable de toda conducta, el ajustarse determinado sentido moral. El país se ha visto y se ve gobernado por delincuentes de la peor especie: ladrones, contrabandistas, especuladores, agiotistas y hasta asesinos vulgares, vienen controlando las posiciones claves del gobierno, empezando por lo que debería ser la primera magistratura del Estado.

En este aspecto de la cuestión cubana se proyectó fundamentalmente la personalidad de Eduardo Chibás, con el lema «Vergüenza contra dinero» creó a su alrededor un poderoso estado de opinión y un gran movimiento político que recogió los ideales de la Revolución cubana y por cuya vigencia y triunfo definitivo lucha el 26 de Julio. Con su pistoletazo mortal el 5 de agosto de 1951 señaló el camino del sacri-   de la glori   tró definitivamen-

Issue number 1 of July 26 Movement clandestine journal, *Aldabonazo,* later renamed *Revolución.* Headline at top reads: "Revolution! The dictatorship staggers."

ing it. That is the only way to draw together the moral forces of the nation. Those who simply strive to "topple the dictator" will not even achieve that, since they lack both serious motives and support from the social forces necessary to stand up to a regime embodying the most negative aspects of Cuban society. The July 26 Movement asserts that the current government is not the cause but the result of the republic's fundamental crisis. And it is working directly to resolve that crisis. It would hardly be worthwhile to confront the dictatorial, corrupt, and mediocre regime we suffer without aiming for a revolutionary transformation of the moral, political, economic, and social causes that made possible the criminal act committed by the seditious group. That is the reason for our revolutionary independence, and the reason for being of our growing force.

The Cuban problem is now so serious that it has become moral in character. The germ of destruction has penetrated so deeply among the ruling minority that there are some who state that morals have nothing to do with politics. As if adjusting oneself morally were not an indispensable precondition for all conduct. The country has been and is being governed by criminals of the worst stripe. Thieves, smugglers, speculators, price gougers, and even vulgar assassins are more and more in control of key posts in government, beginning with what should be the government's highest court.

In this aspect of the Cuban question, the figure of Eduardo Chibás, with his slogan "Honor against money," comes to the fore. Chibás gathered around himself a powerful body of opinion and a great political movement that united together the ideals of the Cuban Revolution. It is to put those ideas into effect and for the definitive triumph of these ideas that the July 26 Movement fights. With his fatal pistol shot of August 5, 1951, Chibás showed the way of sacrifice and glory, and entered into history. In tribute to that gesture of supreme indignation and combat, our clandestine newspaper bears the name of his last speech: *Aldabonazo.*

But the deepest cause of our crisis lies in the absence of a clearly defined revolutionary philosophy, and the lack of an organized will that drives us toward realizable goals of improvement, transfor-

"The Centennial Generation emerged from the youth section of the Orthodox Party."

Eduardo Chibás **(inset)**, leader of the Orthodox Party, which attracted workers and youth repelled by government corruption and subservience to U.S. imperialism. In August 1951, in an act of protest, Chibás ended his weekly radio broadcast with the words: "This is my final *aldabonazo*" and shot himself. *Aldabonazo*—a knock on the door—became a rallying cry for youth seeking to fight the corruption prevailing in the country.
Bottom: march in Havana marking the first anniversary of Chibás's death.

BOHEMIA ARCHIVES

JUVENTUD ORTODOXA

BOHEMIA ARCHIVES

"On March 10, 1952, Fulgencio Batista assumed military control of the country through a coup d'état. With a stroke of the pen he swept away all democratic institutions, assumed autocratic control, and imposed the darkest despotism on the people." RAÚL CASTRO, 1958

BOHEMIA ARCHIVES

GRANMA ARCHIVES

Fulgencio Batista's military coup toppled the Authentic Party regime of Carlos Prío. **Facing page, top:** the day of the coup, a delegation from the Federation of University Students (FEU) went to the Presidential Palace to meet with Prío **(seated at center)** in a fruitless attempt to obtain arms to fight Batista. Shortly afterward, Prío vacated office without a fight. **Bottom:** guards at the palace surrender to pro-Batista troops. **This page, top:** Batista is sworn in as president before his Council of Ministers.

U.S.-backed military coups installed regimes beholden to imperialist interests elsewhere, too.
Right: a 1953 U.S.-organized coup in Iran toppled the government of Mohammed Mossadegh, which had nationalized the country's oil industry. December 1953, U.S. Vice President Richard Nixon congratulates Mohammed Reza Pahlavi, reinstalled as shah.

"With Batista's coup, students and workers burst into the political arena independent of the bourgeois forces."

Initial opposition to the coup was centered at the University of Havana. **Top:** on April 6, 1952, students organized a demonstration to symbolically bury Cuba's constitution. Holding the coffin, clockwise from bottom left, are Manuel Carbonell, Armando Comesañas, Armando Hart, and Juan Pedro Carbó. **Right:** a meeting of the Federation of University Students. FEU President Álvaro Barba is at front left in white shirt; José Antonio Echeverría is in back, wearing dark jacket, with Armando Hart at right, with tie.

Later that year Hart joined the Revolutionary National Movement (MNR) led by Rafael García Bárcena, which sought to organize an anti-Batista uprising within the military. On April 5, 1953—the date chosen for the uprising—García Bárcena and a number of MNR supporters were arrested. **This page, top:** police chief Rafael Salas Cañizares (center) talks to the press about the arrests. **Bottom:** García Bárcena, standing at center left, together with defense attorney Hart, standing at right, at Bárcena's trial for the attempted uprising, held in Príncipe Castle prison, which was converted into a "court of justice."

"The heroism and audacity in attacking the country's second most important military fortress decisively changed the political situation."

Fidel Castro began building a revolutionary movement to oust the coup makers. On July 26, 1953, they attacked the Moncada garrison in Santiago de Cuba. **This page, top:** from left, Calixto García, Raúl Castro, José Luis Tasende, and Ñico López, shortly before the attack. **Facing page, top:** Fidel Castro (center) following his capture; at left is Moncada commander Alberto del Río Chaviano. Under Batista's orders, Chaviano had murdered some 50 of the captured fighters. **Above:** the government suspends constitutional guarantees and establishes press censorship.

Facing page, inset: Tried and sentenced to 15 years in prison, Castro wrote down his courtroom defense speech and organized its clandestine publication. *History Will Absolve Me* became a central organizing tool and program of the July 26 Movement. **Facing page, bottom:** among those active in organizing its publication and distribution following their release from prison were Melba Hernández and Haydée Santamaría, the only women to participate in the Moncada attack.

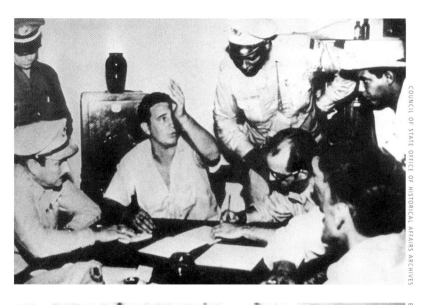

LA HISTORIA
ME ABSOLVERA

DISCURSO PRONUNCIADO POR EL

DR. FIDEL CASTRO

ANTE EL TRIBUNAL DE URGENCIA

DE SANTIAGO DE CUBA

EL DIA 16 DE OCTUBRE DE 1953

"Tyrants like Somoza in Nicaragua, Trujillo in Santo Domingo, and Pérez Jiménez in Venezuela were symbols of oppression and sworn enemies of Cuban youth.

"There was a great deal of activity among Cuban students to protest and condemn the U.S. imperialist intervention in Guatemala."

Facing page, top: Moncadista Ñico López (far right) and other Latin American exiles at a monument in Guatemala for José Martí, January 1954. In June, Guatemala's government was overthrown in a military coup, organized by Washington. **Bottom:** in his prison cell, Fidel Castro reads about the Guatemalan events. Cuban youth saw the fight against Batista as part of opposing U.S.-backed dictators throughout Latin America, such as Trujillo in the Dominican Republic **(top left).** In January 1955 a number of Cuban youth joined forces with others in Costa Rica to resist an invasion of that country by the Somoza dictatorship in Nicaragua. **Top right:** Cuban student leaders in Costa Rica (from left) Juan Pedro Carbó, José Antonio Echeverría, and Fructuoso Rodríguez (kneeling).

Within Cuba there was widespread opposition to the Batista regime's plans to build a canal through the island to benefit U.S. corporations, depicted in a cartoon that appeared in *Bohemia,* **above.**

"The government tried to use the amnesty to present itself as the 'dove of peace,' but its actions revealed this claim to be a total farce. Hunger was growing, unemployment stalked the land, dissatisfaction was increasing."

By early 1955 a campaign to win amnesty for political prisoners had reached such proportions that the dictatorship decided to release the Moncadistas and others. **Facing page, top:** as he left prison in May following the amnesty, Castro was greeted as a hero. **Bottom:** shortly after his release, Castro welcomes Rafael García Bárcena (in glasses) back from exile. Armando Hart is second from left.

In December 1955, over 200,000 sugar workers went on strike to protest government moves to lower their wages. **This page, top:** In Las Villas province, at the height of the struggle strikers and their supporters virtually took control of some towns.

The bourgeois opposition to Batista sought to keep the popular discontent off the streets. In 1955 these efforts were led by Cosme de la Torriente, whose goal, Hart says, was compelling Batista "to agree to a solution acceptable to all the traditional opposition parties." In late 1955, when de la Torriente met with Batista **(bottom),** "the March 10 chief seduced him with words."

> **"Cuba is on the verge of a revolution that will transform the social and political order and will lay the foundations of a socialist and revolutionary democracy. We represent the vanguard of that revolution."**
> ARMANDO HART, 1956

Within weeks of his release, Castro founded the July 26 Movement together with other compañeros, and later left for Mexico to begin preparing an expedition to launch a revolutionary war against the dictatorship. **Top:** Fidel Castro (seated second from right) at a 1955 meeting in Miami, with some of the money raised from Cuban exiles to initiate the armed struggle against the Batista regime. **Bottom:** the Mexico City home of María Antonia González (back row, second from right) became a refuge for the revolutionaries arriving to join the expedition. Next to her at right is Ñico López; in front left is Calixto García.

mation, and progress. It has not been possible to have ideas completely govern individual conduct. The ideas of the Cuban nation, in modern times, are still maintained as a great collective hunger. They are a desire that is scattered. That is, while they exist in the realm of sentiment, emotion, and will, they have nevertheless not been definitively accepted intellectually. When the democratic and socialist idea is spelled out to its final consequence, all action will be directed along this road. At that point a group of men will emerge whose strength lies in their unbreakable unity, men who are united by the same principles and ideas, not by the doctrine of "everyone to destroy," as Antonio Guiteras formulated it in his political testament as he analyzed the causes of the revolutionary defeat.[2] That group will be "the team of men capable of leading Cuba toward its higher destiny" that Eduardo Chibás spoke of. The July 26 Movement aspires to find, discipline, and organize that team of men. And its organ of public guidance, *Aldabonazo*, has the mission of discovering revolutionary ideas and elaborating them. We are not heading to battle without ideas, because war without ideas is a crime, while war with ideas is revolution.

The heroic deed of the Moncada garrison and Bayamo is the unifying factor of our scattered national will. Eighty revolutionary martyrs offer us, through their example and sacrifice, a point of convergence that illuminates the country's future. The most beautiful lesson of that gesture was not only the courage and selflessness displayed by those brave men. It was also their conviction of the importance, transcendence, and power of their example—not to mention their discretion and organizational capacity enabling them to reach the stage of combat. Only a total identification with revolution could write into history the rebel date of July 26, 1953. Cuba must find itself both by looking to the history of the mambises and patriots; and by looking to our generation, with the living example of a legion of contemporary martyrs.

2. Guiteras wrote that in the struggle against the Machado tyranny, the doctrine predominated of "Everyone to destroy; only a few to build." This "terrible doctrine," he stated, "is basic to many of our ills."

A country with human resources and qualities such as ours cannot continue living in the hands of irresponsible and improvising opportunists of the lowest moral character. The world is advancing in the field of science, and technology makes bigger strides every day. Yet we ourselves are not walking to the tune of the times, since we have not succeeded in bringing together all honest, capable, bold, and talented men and putting them at the service of the country. Such men exist, but they're separated, far apart from one another, as if some centrifugal and malignant force were preventing their total unification. It is in the unity of these men—genuine representatives of the people of Cuba—that national unity and true democracy lie.

On the basis of its ideological position, the July 26 Revolutionary Movement for ten months has dedicated itself to publicly proclaiming the need for revolutionary action, and to constructing a powerful underground organization that gathers together and interprets the ideas of the Cuban nation, and the immediate needs of the people.

This strategy has delivered the revolution from small circles of combatants and placed it in the hands of the people. All Cubans have the possibility of participating: not only those who take up arms, but also those prepared to leave work, to contribute financially to buy the rifles, or to extend help to the revolution in a thousand different ways. Large sectors of the population have, for a number of years, felt cut off from the struggle for freedom. The July 26 Movement, with a popular strategy and with insurrectional tactics, is incorporating these sectors into the revolution.

Since revolutionary language has begun to be spoken publicly, large and important gains have been made. The government is staggering in face of the latest mass conspiracy.[3]

In these few months, the March regime has entered its definitive crisis. The crisis has reached the armed forces, undermining internal discipline and breaking its "monolithic unity." On the one hand the *tanquista* elements terrified by their unsustainable situ-

3. A reference to the "Los Puros" military conspiracy.

ation, aligned themselves with the forces of gangsterism and established contact with the Dominican satrap Rafael Leónidas Trujillo. The two most negative forces in our society—*tanquismo* on a military level and gangsterism on a civic level—appear joined together in sinister and insane plots.

On the other hand, the young officers of the army, in face of the imminent crisis and imbued with the democratic and civic teachings of the Higher Academy of War, silently and laboriously prepared a strictly military coup d'état, but one whose aims were undoubtedly democratic and civic-minded. We say this taking full responsibility for our words, and with the moral authority of being the only organization consciously preparing civilians to make a revolution and that is totally separate and apart from the aborted military movement. No one has a right to question the good faith and patriotism of these military men, just as no one has the moral authority to criticize the military institutes for trying to topple the dictatorship. At the same time, no one has a right to wait for the regime to fall through action by forces within the military alone. Men such as the conspirators of April 3 are our brothers in ideas within the army. The words spoken at the court-martial by one of them, that "they did not want soldiers and civilians to look at each other as enemies but as brothers," are, as accurately stated by the central leader of the July 26 Movement Fidel Castro, "the most beautiful words spoken by a Cuban soldier since the end of the War of Independence."

With joy the people have seen how false is the boast by the dictatorship's cheerleaders that the entire army is with them. Within the military institutes, the seed of rebellion has already been planted, and that seed will sprout again when civic action makes itself felt.

All this has created an increasingly violent situation in the country. In this same issue, we present news of the most recent events in Santiago de Cuba and Matanzas, the military occupation of the Universities of Oriente and Havana, the murder of civilians, the tortures suffered by many compañeros, and a whole series of grave events that are putting the country on "the brink of an abyss," to use a phrase by a political commentator. We are in the midst of a terrible revolutionary convulsion that, with a sense of responsibility, we foretold some time ago. We have been led to this convulsion by the incapacity of the political leaders on the one hand, and the intransigence of the government on the other. The economic crisis, aggravated by smuggling, illegal gambling, scandalous embezzlement of the public treasury, and the precipitous fall of business activity due to the most recent events, has already brought us to the inevitable edge of collapse. To try and avoid war at this time, to halt the uncontainable force of the people, is an unpardonable crime. Those who try to do so—who continue talking about peace while the regime has destroyed every possibility for conciliation, every possibility for an understanding even with those who do not want revolution—will have to answer for their crime.

The people have taken their road, and the July 26 Movement is now guiding them. The fulfillment of our program is guaranteed, because the revolution is already a reality, and, as Martí said, "the people are the only leader of revolutions."

In bringing out the first issue of our underground newspaper, we issue a fraternal call to all revolutionary groups and sectors to join the July 26 Revolutionary Movement in an organized fashion. We call on all honest men of the country to make a supreme effort, as the popular classes have already been doing, by contributing funds to the definitive triumph of the Cuban Revolution—a revolution that is not the work of one or another group, but of the entire people.

Open letter
to the president of Mexico

Armando Hart
July 1956

The following was written in response to the arrest in Mexico of Fidel
Castro and twenty-seven others involved in preparing the *Granma*
expedition.

HAVANA, JULY 1956

Mr. Adolfo Ruiz Cortines
Honorable President of the United States of Mexico:

In the interests of good relations between your government and
the people of Cuba, the student and revolutionary organizations
of Cuba consider it extremely useful to send you this message spelling out the thinking of hundreds of thousands of Cubans who have
watched with great concern the arrest of several of our compatriots in Mexico City. Noteworthy among them is Dr. Fidel Castro
Ruz, leader of the July 26 Revolutionary Movement and a pillar
of Cuban youth. We cannot address you through diplomatic channels, since we deny legitimacy to the government set up by the
military uprising of March 10, 1952. We are therefore doing so by
way of an open letter, so the peoples of Mexico and Cuba can become familiar with our views. They will ultimately be the best judge
of a question that creates such anger among us.

Dr. Fidel Castro is a widely acknowledged popular national figure throughout the country. We are not talking about the leader
of a seditious group. Rather, he represents a powerful body of public
opinion that has influence on the course of Cuban political events.

He is a sincere democrat, an honest combatant for freedom, and a tireless fighter for the people's causes. Those arrested with him enjoy indisputable prestige among the student and revolutionary sectors of our homeland. Any assault on them is therefore an assault on us, since we consider their conduct to be correct. For this reason, Honorable Mr. President, your government's position on this incident necessarily has an effect on the present and future relations between Cuba and Mexico. Hence the concern that drives us to explain to you the truth—our truth—which is Cuba's truth.

We know only too well the high sense of responsibility that has always characterized your political leadership at the head of Mexico's destiny. That is why we are certain you will understand us when we assure you that those persons seated at the defendants' bench in a Mexico City courtroom are not just the individuals arrested. Rather, in the dock are the entire people of Cuba and particularly we, the students and other revolutionary sectors.

Mexican democracy cannot and must not ignore this reality, because it would endanger its well-earned prestige among the brother peoples of the Americas.

Cuba, Honorable Mr. President, is on the verge of a revolution that will transform the social and political order and will lay the foundations of a socialist and revolutionary democracy. We represent the vanguard of that revolution. Due to circumstances that can no longer be denied, we have the patriotic duty to lead the people during this uncertain moment when the government has driven them into a seeming blind alley. We don't need to explain to you the reasons we have taken this route. . . .

In Cuba there are political, social, economic, cultural, and even legal reasons that lead us to take the unavoidable road of violence. By doing so we are doing nothing else but following the example of Mexico, among others. Neither you nor your government—which arose during the stage of the Mexican Revolution's institutionalization—can ignore the fact that Fidel Castro and his arrested comrades are fulfilling the same duty as the men who in 1910 made possible the overthrow of Porfirio Díaz's one-man regime. How great is the resemblance between that regime, in its origins and policies, and the one endured today by our homeland! At the time of the fall of President Lerdo de Tejada, José Martí—who was then in Mexico—prophetically stated that the Aztec people had thirty years of tyranny ahead of them. Indeed, up until 1910 it was not possible to break the ring of plutocratic interests that kept in power those who forgot the people, drowning the Mexican impulse. Your government—the offspring of that revolution—should not deny us the right to prevent a recurrence in our land of what we today observe in the sister land of Santo Domingo, where to the disgrace of the Americas an oppressive system has been in power for more than thirty years. We must not permit the thirty-year regime of a Juan Vicente Gómez and so many other cases, such as those of Rosas in Argentina, Francia in Paraguay, and Ubico in Guatemala. We would be betraying the history of the Americas if we stopped this fight, just as you would have betrayed it forty years ago had you chosen the easy and comfortable option of accommodation. Accommodation! That, Mr. President, is what has caused so much harm to the Americas and particularly to Cuba.

We know only too well that in international practice, where so many different interests come into play, it is necessary to view these problems from a different angle. But international practice cannot pass over the reasons that brought you to the head of the Mexican state, i.e., democracy, the people, and the law.

We are not going to demand that Mexico side with us, because we know the international commitments it must fulfill. We are not requesting that your government adopt the same stance as taken by Eloy Alfaro, president of Ecuador, who [in 1895] officially recognized Cuba's independence in the very midst of war. That would be a heroic act, and heroic acts, while laudable, cannot be demanded. What we want from you is understanding.

A Mexican newspaper stated that Fidel Castro had turned his asylum into a lair. It is understandable that those who have not known liberty may hold that opinion. But those who have been able to study our history and learn the principles that took our liberators to war have no moral justification for such nonsense. If the attitude of our fellow countrymen is to be judged, Mr. President, this should be done bearing in mind that they are not holed up in a lair, but are selfless fighters for Cuba's freedom.

No serious evidence has been submitted that they violated Mexican laws. Press dispatches reporting the news are filled with contradictions, such as the report that Fidel Castro left Cuba several months ago with a passport obtained by various communist leaders. The truth is that he departed for exile in July 1955 with a Cuban passport, in broad daylight and in public, after the doors of all newspapers and radio programs had been closed to him by government decree and repression had been unleashed against him and his friends. Yet these compañeros are still being held in prison with no other explanation than the fantastic accusations, which no one believes, of ties to communist organizations preparing to assassinate Batista.

No, Honorable Mr. President. Your obligation is to feel yourself together with your people and with us, and for that reason we respectfully request you to act in this case.

No arguments can make you remain with arms folded in face of such violations of Latin America's norms of life. Or is it perhaps, to Latin America's disgrace, that once more "the full dignity of man"—placed by José Martí at the very center of Latin American political thought—is to be ignored?

Mexico, which set an example for the world by sending the intruding Prince Maximilian of Austria to the firing squad, cannot allow the tyrant of a sister land to intrude in its domestic policy. . . .

As the magazine *Bohemia* put it—one of the loftiest voices of the continent—all of America is attentively watching Mexico's actions.

The decision is in your hands, Mr. President. Save the prestige of the Mexican Revolution, which some have attempted to cast aspersion on. The brother peoples of the continent have their eyes focused on the Aztec capital. From there, the scene of so many struggles for Mexico's redemption, a word must come forth to end this irritating incident. And that word must be *freedom*.

Yours in revolution,
Armando Hart Dávalos

Chapter 6

'The most important thing in a revolution is decisiveness'[1]

By mid-1956 I realized that an effective action in support of the landing would occur only in Santiago de Cuba. The level of organization and the capacities of the leaders in that city were very high. These included Frank País, with whom I was united by old ties of friendship and a very deep personal attachment. I decided to head to Santiago, the decision I am proudest of during that period. I arrived with Haydée on November 14, 1956, and we immediately went to the home of Cayita Araújo, who from then on became an inexhaustible source of optimism for us. From there we were taken to a boarding house on San Agustín Street.

On Tuesday, November 27, Frank brought us the communication from Fidel: "Edition requested, sold out." That was the coded message informing us they had departed Mexico and were heading to Cuba. Frank jumped with joy at the news.

The work had to be accelerated, and the houses to be used on

1. Fidel Castro at the first joint meeting of combatants of both the Sierra and the Llano, February 1957. [AH]

Friday, November 30, had to be prepared. That was the day we had estimated the expedition commanded by Fidel would arrive on our coasts.

News reached us of the arrest in Havana of Aldo Santamaría, who also knew this information. The circumstances made us fear for his life, but Aldo swallowed the cablegram he had received and held firm, with the news locked away in his mind. I thought I would never see him again. The tyranny had arrested someone who had the information, but could learn nothing.

I proposed to Frank that we seize a radio station to call people out on strike. He argued that since we did not have enough weapons, it was better to record a message and assign the compañeros to get it broadcast.

The house at 463 San Jerónimo Street, where Vilma Espín's family lived, had been turned into a planning center and the headquarters of the Movement's leadership. There we drafted the message, recorded it, and handed it to the radio station's owner, with whom we had contact. The man was opposed to Batista, but was incapable of taking a step like the one we were asking. Given the outcome of events, I later realized this was undoubtedly for the best.

In a 1975 interview published in the magazine *Santiago*, Vilma explained what happened to the recording:

> I had to stay home so I could deliver a recording we had made the night before to the man who was to relay it nationally. It was a call for all the people to rise up, and it announced Fidel's arrival.
>
> That recording was only broadcast within the studio, because the man who was supposed to relay it nationally became so frightened that he burned the tape. . . . There is always someone who fails, but in the end almost everything was carried out exactly as had been laid out. Our mission was to deliver the tape, inform compañero [Carlos] Amat at the Telephone Company so he could organize its broadcast over those channels, as had been decided, and then go immediately to the house at San Félix

and Santa Lucía Streets, where the general command post was located.

In this regard, Carlos Amat comments:

A week before November 30, Vilma called us together at her house. When we arrived we found Armando Hart and Haydée Santamaría. There we were informed of the preparations for Fidel's landing, and that Santiago de Cuba would support him with a general uprising. For me there was a specific task. But first I must explain something. Vilma knew that in the department where I worked there was a section that handled the broadcasting lines. That is, the radio stations transmitting from Havana reached Oriente by telephone line, and there was a relay station in Santiago. The lines of those stations and of the local ones—CMKC, CMKW—ran through the switchboard I was talking about, which could be monitored. Well, they had recorded a call to the people that was to be broadcast by radio to the entire country on the day of the uprising, and it was possible technically to do this. The recording was to be played at a local radio station that would act as the master station, while at the department where I worked we would make the necessary technical arrangements so it could be heard simultaneously on the local and national stations.

Naturally, no one knew on what day the uprising would take place—a message was to arrive informing us. So starting the following day, every morning at 5:00 a.m. I was to go to a place near the Telephone Company, and wait for someone who would tell me to carry out the operation. Armando Hart had written a phrase on a paper that he later ripped into two halves, in a jagged way, and gave me one half. "I'll keep the other half. Unless the person who brings you the message carries this other half, which will complete the sheet of paper, you should not do anything, no matter who tells you. He has to bring this paper with him." That was the password. After I had received it, I was to await the first shots. Then I was to run to the Telephone Company and phone a man at the station who already had the recording, telling him to play it, and I would then retransmit it.

I went to that post for eight or nine days. Then, when I least expected it, I saw Vilma and Asela de los Santos driving up in a car. When they reached where I was, Asela stuck her hand out the window, gave me the paper, and said to me: "Look, this message is yours. The thing is today. When you hear the first shot, call this number—and she gave me the number—and ask for so-and-so." She gave me a name. "This is a radio station; he's the one who is to play the recording.". . .

I ran to the phone company. When I got there a policeman was sitting at the switchboard. The dictatorship had already placed guards at the phone company, and we were supposed to teach them how to monitor the calls. Of course, there was passive resistance to doing this. We made the technical aspect of their training as difficult as possible. . . .

Well, when I saw the guard I called Rogelio Soto. Once, when I had seen him leaving Vilma's house, I had asked him—without telling him why—how one could connect up the local stations to the national ones, and he had shown me how. Up till then we had not identified ourselves to each other, but when I called him I noticed he was nervous; he had also been informed of what was up.

"Listen, something's going to happen today," I told him.

"Yes, I know," he told me.

"Get this guard out of here on any pretext," I said, "because I have some work to do."

Then Rogelio called the guard over. . . .

I took advantage of this to set the connections. When the shots were fired, around ten minutes to seven, I phoned the number Asela had given me, but it was busy again and again. The guards had already become alarmed with the shooting and were running around everywhere. I had to call Rogelio and ask him to interrupt the call. At last I was able to speak to the man and I told him: "Hey, you have to play the recording."

"I can't, I can't," he said.

"Play it!"

"I can't," he said.

I started cursing at him right on the spot: "You miserable
————, play the recording! You have to play it!"

The guy did not want to play it, and he didn't. So the mission was not accomplished because of him.

＊

The night of the 29th we went to sleep at a house at Punta Gorda, which was one of the places where strongly armed groups had gathered. Vilma, Frank, and others were there.

Before 7:00 a.m. we left for a house at Santa Lucía and San Félix Streets, where the operations were to be directed from. This house became general headquarters and seat of the general staff. We arrived in a car—Frank (who was driving), Vilma, Haydée, and I; the rest came in other cars. There was a row of vehicles, of armed people whose aim was to attack the stations of the National Police and the Maritime Police. That historic day we wore for the first time the olive green uniform. María Antonia Figueroa explained the details:

> Frank and Taras [Domitro] brought the olive green uniforms. The Durruty sisters had made these uniforms in Palma Soriano. Tina Esteva and Nilda Ferrer had taken them to Vilma Espín, who had delivered them to Frank. The olive green color was chosen by Frank—as well as the flag and the armband—and approved by Fidel in Mexico.[2]

Five women participated in the uprising: María Antonia Figueroa, national treasurer of the Movement, descended from Santiago's patriotic tradition and from Cuban teachers; Gloria Cuadras, who came from the Orthodox Party and the fights of

2. This quote, as well as those that immediately precede it by Vilma Espín and Carlos Amat, were taken from the previously mentioned magazine, *Santiago*. [AH]

the 1930s; Vilma Espín, the foremost representative of the women of Santiago in the Centennial Generation and irreplaceable assistant to Frank; Asela de los Santos, the inseparable compañera of the underground combatants who played an outstanding role in the struggle; and Haydée Santamaría, the representative of Moncada.

The plan had been to torch and assault the police stations, to fire mortars at Moncada, and then to advance on them. These actions were to be signals for calling the general strike. The general staff would know the results of the attacks by the smoke.

The minutes passed, seeming like hours, and we had no news of the mortar that should have been fired at the old garrison. Later we learned that Léster Rodríguez, in charge of this mission, had been arrested at dawn on the 30th. More discouraging news arrived from one place after another: Pepito Tey was dead, the police stations could not be taken, nor could the Moncada garrison. By noon we knew the operation had failed.[3]

We worked out with Frank that Haydée and I would go to the house next door to hide the weapons. But that attempt was unsuccessful. A dangerous confusion occurred when we went to the house–command post. Those inside thought that we were Batista guardsmen, and we could not convince them to open the door. We then went across the street and signaled them, but they thought we were warning them that it was the police. So we insistently knocked on the door. Frank País suddenly appeared at the old gate, gun in hand, pointing it at us. "It's us!" I yelled at him with my arms raised. I'll never forget that moment.

We immediately met to discuss what we should do. Some proposed we march to the Sierra to meet Fidel. That was not possible, since we were hundreds of kilometers away. Haydée, with the experience from Moncada, advised us to disperse

3. See page 149, "The Valiant Action of Santiago de Cuba" by Frank País. See also page 158, "Support Actions in Havana for the *Granma* Landing" by Héctor Rodríguez Llompart.

around the city. She said that after the action of July 26, 1953, those who fanned out around Santiago received the support of the population and were able to escape. We finally decided to abandon the dwelling that had been turned into a garrison. The last ones to leave were Vilma, Haydée, and me. We went to Vilma's house, on San Jerónimo Street. Mariano Feijóo *(Papucho)*, a young man of fourteen or fifteen at the time, arrived there. He had been in jail at the police station when the assault took place, and the fire had almost devoured him behind bars.

Pepito Tey's body was laid out at the San Bartolomé funeral home. Several of us, his compañeros, were there. While the body was being carried to the street we stood at attention before the body of that martyr of the homeland. The army fired a burst with a machine gun to frighten us, but achieved nothing.

We were also living through uncertain and worrying moments due to the lack of news about the *Granma* expedition. We even feared a shipwreck, since by our calculations they should have been on Cuban soil by that time.

On Saturday, December 1, between 3:00 and 4:00 p.m. we met again with Frank, who we found at Vilma's playing the piano. The operation of November 30 had failed. His very close friends Pepito Tey, Tony Alomá, and Otto Parellada were dead. And we still had no news from Fidel.

In spite of the setback we continued our fight. We knew that these were tactical reverses while we were winning strategic victories.

Our first objective was to make contact with Fidel, which could be accomplished through Celia Sánchez. Frank secured a mimeograph machine and prepared a bulletin to provide information to all Movement cadres in Oriente province.

By the evening of Sunday, December 2, indications of the landing began to arrive. But that was all they were: indications. The days that followed were dramatic, but our activity kept growing. In short, every one of the cadres of the July 26 Movement in Oriente province passed through Santiago.

Prior to December 24 news from Fidel finally reached us. We

had agreed with Cayita Araújo that as soon as she learned Fidel was alive, she should notify us urgently in code and by phone. The code was: "María, come eat meringue." One day we heard the sweet and clear voice of Cayita, who had become our guardian: "Yeyé, meringue! Little meringue! Big meringue!" All of us were ecstatic; confidence grew.

A few days earlier we had picked up information from radio reports about those who had fallen, and among those mentioned was Faustino Pérez. For a while I thought I would never see him again, but around noon on December 24 we spotted him, about one block away, coming toward Vilma's house along San Jerónimo. We all hugged in the middle of the street—that block was ours.

During the following months the Movement's headquarters remained there. All the neighbors knew it, and not a single one informed on us. The homes of Vilma, Cayita, and Arturo Duque were the places we stayed at the most during those days.

Faustino's arrival with news and instructions from Fidel gave a boost to all our work. It was of decisive importance to get out the word that the Movement's leader was alive in the Sierra Maestra. Our greatest concern was the need to restructure our organization nationwide. We decided that Faustino and Frank would travel to Havana for that purpose and to seek financial support.

Around that time I began to use the name *Jacinto* to work with the underground movement.

Days later, on January 2, 1957, the body of William Soler, a teenager, was found in the streets of Santiago. This crime caused great popular indignation, and Santiago became a boiling pot. The idea was raised of holding a women's demonstration along Enramada Street at the beginning of 1957, to protest the murder, and we all went to work organizing it. It was an event that showed the strength the July 26 Movement already had among the masses. The men lined the sidewalks, and the women marched through the streets. There were huge banners denouncing the intolerable situation and demanding there be no more murders. The march stepped off from Dolores Church. In a letter to my family I described those memorable events:

SANTIAGO DE CUBA,
JANUARY 4, 1957

Dear all:

I am taking advantage of a friend's trip to write you.

We are still under the effect of this morning's beautiful events. Nearly three thousand women marched through the streets of Santiago in a silent protest against the recent brutal human butchery—outrageous to even the most timid spirit—of a fifteen-year-old boy who was tortured and had his limbs torn apart by the agents of oppression. In less than twenty-four hours an immense crowd of women was mobilized. Many of the men were moved to tears by their impressive march. Stores closed their doors, and I saw an officer of the U.S. Army, eyes wide open, overcome with emotion. The store employees gradually joined the march at the initiative of the owners themselves. The soldiers sent to disperse that wave of women, who cried with dignity and courage, were also moved. Many of them were as young as us, and I think that as a result of these events—and perhaps so many others!—their souls were shaken in face of right and justice.

My words are pale compared to this event, which shows how deeply the people here have become imbued with the purest ideas of justice. The civic quality of the people of Oriente is exceptional in all respects. The wealthy classes, certainly the most reluctant, will understand us. Here they are practically linked to the fight for freedom.

I have found here the essence of what it means to be Cuban. In Havana opposition sentiment is unanimous, but in many cases it is merely a resentment against someone in particular. Here, however, that feeling gives birth to righteous indignation, and it is so pure and deep that it takes on a militant attitude. In these parts, the indispensable psychological conditions are perfectly ripe for the triumph of a truly revolutionary upheaval. It is very far away from the great centers of infection emanating from the leaderships of political parties and social groups, and therefore people are better disposed to a truly new idea.

Today, closely and deeply thinking about the best values of the Cuba we dream of, and at the same time somewhat distant in space and time (measuring the latter by the events that shook our lives), my feeling of revolutionary urgency is reaffirmed. And I believe it is definitely on the march. What's more, paraphrasing someone, we might say that if a revolution was not already under way in the rebellious conscience of Cubans, we would have to create it. But it is not so, we are marching toward it. We Cubans will only have to guide it, since we already have it in the form of an immense discontent among the majority and a firm and maturing sentiment among the smaller layer remaining. In the end the latter will be the ones who will most determine the outcome.

Were it not so, Martica, Enriquito, Liliam Teresa, Mariló, and Marinyn would have to live in a country totally colonized, in practice or even formally, by one or another foreign power. Yes, because if we do not solve our essential problems in a short period (and the most vital one is for the nation to find itself), twenty-five years from now the great power concentrations will take place without our contribution or influence. And this is equivalent to liquidating the work of the founders and forgers of our political independence.

There, Gustavo, you have a Marxist reason for the need to establish revolutionary foundations in less than ten years and a concrete explanation of why we must act quickly. Yes, because there is not one second to lose.

We must therefore hurry up. I have faith in the people, upon whom those who regard themselves as very mature heap hollow words every day. It is hard to find more hollow words than those of the recent editorials. I have faith because if I, full of limitations, am capable of giving what little I have to attain a higher life (one that is lived in the service of history), then what are the immense legions of compañeros who are capable of greater sacrifices and higher virtues achieving? And I have seen them in flesh and blood in these emotion-filled days that my poor destiny reserved for me, in the midst of so much pain. Pain for the anguish caused by the knowledge that the best Cubans have been lost forever, and that the wicked continue to obstruct us. Pain because it is sad to see persons fall with whom we had become so close through months of joint work. But everything has its good side: without those great emotions, life would be worth nothing to me.

As you can see, this is entirely my own letter: the text, the contents, the apparent remoteness of what is concrete, etc. It is so beautiful to find in the abstract the concretes of oneself! But it could not be otherwise. What better present for the twelfth day of Christmas than a part of myself? It is the only thing I possess, ultimately, since for some time now I have been able to show great passion to those outside of myself only when it's found deeply inside my ideas. That is the case with Yeyé, whom I could reach only because she was in the center of this world.

As for all of you, for some time now I have only been able to think of the pain I'm causing you and I ask for understanding. I want you to feel that pain and to understand that the first duty of a man is to be faithful to his conscience. I know this is so, even if a natural self-centeredness may predominate in him.

Do not think that something may happen to me that will sadden you. I have always believed that if the lion escapes from its cage, the most prudent thing is to get into the cage. All of us—absolutely all—are in danger.

This is what I was thinking and feeling in mid-February 1957 when we were called to the Sierra to meet with Fidel. Frank had already returned to Santiago; so Haydée, Vilma, Frank, and I set out for Manzanillo. Faustino, who was returning directly from Havana, would be waiting there for us.

When we reached Manzanillo we received good news: Faustino was bringing an important journalist from the *New York*

Times who wanted to interview Fidel. One has only to imagine what that meant for a small group of revolutionaries who were working to find a way for Cuba to know Fidel Castro was alive and still fighting. Due to the political cowardice of the newspapers in Havana, it seemed it was going to be very difficult to get out the news that Fidel was alive. Suddenly we found out that a journalist of such an important U.S. daily had agreed to interview Fidel.

Faustino and Frank had the assignment of making contacts in the capital to make Fidel's presence in the Sierra known. Some contacts informed them of Herbert L. Matthews's aim, and everything was organized to facilitate his arrival.

The first meeting between those in the Sierra and those in the Llano—that is, the first meeting of the combatants of November 30 and those of December 2—was to coincide with the political and propaganda event of an interview with Fidel published by the *New York Times*. The two main scenes of the revolutionary struggle that was to culminate with the victory of January 1, 1959—the Sierra and the Llano—were born at that moment.

Celia was the main contact with Fidel, although she did not yet know him personally. She and Frank went on ahead. Faustino, Haydée, Vilma, and I left the following morning. At last, at dusk on February 16, we reached the place where the above-mentioned meeting between the Sierra and the Llano was to take place. The historic significance of this meeting, held on February 17, 1957, can also be appreciated from the decisions we made, including to send a group of armed combatants from November 30 to support the guerrilla struggle in the Sierra Maestra.

On that occasion I said to Fidel: "I didn't think you could get this far." He answered me: "The most important thing in a revolution is decisiveness."

In addition to Fidel and Raúl other combatants were present, including Ernesto Guevara, Juan Almeida, Camilo Cienfuegos, Ramiro Valdés, and Guillermo García. They formed the essential nucleus of the guerrilla war that had begun in the Sierra Maestra.

Fidel, Raúl, and Che were the highest symbols of this entire history. Camilo was to become the legendary warrior who, together with Che, advanced westward and triumphantly entered the Columbia military garrison. Almeida was Fidel's close collaborator during the entire war and the organizer of the Third Front, which surrounded Santiago de Cuba and paved the way for victory. Ramiro was at Moncada, on the *Granma*, in the mountains, and participated in the westward invasion together with Che and Camilo. Guillermo, a peasant from the region, rendered decisive support to the expeditionaries from the start because of his knowledge of the territory. He was one of the most effective and reliable combatants.

A shot rang out while Fidel was drawing up the first document issued from the Sierra, which he entitled "Manifesto to the Nation." In that manifesto he informed the people of Cuba that the guerrilla group was alive and fighting, denounced the abuses committed by Batista's military, and confirmed that the fight was to continue until the final victory. We all scrambled because we were expecting an enemy attack. Faustino collected the papers. We were ready for combat but immediately learned that the problem was not with the army—it was just that someone had fired a shot. José Morán was guilty of that incident, in which he wounded himself in the leg. Days later it was confirmed that he had betrayed the Movement, and he was later executed during the underground struggle in Guantánamo. We came to the conclusion that the shot fired that day had been the intentional stratagem of a traitor so he would be taken out to Manzanillo and could abandon the guerrilla unit.

During the meeting referred to above Eutimio Guerra appeared, returning from town. He had met with the army with the aim of continuing his work as a miserable traitor, and he had told Batista's henchmen of the guerrillas' movements. But there was very clear information already of his plans, and he was captured with the army's safe-conduct passes in his possession. He was shot.

After a long visit with Fidel, we returned to the cities by way of Manzanillo. I went with Celia, Faustino, Frank, Vilma, and Haydée.

I was happy because I was fighting, and there is no greater satisfaction than that of fighting and working for the future. That is the nature of those who have decided to be revolutionaries. It is also true of peoples in revolution.

The valiant action of Santiago de Cuba

Frank País
February 1957

This account of the November 30, 1956, uprising in Santiago de Cuba was printed in *Revolución,* the clandestine publication of the July 26 Movement, during the first half of February 1957.

On November 23 the leadership of the Movement assigned each group leader to study and submit a definitive report on its military target. Three days later it was decided that the basic targets were to be the Maritime Police, the National Police, and the Moncada garrison.

On the 28th we met to finalize details and discuss plans. We had already received the message saying that Fidel and the compañeros from Mexico had left for Cuba.

"Fidel arrives tomorrow," Pepito Tey stated. "We have only one night to prepare everything."

"Does anyone object?" he then asked.

"No!" we all answered.

When we were later informed we had another day for preparations we were very happy. On the 29th we worked frantically to prepare the houses and distribute the arms and uniforms.

In the evening we settled down in barracks. The city seemed normal. But during the night many families began noticing the absence of their sons, husbands, or brothers, and the population was overcome with fear, with the premonition that "something" was about to happen.

The attack had initially been set for 6:00 a.m., but it was postponed until 7:00 to avoid the changing of the guard. At 5:00 the alarm clock rang, although almost all the combatants had spent the night wide awake and were understandably nervous. Café con leche and biscuits were distributed, but almost no one ate or drank a thing. With intense emotion we put on for the first time our July 26 uniforms—olive green, black armbands with red letters on them and military insignia.

Needless to say, the moment was dramatic and we were all so moved by this beautiful crusade for freedom that our fervor grew and overcame us completely. In my group the weapons were divided up. We were informed that since there were many more men than weapons, the leadership was ordering married men or those with family responsibilities to stay in the reserve force until called.

"No one can deprive me of the right to fight for Cuba!" Tony Alomá shouted nervously. "I've waited too long to remain still now."

"No, Tony, you've just become a father this very night. If we fall, you'll take our place."

"Then how come Otto's going?" he said, referring to Otto Parellada, married just like he was and with children.

"He's a group leader."

"One way or another I'm going," said Tony.

We sang Cuba's National Anthem. Pepito spoke a few fiery words to us:

"We're going off to fight for Cuba! Long live the revolution! Long live the July 26 Movement!"

Our group was composed of 28 men. This included 20 in uniform headed by Pepito Tey, who were to attack the police headquarters from the front. Prior to the attack, eight men in civilian

¡NO HABRÁ PAZ CON BATISTA!

Revolución

★ ÓRGANO DEL MOVIMIENTO REVOLUCIONARIO 26 DE JULIO
Impreso en algún lugar de Cuba · Primera quincena de febrero 1957 ★
PRECIO DEL EJEMPLAR: 10 CTVS.

La Valerosa Acción de Santiago de Cuba

El 23 de Noviembre la Dirección del Movimiento encargó a cada jefe de grupo que estudiaran y rindieran el informe definitivo de su objetivo militar. Tres días después quedó decidido que los puntos básicos eran la Policía Marítima, la Policía Nacional y el Cuartel Moncada.

El día 28 nos reunimos para ultimar detalles y discutir los planes. Ya teníamos el aviso de Fidel y los compañeros de México habían salido hacia Cuba. Pepito Tey aseguró: «Mañana llega Fidel; tenemos solamente una noche para prepararlo todo»; preguntando luego: «—¿Alguien tiene alguna objeción que hacer?».

—¡No!, contestamos todos.

Cuando después se nos informó que teníamos otro día más para los preparativos nos alegramos mucho. El día 29 trabajamos frenéticamente en la preparación de las casas y la repartición de las armas y los uniformes.   ·nie

Por la noche, nos acuartelamos. La ciudad parecía normal, pero por la madrugada muchas familias empezaron a notar la a___ __ de sus ___ios, esposos o herma___ ____ sobre____ ____ te-

combatientes habíamos pasado toda la noche despiertos y naturalmente nerviosos. Se repartió café con leche y galletas, que casi nadie ingirió. Con intensa emoción, nos pusimos por primera vez nuestro uniforme del 26 de Julio, color verde olivo, con brazaletes negros con letras rojas y con arreos militares.

No es necesario afirmar que el momento era dramático y todos nos hallábamos impresionados de tal manera por esa hermosa cruzada libertaria que el ánimo crecía y nos dominaba íntegramente. En mi grupo nos iban repartiendo las armas. Se nos informó que como éramos muchos más hombres que armas, la Dirección ordenaba que los hombres casados o con responsabilidades familiares se quedaran en reserva hasta que se les llamara.

Tony Alomá, nervioso, gritó:

—Nadie puede quitarme el derecho de pelear por Cuba. He esperado demasiado tiempo para ahora quedarme quieto...

—No, Tony, tú acabas de ser padre esta misma noche; si caemos tú tomarás el lugar de nosotros...

___ mo Otto va___ ___cía refiriéndose a

Revolución, with Frank País article on November 30 Santiago de Cuba uprising. The slogan at top reads: "There will be no peace with Batista!"

clothes headed by Parellada were to move in and take positions behind the building.

Time passed at a dizzying speed. Before leaving we embraced one another. We carried hand-held machine guns, rifles, grenades, Molotov cocktails, and a .30-caliber machine gun. We had some cars but we needed more. So we stopped several that were passing in front of the place we were leaving and told the owners:

"At this very moment the revolution in Cuba is beginning. The homeland asks you to sacrifice your car. On behalf of the July 26 Movement, we're going to fight the dictatorship. We're sorry, but it's necessary."

Amazed, naturally, they gave us their vehicles. I remember one man said to me: "Be careful, boys. Cuba greatly needs you."

The first battle begins

Parellada's group came down Padre Pico Street, entered the School of Visual Arts, crossed the courtyard, and reached the roof overlooking the rear of the police station. But a sentry saw us and opened fire, starting the unequal battle: 28 revolutionaries against 70 policemen and 15 soldiers.

Those of us with Pepito were going up the hill toward the station when the enemy opened fire with a machine gun they had set up on top of the building, preventing us from reaching the door in the cars we had seized. Pepito jumped out of the car, shouting fiery words to us. We took positions and began firing. A tremendous machine-gun duel ensued. Our war cries were heard in the midst of the intense exchange of fire:

"Long live the revolution! Down with Batista! Long live the July 26 Movement! Long live Fidel Castro!"

Moments later, uncontrollable flames swept through the headquarters building.

In silence the enemy fired back. The compañeros at the back of the building inflicted several casualties on the policemen running in the courtyard. Smoke and flames began to rise very slowly. Pepito saw Tony Alomá fall with a shot to the head and became very agitated, since he had been the one who had tried the hardest to stop Tony from coming. In this state, he got up and gave the order to advance. As we followed, Pepito fired his m-1 to protect the rest of the column behind him. When he turned the corner, a burst of fire wounded him in the leg. Leaning against the wall he continued advancing, firing nonstop. Another burst knocked him down forever.

In the meantime, Parellada, seeing that we had not been able to reach the main door, tried to draw the enemy's fire onto his group. He attempted to reach the courtyard, but fell to the ground face up, with a shot in the head. Having lost the surprise factor, with heavy fire raining down on us and two leaders killed, we began an organized retreat, with cover provided by the firing of our .30 machine gun. Three of our comrades had fallen. The enemy had lost five.

Moments later, the uncontrollable flames swept over the station completely. Had we waited before advancing on the station, we would have wiped out all the defenders of the Batista stronghold.

Something occurred at the police station that we do not wish to pass over. A policeman who was retreating while the flames were gaining force wanted to open the door to the jail where several young men from Santiago had been kept since the previous night. The cop wanted to prevent those arrested from being burnt to ashes. But Lieutenant Durán, expelled from the army for being a criminal and restored to his post by Batista, gave the following order:

"Retreat! Let them all burn so they won't make any more revolution!"

In desperation, the young men watched the flames do their macabre dance around them. Abandoned by the policeman who had the keys, they began to be burned. In terror, with legs, arms, and other parts of their bodies covered in flames, some tried to force open the padlock, already reddened by the fire, while others prayed. Endless minutes went by until the firemen arrived and opened the cell door.

The harbor master's office falls

We were more fortunate in the action at the harbor master's office. Several armed compañeros, wearing workers' clothes, took three posts by surprise and disarmed them. Wearing uniforms, the rest of the men drove cars right up to the very door of the office and went in. When the sentry attempted to open fire, he was cut down by a burst of our fire. Two more cops fell dead. The lieutenant in charge, wounded, shouted:

"Don't shoot, boys, we're with you!"

"Down with Batista!" shouted other frightened policemen, in unison with us.

We had instructions from our general command to respect the lives of our prisoners. We took the weapons of those we captured. Meanwhile, on the ground floor the police opened fire but were silenced by our sharpshooters, stationed on nearby roofs.

Finally they surrendered and the position fell into our hands.

Amid cries of happiness and revolutionary curses against Batista and the tyranny, we began to pick up the ammunition, the weapons—some 20 rifles—and to take care of the wounded cops. They had 4 dead. We came out unscathed from this first encounter, but two trucks arrived with 70 soldiers from the Moncada garrison carrying heavy weapons, and an unequal battle began. Finally we retreated, under the cover of a curtain of lead. We withdrew to our command post. The barrel of one of our machine guns nearly melted, such was the trial by fire to which it was submitted. The leader of our group fired nonstop while another fed it more ammunition.

After retreating two blocks, a brave comrade realized he had left behind a handkerchief of his girlfriend and other documents. So with the .30 machine gun loaded and blazing he returned to the line of fire. He recovered the items, and withdrew once more. The army was so frightened they did not pursue us. . . .

At Corona Street there was another battle when a group of compañeros attempted to reach us, amid intense fire from the army. Several soldiers were wounded and picked up in military trucks.

A fundamental objective: Moncada

With our mortar battery failing to fire, and having been located by the enemy, it was not possible to carry out the assault on the

Moncada garrison, where the Cuban revolutionary youth wrote a beautiful page of courage and idealism on July 26, 1953.

The plans for the attack were to blockade it, torch it, and carry out other simultaneous actions. As the army fought to break through the blockade at several points, an intense exchange of fire occurred between our forces and Batista's. Our people, posted nearby, intercepted the soldiers who fell wounded or dead facing our barricade.

Many soldiers at Moncada refused to fight against the revolutionaries. Sixty-seven were arrested and court-martialed afterwards.

A .30 machine gun was set up opposite the frigate *Patria*, which was in port. The ship withdrew to the entrance of the bay, with its crew at battle stations.

The people of Santiago

Four compañeros arrived at the Dolores hardware store and pointed their guns at the owner, saying to him: "Pardon us, but we need these weapons to fight for Cuba's freedom."

A soldier who was having coffee at a nearby cafeteria threw himself to the floor on his stomach.

The streets were being guarded by members of the Revolutionary Army. A citizen asked:

"Can we get through?"

"Of course. Just stay close to the sidewalk. This is yours!"

A soldier who was traveling in a bus attempted to fire at the revolutionaries standing guard, but they closed in on him. Without our having to fire, he decided to flee.

We installed our command post at an appropriate location. We surrounded a house and asked to speak to the owner.

"We need this house for the revolution. We're sorry to bother you, but we want your permission and we ask you to leave with your family. Take all your jewelry and money. We trust our comrades, but if we have to withdraw, these things could be in danger from the other side.". . .

Those were hours of enormous tension. With guards stationed

outside, we prepared all the details in that house. After 6:00 p.m.
Santiago became a hell. The city became a generalized crossfire.
Weapons of all calibers spewed out fire and shrapnel. Alarms and
sirens from the firefighters at the Moncada garrison, and at the
Navy. The sound of low-flying planes. Fires all over the city. The
Revolutionary Army controlled the streets, and Batista's army intended to take away that control. The shouts of our comrades, repeated by the people, and a thousand other indescribable events
and emotions.

The entire population of Santiago, emboldened and allied with
the revolutionaries, cooperated with us as one. They cared for the
wounded, hid the armed men, safeguarded the weapons and uniforms of those being pursued, encouraged us, lent us their houses,
and watched out from place to place, letting us know of the army's
movements. The sight of a people cooperating courageously during the most difficult moments of the fight was beautiful. When
the first plan basically failed—due primarily to the fact that the
mortar battery would not fire, preventing the attack on Moncada—
our forces began to retreat to the command post.

These were difficult and anguished moments. Three of our best
comrades, brothers of ideals, had left their generous blood on the
streets of heroic Santiago. We were no longer nervous or frightened, as we had been before going into combat. We were now battle-
hardened, and inside us burned the desire to continue fighting, so
that our goal of liberation would not be cut short.

Plan no. 2

We put Plan no. 2 into effect, which we had studied beforehand
in order to take contingencies into consideration. It consisted of
withdrawing, taking control of the city's heights, and beginning a
war of snipers. There was a battle at the high school, where our
comrades fought heroically. All day Friday the shooting was intense. Planes flew very low. We fired at them from wherever we
were, and pierced the gasoline tank of one that had to land, damaged.

On Saturday the battles continued. The army, frightened, fired at anyone, killing several passersby, as in the well-known case of the two cars that collided.

On Sunday, given the uselessness of continuing the fight under such disadvantageous conditions, we ordered a retreat. Weapons were to be put away. We would await another opportunity to relaunch the struggle until victory or death.

In Guantánamo

At the Elia sugar mill our comrades captured the Rural Guard garrison, taking it by surprise, setting the prisoners free. Singing revolutionary songs and shouting revolutionary slogans, they walked through the town shooting at the Guantánamo garrison and then withdrawing to the countryside. The city backed the general strike, stopping all activities, closing shops, and reviving its tradition as one of Cuba's most combative towns.

Meanwhile, our armed fighters took over the hills, interrupting public services. When the army arrived with workers who had been brought in by force to work or restore the services, our comrades' gunfire forced the soldiers to retreat.

In the hills our fighters set an ambush, killing several members of the military by throwing hand grenades.

Plan no. 3

Plan no. 3 began to be carried out immediately: sabotage of public services, burning of sugarcane fields, setting fire to large estates, etc. Fifty days after the heroic November 30, the situation is extremely violent in Santiago de Cuba and throughout the eastern province. The forces of public order, incapable of controlling the situation, began to carry out a barbaric massacre. More than thirty murders are public knowledge, making the entire citizenry tremble with rage. They protest not only the Batista regime's fury, but have together risen up against the acts of the vandals and of the tyranny that provokes and directs them.

In Oriente even the women have gone out into the street ready for battle. The mothers, just as in the great demonstration of days past, marched in a challenge to the janissaries represented by the evil officers Díaz Tamayo, Cruz Vidal, and Cowley. The mothers of all Oriente shouted with all their might:

"STOP THE MURDERS OF OUR CHILDREN! DOWN WITH THE MURDERERS!"

And when the mothers raise their voices like that, it does not take long before they see their promises fulfilled.

The eastern rebellion will not end until the tyrants have disappeared.

Support actions in Havana for the 'Granma' landing

Héctor Rodríguez Llompart

This account by a member of the July 26 Movement's underground in Havana, in which he describes the different actions that took place there in support of the *Granma* landing of December 2, 1956, was written specially for this volume.

Enrique Hart contacted us prior to November 30. Although I cannot say with certainty that he told me about Fidel's departure, he did insist and repeated vehemently that it was necessary to carry out, beginning then, "as many actions as we could, and with whatever we had" against the dictatorship. He used the latter words, since he knew our limitations in terms of arms and resources needed to carry out large-scale actions.

Along these lines Bebo Hidalgo has referred to how Enrique, Pepe Prieto, and Julio Alom threw Molotov cocktails that same November 30.

Héctor Ravelo found out from Enrique about Fidel's departure from Mexico, and together they began to mobilize the [action cells in the] municipalities surrounding Havana.

Pepe Díaz received Enrique's order to carry out a sabotage attack against the Modelo brewery as soon as news of the landing was received.

René de los Santos—who was hiding at the home of Alfredo Donate in Víbora—together with Enrique tried twice to blow up the liquified gas tank on Paso Superior, both times without success.

On December 4 we held a meeting in Centro Asturiano, organized and inspired by Enrique—who at that moment did not hold a leadership position in the Movement. In addition to Enrique and myself, also present were Héctor Ravelo, Bebo Hidalgo, Julio Alom, René Verdecia, Julio Bauta, and Fico Bell-Lloch. There we discussed the current situation and decided to carry out a series of actions that very day. . . .

That night the participants in the meeting, who were part of various action groups, began to carry out a plan to sabotage the electricity cables and phone lines. In most cases, this was done using 81 mm. Brazilian mortars that Faure Chomón had given us at the request of Enrique and Bebo.

Chapter 7

1957: From the Llano

If after Moncada Fidel became the undisputed leader of Cuban youth, after November 30 and December 2 the July 26 Movement came to be the main political center of opposition to Batista. In the country's eastern region this had been the case in some ways even earlier. But now we were able to organize and carry out large-scale action there by the people.

The unity of revolutionary forces in the eastern region developed with undisputed authority under Fidel's leadership, and under Frank's immediate command in the Llano. It was not a question of exercising political control in an absolutist manner, since the population there had been radically Fidelista ever since the days of Moncada. In late 1956, however, and early 1957 Oriente assumed a national political authority it had not enjoyed since the time of the 1868 war. Santiago and the Sierra became the capital of the revolution. After the great events that had occurred, the political upsurge seething in the eastern region took on profound and radical revolutionary characteristics.

In those days the two decisive fields of action in the struggle—the Sierra and the Llano—began to be precisely demarcated. Events leading up to this included the meeting described previously in the foothills of the Sierra Maestra between representatives of the combatants of November 30 and the *Granma*; the initiative that created the Civic Resistance Movement based in Santiago de Cuba; the ideas drawn up to restructure the July 26 Movement nationwide and the initiation of that work; the trip made by Frank and Faustino to reorganize the Movement in the capital and the first steps in that direction; the efforts to publicly spread the news that Fidel was in the Sierra and was initiating a guerrilla war; Faustino's ideas and initiatives to form a guerrilla front in the Escambray mountains and Frank's ideas to develop the guerrilla struggle in the zone that would later become the Second Eastern Front under the leadership of Raúl; and lastly—what was most urgent then—the sending to the Sierra Maestra of an armed group composed of the November 30 combatants.

For us in the Llano, it was vital to maintain the Sierra. That was considered our first, our fundamental revolutionary obligation. The triumph of the revolution depended on the success and maintenance of the guerrilla nucleus operating in the mountains.

In those days Frank described to me the process that would be unleashed starting with the combatants in the mountains. He had a very clear idea of how the victory against the tyranny was going to be achieved.

Two individuals, Celia and Frank, were to play key roles in the relations between the Llano and the Sierra as this history unfolded.

I remember the first time I heard someone speak of Celia, many months before the *Granma* landing. Compañeros Pedro Miret and Ñico López had traveled to Santiago to make contact with Frank, tour Oriente province, and analyze possible areas we could turn into zones of revolutionary combat. The decisive point of that trip was the Manzanillo region. They returned happy about the possibilities they found there, where Celia and other compañeros had organized insurrectional groups and were promoting the popular movement against the tyranny.

Deeply involved as we were in our underground work, giving priority to the problems related to obtaining weapons for the struggle, Ñico and Pedro brought us their impressions on an emerging popular movement in Manzanillo with highly advanced ideas. And the compañeros brought Fidel useful information for the successful development of the struggle.

The first time I saw Celia was in Havana, when she came asking us to give authorization and help find her a way to travel to Mexico, so she could be part of Fidel's expedition. But Frank wanted her to remain in Manzanillo and organize support for the landing. Afterward it was confirmed that her work in the zones of Pilón, Niquero, and Manzanillo was invaluable in enabling the expeditionaries to penetrate the Sierra.

Before she began working directly with Fidel—and thus before she could show her qualities as an organizer and her exceptional executive capacities at his side—she was already one of the most outstanding leaders of the underground movement in Oriente, and was regarded as a valuable pillar of the July 26 Movement.

From the months prior to the *Granma* landing up until her death, there was not one episode in the revolutionary struggle led by Fidel in which Celia did not appear in the front line of combat.

Not only did she draw close to the Movement. The Movement drew close to her. Celia exerted a remarkable and growing political influence in those days among the poorest sectors of the population of Manzanillo.

Her intense organizational activity in support of the expedition in Manzanillo, at the gateway to the Sierra Maestra, helped organize the rearguard for the Sierra. And she became the main contact between the rebel groups commanded by Fidel and the underground movement that operated in the rest of Cuba, especially in Oriente.

Her capacity to get things done, her gift for turning the most daring project into reality, her formidable concern for every detail was evidenced from those moments on.

It's true that Celia had great influence in Manzanillo among various popular sectors, which was extraordinarily useful for the work she did. But the value of her efforts lies in the fact that, although known by wide sectors of the population, she always managed to work clandestinely in the zone, prepare audacious operations, and not be discovered.

Once the rearguard was assured, she started working in earnest with Fidel in the Sierra, and she emerged as one of the most important bulwarks of the guerrilla movement. She came to be the main link between the Sierra and the Llano, Fidel's top assistant, and a symbol. In the Sierra she was not only the heroine of the war. She was also the heroine of work. In her, legend acquired real form and content.

She had lived intensely the clandestine life in Oriente and was closely acquainted with the feelings and problems of the underground combatants. She was one of them! From the Sierra she fulfilled the role of compañera to all and offered her fraternal help. She worried about the smallest details and personal concerns we faced.

She had the capacity for giving, personal selflessness, human sensitivity, and the great gentleness that only women are capable of. Every injustice to be righted, every problem to be solved, every question of revolutionary concern that needed her involvement was taken on by her with firmness, modesty, love, determination, and a fervent revolutionary spirit. She was like justice itself: human yet demanding. Perhaps it was this combination—which life shows to be exceptional—together with her popular sensibility and her modesty, that helped her identify herself politically with Fidel so completely and deeply.

She was a typical Cuban in her joyfulness and dynamism, in her outgoing, open, fraternal, human, yet demanding and rigorous character. She never ceased being the *guerrillera* of the eastern mountains, who liked to sleep in a hammock or follow a mountain path. Her roots among the people, which molded her consciousness as a combatant, were a weighty part of her very nature.

And in this she was an example. Her devotion to the cause knew no bounds. She was also a creator who focused on carrying out concrete tasks useful to the revolution. She worked without rest and gave herself fully to her country. She had a passion for history. But more than any other virtue, she was great because of her simplicity.

She should be regarded as a genuine representative of the people during the stage when Fidel and our movement changed the course of history of the Americas. She is like Che and Camilo. She passed into history as they did, as one of the purest symbols of the Cuban people.

Her absolute commitment will remain forever in the hearts of the people as an example of unsurpassed loyalty. This most native flower of the revolution is undoubtedly an essential thread for understanding its history.

There are three important milestones through which Celia began to leave her imprint on the history of the revolution: First, the organizational work accomplished in the zones of Manzanillo, Pilón, and Niquero prior to the landing, through the vast underground network she created there prior to the *Granma*. Second, the tenacious work of the revolutionaries in the zone in the weeks from December 2, 1956, to February 17, 1957, when the interview with Matthews mentioned earlier took place. And third, the successful operation she helped organize to bring an armed detachment up to the Sierra.

That operation, carried out in the early months of 1957, consisted of moving an armed contingent of some sixty men from Santiago and other parts of Oriente to Manzanillo, sheltering them in *marabú* thickets for over two weeks a few kilometers from the entrance into the town and just steps from the Bayamo-Manzanillo highway, and then moving them to the Sierra. These were tasks that demanded courage, organizational ability, handiness, talent, and audacity. Without a doubt, that first enlistment of men and weapons from different zones of Oriente to the Sierra was of extraordinary value in sustaining the guerrilla nucleus and allowing it to develop later on. For weeks, Celia, together with Frank and several other compañeros, worked without rest in that endeavor. In fact, the two of them were the heart and soul of that operation.

Three North American boys who lived at the Guantánamo Base—Victor Buehlman, Chuck Ryan, and Michael Garvey—participated together with the young men from Oriente province in that first armed reinforcement to the Sierra.

On several occasions I was in the *marabú* thickets with Celia, talking to the compañeros about different organizational questions and giving encouragement to the combatants.

※

Seldom have I felt so good as I did when I was able to help Frank take the initial steps to restructure the underground movement after November 30 and December 2.

The objective we longed for was to organize a general strike in the country and unleash a nationwide insurrection, which—according to the conception we had at that time—would enable us to devote ourselves to attacking the garrisons and plunging the tyranny into crisis.

We looked for young men who did not have links to the past, as well as professionals, teachers, and intellectuals. We tried to establish links with the workers. None of us conceived of a Movement leadership without the presence of a leader or representative of the workers.

Our perspective was to organize a national workers' front in order to develop a broad mass movement among the workers. Participating in the initial foundation work for such a front were, among others, Ramón Álvarez, of the workers section of the Orthodox Party, along with Octavio Louit *(Cabrera)*, Gustavo Fraga, and Antonio "Ñico" Torres, who came from an active trade union movement in Guantánamo. In Havana we worked with David Salvador.

＊

Rereading some of Frank's letters and various circulars from those days confirms the high level of political development and revolutionary value of the organizational ideas prevailing among us, which we had reached by ourselves.

In those days, on behalf of the leadership of the Movement in the Llano, I held a wide-ranging discussion with Carlos Rafael Rodríguez, who represented the Popular Socialist Party and had come to discuss with us the new political situation that had been created.

＊

After the events of November 30 in Santiago de Cuba, the idea arose of organizing the Civic Resistance Movement nation-wide. With a leadership made up of the most progressive elements, under the guidance of the July 26 Movement, the new formation received the support of broad professional sectors, of the urban middle class, and of the great mass of the population. It was later extended to Havana.

The Civic Resistance Movement was different from the professional institutions and organizations that functioned as part of what we could call prerevolutionary civil society. The idea we sketched out in Santiago and on which we started working had a much more profound social character, since it involved a mass organization that served as support to the underground struggle, an arm of the Movement structured on the rank-and-file level through groups of cooperation for different purposes. It developed this way throughout the country. It had the support of important sectors of the bourgeoisie and of professional sectors in Santiago that had a marked patriotic character.

This movement was formed to bring together many honest men

and women with whom we might have disagreements of a programmatic nature or over tactics of struggle, but who at the same time were without question a force against the tyranny.

Along the way, almost all the members of the Civic Resistance joined the July 26 Movement, but for class reasons there were some who abandoned the revolution. The Civic Resistance Movement was not the July 26 Movement, but a force supporting it.

Starting from the guidelines and work of the Civic Resistance Movement, we encouraged the development of citizens' consciousness against the regime and in favor of our cause throughout the country.[1]

※

In the meantime, Faustino insisted on opening up a guerrilla front in Las Villas. In February, when we met with Fidel, the initiative was approved.

I was working hard to reorganize the July 26 Movement, the Civic Resistance, and a Student Front. We began to create the latter starting in Oriente, since we had relations with different high schools; among these was a nucleus that functioned inside the School of Commerce. There we dealt in particular with Joaquín Méndez Cominches.

In Santiago, the home of Arturo Duque de Estrada had become an important center of the July 26 Movement. Duque acted as Frank's secretary and was in charge of the organization's most important papers.

In those days, the places I stayed at most were Vilma's house on San Jerónimo Street, Arturo Duque's home, Santos Buch's laboratory and his private residence, the home of Cayita Araújo and María Antonia Figueroa, and Silvina's boarding house in San Agustín, where underground combatant Agustín Navarrete

---

1. For a more detailed view of the Civic Resistance Movement, I recommend the book by José María Cuestas, *La Resistencia Cívica en la Guerra de Liberación de Cuba* [The Civic Resistance in Cuba's Liberation War]. [AH]

(Tin) lived in addition to Yeyé and myself.

The Movement's authority was growing; it increased day by day. In Santiago there was such an abyss between the people and the army that we moved as we pleased throughout the entire city, we visited and held meetings in various parts of Santiago. Many times I went from San Jerónimo Street to Arturo's house, covering several blocks by foot. On the way I passed right by the provincial government, a place guarded by many police. It's amazing that the police did not identify us; it also seems miraculous that in spite of the large number of inhabitants of Santiago who knew us and collaborated with us, it was not until later that the regime learned of some of these places. In reality, Santiago and its population belonged to the July 26 Movement, and the army was isolated.

Faustino and Frank arrived in Havana to carry out the missions entrusted to them after the *Granma* landing, and they started restructuring the Movement. In the capital the organizational work was more difficult due to Havana's complexity as a big city, and the situation became further complicated since there were many different tendencies and interests.

On January 3, 1957, I sent the following letter to my brother Enrique to explain my viewpoint and assessment of the Movement in Havana:

Dear brother:

This is for you and for all who have truly worked there. . . .

In general, as you may already have learned from Luis's trip, we have reason to feel optimistic. Particularly those of us who viewed the effort made as the beginning of the end. Our joy is only dampened by the pain of certain losses, and the anguish of seeing the dramatic situation the country is unfortunately going through. It is terrible to realize that Cubans with whom we came to identify as brothers during months of work are now gone forever. That is the case with Ñico [López], Raulito [Suárez], Cándido [González], and so many others with whom— even if we did not deal with them directly—we were united by powerful bonds of common ideals and social objectives, the first element of all patriotic sentiment. In them, Cuba had great and beautiful reserves without knowing it precisely. There are so many petty politicians, so many useless beings, so many individuals young in age who wander about the cliques of fashionable politics in pursuit of bastard aspirations. Meanwhile youth in full bloom plunge into the revolutionary struggle out of a sense of historical duty, and fall in the struggle or gradually lose parts of one's life itself in order to identify themselves more and more with the ideals and the most urgent needs of the people. That blood leaves a deep mark on each one of us—whether we want it to or not—and makes firmer our duty to continue along the road we have set out on.

My optimism regarding the future of the revolution comes from seeing thousands and thousands of men and women willing to make all the sacrifices and work tirelessly for a cause that does not belong to anyone in particular but to all in general. It also comes from seeing how—at least in this province and I hope in all of Cuba—the Movement is definitively rooted in the people. It comes, above all, from the appreciation that this time the best elements of our generation remain and possess a force that can determine the course of events.

A new generation has taken root in history once and for all. Its cadres are intact, its desire to fight is stronger than ever, and its influence on the future of our country is on the rise. All that is lacking are the material instruments—which a growing movement will easily obtain, and which, given our popular strategy, it will be possible to secure in many different ways—and for the organization and social conditions of the revolution to mature a little more. In reality, only the first two aspects were lacking for the immediate triumph. Because for the latter, our objective was to give an impulse to and specify the change in social conditions that an immediate victory would have on the majority of Cubans. Besides, when it comes to material instruments, with the organization's greater maturity we can be ready and prepared to use effective means to obtain them.

As a result of the events and the painful experience of certain deficiencies, the Movement's cadres can now close ranks to make those means truly effective. Our sacrifice, our strategy, and the immediate policy we are going to follow will give an impulse and consolidate the conditions of the revolution that are external to us. From this experience, and thinking about all the work carried out throughout the island, I have drawn the following lessons:

1. One weakness can wipe out months of persistent effort. . . .

2. Only those persons who are willing to commit themselves fully are to be counted on for leadership responsibilities. . . . I know that some of you already realized this truth years ago. . . .

3. The dissemination of doctrine among the membership and leadership is posed more than ever as a fundamental question. It is essential to turn the newspaper into a necessary part of our functioning. Revolutionary schools must be organized immediately. The exchange of ideas on each of the vital questions we are analyzing and on the events that are taking place is something to which we must devote time in our work. Reality has shown that we are now in a position to focus our energy along these lines.

One of the objectives of this letter is precisely to initiate the exchange of ideas I refer to. . . .

We must publish as soon as possible the ideological pamphlet—for which I have already raised part of the money. . . .

4. Propaganda should be directed not only to the people but also to economic classes, political leaders, etc. In practice we have always somewhat underestimated these types of people whom we have to try to influence with our position, with our firmness, and with the concrete explanation of our true aims, because they will only act in a way useful to us the day they fear us in recognition of our strength. . . .

That is my aim in the two public letters addressed to the press and the political organizations. We must skillfully cause these people either to become completely inhibited or else to confront us openly. It would be a fantastic propaganda device to drive them to hysteria in face of our firmness. I think every single crime, every single murder must be denounced, so that they will be turned into accomplices if they too do not denounce them. Of course, this should be accompanied by propaganda directed to the people, in which they are told of everything that is being done. . . .

We are writing a public letter to the main U.S. magazines explaining to them what is really happening in Cuba and sending them our proclamation. We can have an influence on them. Remember that *Life* published very important things in the recent past. Even the *New York Times* has published editorials favorable to us, if you analyze what this newspaper represents. It goes so far as to refute Batista concretely when he called us mercenaries. If that's the case, why can we not influence those important media organs with our propaganda? And the effects of this influence—however minor—are so great that they cannot be appreciated at first sight.

5 Discipline is indispensable; it is preferable to have an excess of discipline than a shortage of it. It must arise from the respect inspired by those who lead the revolutionary tasks. Where there has been discipline, as in Santiago, the organization has turned out to be more effective.

All right, compañeros, these are my conclusions—perhaps somewhat lengthy—on our current situation and the immediate future of the revolution. I intend to organize here one of the schools I've spoken to you about. I think that others should be organized there and elsewhere. I propose the name "Antonio [Ñico] López" for the revolutionary school in Havana. No one deserves it as much as he, a true lover of the revolution—as Luis described him—and someone who was truly convinced of the imperative need for these schools. We should remember him especially when we consider that it was he of all the members of the leadership who was most correct theoretically when it came to the strategy to follow and the form of the struggle. The present reality has proved him right. It's a pity he cannot see it.

With all my affection,
Yours as a revolutionary,
Jacinto

In western Cuba a new force began to emerge that showed great capacity for action and developed an intense process of political agitation.

After November 30 another stage began in the capital, with very active revolutionary combatants who distinguished themselves as great leaders of armed actions. Many became martyrs of the revolution, among them Arístides Viera, Pepe Prieto, Sergio González *(El Curita)*, Gerardo Abreu, and Enrique Hart.

In those days the repressive forces located an important center of the recently restructured July 26 Movement in Havana. It was the apartment at 5th Avenue and A Street in Vedado, which had been rented by Enrique as an arsenal and depot for dynamite, petards, and bombs, and for preparing materials to be used later in actions by the underground movement in the city. Enrique was arrested. I heard the news through the commotion it caused in the press, and we confirmed it because one of the photos in the newspaper showed pieces of furniture from the room that Pedro Miret and his wife, as well as Yeyé and I, had used several months earlier.

The house at 5th and A Street became a symbol of the relaunching of the underground struggle by the July 26 Movement in Havana. Despite this setback, there were more and more actions in the city, and the work of the July 26 Movement, which had organized an important center of action and sabotage, began to be felt.

In those days also some negative currents began to appear, however, exemplified by those who went into exile after the revolution.

In the meantime Faustino had become the real leader of the underground struggle in the capital. He was respected by the action groups and had a great capacity for establishing relations with all social and political groups. Frank in Oriente and Faustino in Havana, as I see it, are the highest symbols of the underground that supported the Sierra Maestra.

I was linked to Faustino by a deep friendship, since we had been together in the MNR, in the events of 222 Salud Street, and we had participated in various actions sharing the exact same political conception. We had both been involved in organizing the July 26 Movement since mid-1955.

Faustino was a man made of a single cloth, revolutionary and patriotic. Clean, authentic, astute. He was calm when speaking and listening to others, but inside he had the fire of a rebel temperament, intransigent against all injustice.

If in Ñico that fire burst out in formidable political and social agitation, in the case of Faustino, with the same human passion, the flames came out gradually from the soul, and he transformed them into facts and deeds, as well as calm speech.

He had the human fiber needed to deal with others, and this was at the center of his revolutionary calling. He was a genuine politician along the lines of Martí. Though he might have disagreements with others, he was capable of discussing, acting, and understanding them. His conduct and life as a revolutionary were devoid of any sectarianism. At his gravesite, Pedro Miret characterized him, in an eloquent phrase, as "humble yet defiant." How difficult it is to unite those two virtues in one soul! Behind these values is a humanistic sense of life, which he possessed with tenderness and firmness.

A complete man in the strictest sense of the word, his passion for working with people was one of his principal merits. It is difficult to find in a single person one who combines a combative character with the capacity to understand people in all their variety. That combination is achieved only by those who have a concrete sense of what is human, as the first and most important thing that revolutionaries must defend.

✳

In those days I traveled a lot between Manzanillo, Bayamo, and Santiago on organizational assignments, particularly for the Civic Resistance and to organize propaganda. In Guantánamo there existed an underground movement inside the naval base, from which even weapons were removed. Once I traveled with

Frank to that city and held various meetings. That was the last time I saw him.

I will always remember Frank as quiet and responsible, with the characteristics of a playful young man and an impressive youthful spirit. He was a tireless organizer, a man of few words but with developed political ideas and a great ability for handling human relations. Meticulous in details, of a particular sensibility and a refined temperament, with a passion for ethics and Cuban revolutionary history, he had a very precise grasp of the matters he was responsible for. I felt closer and closer to his personality in a revolutionary way.

On March 13, 1957, we were meeting with José Aguilera Maceiras, the recently appointed president of the Civic Resistance Movement, and other representatives of it, when shortly after 3:00 p.m. we were all shaken by news that the Batista government had been overthrown. The courageous summons by José Antonio Echeverría over Radio Reloj, and the heroic assault on the Presidential Palace, had aroused the admiration of the people of Santiago. We urgently left the meeting in search of news. The population was out in the streets moving about, interested in obtaining information and in a mood to celebrate the event.

Soon it became known what had really happened. A group of brave compañeros fell in the assault, and José Antonio was gunned down beside the walls of the University of Havana. I would like to pay tribute to those heroes by recalling the image I have of this great student leader.

A genuine mass leader, generous, courageous, with an outgoing personality, José Antonio Echeverría was the type of individual who was immediately liked by others. When you spoke with him, you felt that nothing was being hidden.

Since 1952 he had belonged to the FEU leadership as vice president in the School of Architecture, and he had wide support among the students. I met him there. When it became necessary for this organization to take on a revolutionary character and a stronger insurrectional dynamism, José Antonio emerged as the undisputed leader of the students. He stamped the organization with the force and revolutionary character of his fighting temperament.

He was greatly preoccupied with fulfilling the commitment he had made to Fidel in the Mexico Letter, and the main passion of what were to be his last days was to work to be true to it. José Antonio was one of those revolutionaries who not only makes a cold analysis of his duty and political activity, but also feels bound by it once he has given his word. He holds an outstanding place in the history of this revolution as the highest example of the students of the 1950s. The image of the best of the new revolutionary generation that was coming forward found expression in José Antonio's happiness and vitality, and the oath he had sworn to his people.

The twin dates—although different on the calendar—of November 30 and December 2 did not coincide in time with the heroic March 13 of 1957. Ideally the three events related to each other by history and by the revolutionary force they carried might have coincided in time, but reality does not occur in an ideal form; it does not happen the way we revolutionaries often dream. The important thing was that the strategy and leadership of Fidel tied together the significance of those far-reaching events for all time.

✳

At the end of March, Haydée and I were preparing to leave for Havana. On the eve of our departure, at the home of the Duque Estrada family, they dyed my hair to try to disguise me. We took the bus late at night, and when the first rays of sunlight began to appear in the morning, the effect—far from fulfilling its purpose—was just the opposite. We were very noticeable, and it made us conspicuous to those riding the bus; we were the center of attention. We decided to stay in Santa Clara in order to restore my former look, which, of course, we did not achieve completely. Weeks later I still had traces of that attempted change of appearance, done to avoid recognition by the police.

We arrived in Havana and discreetly went to my sister Marina's home. From there we began working with the compañeros and carrying out the tasks of reorganizing the July 26 Movement. One of our meetings took place at a laboratory in Vedado. We had a meeting with Faure Chomón, Julio García Oliveras, Fructuoso Rodríguez, and other leaders of the Directorate with the aim of having the two organizations close ranks. There they told me that the action at the Palace had been carried out to fulfill the commitment made in the Mexico Letter.

We had to strive to continue the effort begun by Frank and Faustino. The latter had been imprisoned around March 20. We began to organize the Civic Resistance Movement and to carry out propaganda activities. We now enjoyed great authority in the capital; we were respected and acknowledged as the main opposition force to the regime. Available to us were houses and relations with well-to-do people and those from the most diverse strata of the population.

In mid-April I received a message from Fidel through Celia. The text read as follows:

> . . . Tell Jacinto that the Movement's National Directorate has all our confidence; that it should act with full powers as circumstances require; that in many cases it is virtually impossible to consult each other in time; that I trust in his talent to find a way out of difficulties and to take the steps most appropriate for the definitive triumph of our cause. In short, tell him that the National Directorate may act as a representative of our Movement. I believe as he does: that nothing will stop the Cuban Revolution. . . .

❋

After a short time in the city, we established links with the U.S. journalist Robert Taber, an independent reporter hired by the Columbia Broadcasting System (CBS) television network, and with that network's cameraman, Wendell Hoffman. They were willing to prepare a wide-ranging report on Fidel in the Sierra Maestra. Haydée and I prepared to return to Oriente to carry out this mission.

It was almost nighttime on April 18 when we went to take the bus to Bayamo. Dr. Julio Martínez Páez had driven us in his car. He had helped us make contact with numerous people in Havana, since as a respected physician he had friends in broad sectors of the population. When we reached the station, Martínez Páez and I stayed in the car and Yeyé went to buy the tickets. At that moment, forces of the Bureau of Investigations appeared and, without giving us time to do anything, they arrested us. We knew it was them; by that time we could spot their people to perfection.

Yeyé realized immediately what was going on and managed to escape the henchmen by hiding in a nearby parking lot. From there she observed what happened.

Paradoxically they arrested us at a spot where it was easier to travel without being identified—the Virgen del Camino station—whereas at the bus terminal it was more difficult to elude the police.

Days later, when I was in jail, I learned with great satisfaction that Haydée, in addition to escaping, had been able to quickly inform our families of what had happened, which made it possible for them to denounce the arrest at once—because if you did not act quickly after an arrest, the price to be paid was murder. She also sought to immediately make contact with Marcelo Fernández, who had been entrusted on this mission with picking up the North Americans at the airport; she explained to him the new situation. Haydée traveled along with them to the Sierra, and was present throughout the reporting trip. Despite what had happened, the task was carried out successfully, and she was also able to deliver to Fidel five thousand pesos that had been collected.

Martínez Páez and I were taken to the Bureau of Investigations. I was accused of carrying firearms at the time of my arrest. The regime was so incompetent that it had to make up a story about firearms, even though they had arrested someone who had participated in the events of November 30, who was carrying out underground work in Oriente, who had gone up to the Sierra and come back down, and who had worked together with Frank País in sending the first armed groups that reached Fidel in the initial months of 1957—events that have all been described already in this account.

My family submitted a habeas corpus petition and took countless steps to try to have me brought before the court. In less than seventy-two hours I was taken to the Havana municipal jail. There I found a wide-ranging mass of youth and workers, among them Faustino, my brother Enrique, and many other members of the July 26 Movement. As the weeks passed following March 13, the political upsurge was growing, and we were already considered extremely dangerous.

As long as Batista maintained "constitutional guarantees" and "freedom of the press," we at the jail were able to carry out broad political agitation denouncing the regime during the many times we were brought before the Urgency Court.

*

As a political personality, Fidel's influence continued to grow. In those months Raúl Chibás and Felipe Pazos were in the Sierra to talk with him. Felipe Pazos had been president of the National Bank of Cuba during the constitutional government. He had links with the Authentic Party and particularly with everything that Carlos Prío Socarrás represented. Raúl Chibás at that moment was at the head of the Orthodox Party, but this was obviously due neither to political capacity nor revolutionary conviction—unlike his brother Eddy. Chibás and Pazos were both conjunctural allies of the July 26 Movement in the confrontation with Batista and in the framework of certain democratic political principles. But their interpretation of democracy did not coincide with our deeply popular conception.

*

On April 20 a large gang of police thugs headed by Col. Esteban Ventura Novo broke into the apartment at 7 Humboldt Street where compañeros Joe Westbrook, Juan Pedro Carbó, Fructuoso Rodríguez, and José Machado Rodríguez *(Machadito)* of the Revolutionary Directorate were staying.

Although the compañeros managed to get out of the apartment, they were surrounded and unable to escape. They were hunted down and murdered.

To protest this crime, all of us in jail decided to go to our trials wearing black ties and singing the National Anthem. On one of those occasions an altercation arose with the guard who was taking us, since he did not want to let us leave the jail singing the anthem. We resisted, and the Batista agent slapped me in the face. I kept singing and we immediately denounced the abuse in court. I knew very well that this complaint would have no legal effect, but what interested us was the political scandal we were creating with it.

Insurrectional activity was growing all over the country. From the old castle where the jail was, we heard the explosions of bombs that the July 26 Movement set off in the city as a popular response to the vicious tyranny.

Several times a week, we were transferred in the cage from Príncipe Castle to the courthouse. This was for hearings related to different trials at the Court of Exception, which they called the Urgency Court. The route was from the old castle up to 23rd and the Malecón, and from there to the old courthouse—later torn down—located behind the Palacio del Segundo Cabo (at that time the Supreme Court).

The courthouse was two stories high and all the hearing rooms of the Havana provincial courts were located there. It was a center where the tyranny passed "justice" on revolutionaries and where penal and civil "justice" was dispensed. On the way there, when we encountered people, we were greeted warmly and received expressions of solidarity that strengthened our revolutionary morale and our absolute faith in the justice of our cause.

In the back of that building was a staircase used by the line of prisoners to get to the second floor. There they were put in a room that had previously been a civil court and had become a waiting room for the accused.

I knew those buildings because of my participation as a lawyer in some political trials and legal complaints I had filed on numerous occasions. My father, who was a judge of the Civil and Administrative Court, also worked there.

During those transfers I observed that one of the guards remained below—at one end of the line of prisoners—while the other one went up and stayed at the front. For a few seconds he opened the hall and inspected it. I realized that by taking advantage of that brief moment I could leave the group and reach the nearby hall to the right. In that way I would be able to advance without being seen along the hall which would lead me to the main stairway that led to the big front door of the building, and also to a side door through which cars entered.

If not discovered immediately, someone could get away from the group, since they usually counted the prisoners inside the room—time enough to get out of the place. Of course the person would be seen by the compañeros and the few personnel on the premises of the courthouse at that hour of the morning. But I realized I had at least two or three minutes to get out of the building and disappear into Old Havana. When I was first thinking about all this, I had not yet been convicted and was taken to court in civilian clothes.

This idea was hammering unceasingly in my mind when I was sentenced to two years and transferred to the zone of Príncipe that was reserved for those convicted.

At the trial I rebutted the witness—an officer from the Bureau—and the court with the following statement: "I consider that I have the right to have weapons, because rising up in arms against this government is a right. But in truth I was not bearing arms, and you know that well." I was being convicted for something that was not true, since they lacked the courage to convict me for my actions, positions, and membership in the revolutionary movement.

Once sentenced, I was made to wear a prisoner's uniform. There was a protest against that, and they proposed to make an exception for me because I was a lawyer. I refused, however, since I was proud to wear the uniform of a prisoner of that government, despite the fact that being dressed that way made escape more difficult. I nevertheless kept the idea fixed in my mind, and decided to escape by taking advantage of the situation already described, as long as I could change clothes first. It was a simple matter. I asked my family to bring me a sweater, which I said I needed in the jail's cell block and they sent it.

On the morning of July 4—my brother Enrique's birthday— I again made the trip to the trial. As we had done many times before, we climbed the rear staircase and were taken to the waiting room upstairs. When we arrived, the guard went in to check it, while a group of us remained waiting outside. I calculated that I had only a few seconds, and kept walking along the adjacent corridor. One of the compañeros said to me: "It's not over there; it's to the left." I answered him: "I know where it is."

I advanced to the right of the second floor, took off the prisoner's shirt, and threw it to the floor. I headed toward the staircase that led to the front entrance, left through one of the main doors, and walked along the side of the Palacio del Segundo Cabo toward the old City Hall (today the Museum of the City of Havana). Behind this building I walked fast, but without running, until I got deep into Old Havana.

A few blocks away lived a family I knew. When I came in, the lady of the house became frightened and I said to her: "Don't worry. Give me some civilian clothes and some money. I'll leave immediately."

So dressed in a shirt and tie and with ten pesos in my pocket, I headed toward the building of the Ministry of the Treasury—

where the Ministry of Finance is located today. I took a cab and went to the home of a woman I had known for years as a student and in whom I had great personal trust, near the corner of Acosta Avenue and Dolores Street, in the Lawton neighborhood. But at my friend's house I found only the maid, who luckily did not know me. So I walked a few more blocks until I reached an apartment that I had frequently visited prior to the *Granma* expedition, where the family of one of the Moncada martyrs—Ramón Méndez Cabezón—lived. There I found his mother, sister, and other relatives. They were dumbfounded, because they had visited me in jail just a few days before.

From there I sent the following message to Yeyé and to the Movement through my uncle Gabriel Dávalos, who had a pharmacy on Dolores Street:

> Don't be alarmed. I'm all right. I beg you to do as I tell you below, and not mention it to anyone at all. My life is at stake. I entrust it to you in relation to this important message.
>
> Find Marinita's husband immediately. Ask him to notify right away the one he knows, telling him that I am at the home of the person who used to do typing for me. They should send for me urgently. Also tell him they should send a message to my home saying I'm all right.
>
> No one should know that you transmitted the message to this gentleman. You must go right away.
>
> I don't need to beg your pardon, because you understand me. I don't need to say thanks, because you love me.
>
> Tear this up.
>
> Yours,
Rogelio

My cousin Fernando Dávalos—Gabriel's son—went to my parents' house on 25th Street, almost at the corner of Paseo in Vedado. There, everyone was anxious and concerned. He informed them of the message he had received, and they got in touch with my sister Marina and her husband, who were in contact with Haydée. In the meantime, I heard on the radio about the big commotion my escape had caused. I thought there was no reason for such a fuss.

I recalled that several times I had been together with Ñico López at the house where I now found myself. There we had written proclamations and denunciations, a task in which Marta Méndez had helped us.

A few hours later, my sister Marina and her daughter, who was not yet a year old, arrived in a small car accompanied by María Angélica Álvarez and Marcia Leiseca. Through Yeyé they were both contacts of the underground movement.

We left the Lawton neighborhood, crossed the city, passed by the Bureau of Investigations, went over the Almendares Bridge, and arrived at a place in Miramar. There Germán Amado Blanco was waiting to take us to the residence they had prepared for putting up Haydée and myself. We could not stay there very long.

During those weeks we had to move to different safehouses, from which we kept on carrying out our work for the Movement.

The newspaper *Revolución* published in its "Latest News" section a statement I made regarding the escape:

> . . . Only the anguish of not being able to continue fighting actively for the Cuban Revolution made me run the risks of an escape. When all avenues were closed to defend in court the cause of the July 26 Movement, my spirit was filled with healthy indignation and I was driven to escape at a propitious moment.
>
> I am sorry for the guards, who may go through bad times on account of something that was not their fault or responsibility.
>
> I still accuse the members of the Urgency Court of Havana of convicting me when they knew that the crime I was charged with was false. I cannot take the case to the Supreme Court, but I affirm this before public opinion. I swear it before the martyrs of the revolution!
>
> Besides, all the people know how the Urgency Court proceeds. I simply report it so that the honest judges of Cuba may

know that this court denies due process and convicts defendants knowing that in most cases the accusers lie.

On the other side, despite having hard proof of my revolutionary membership in the July 26 Movement, the accusers still had to resort to lies. A government that cannot face the truth is a failure. The July 26 Movement has never lied because it faced the truth a long time ago: the need to take up arms and fight the tyranny. And with that great truth the Movement will conquer freedom.

During this time, on leaving a meeting of the Movement, I was about to get in a car, but I made a mistake and started to climb into the wrong car. From behind, Yeyé shouted at me: "That's not it!" I looked up and saw a police car surrounded by cops. A man, in an imperious tone, said to me: "Don't make a mistake." I apologized to the owner, continued ahead, and got in the right car. The other car was for Rafael Díaz-Balart's bodyguards. Had they recognized me, I would not be recalling these events now. From there, Yeyé and I left for a house near Colón Cemetery.

On another occasion, when I was staying at a residence in the Nuevo Vedado neighborhood, one after the other the whole family left for one or another reason. Only the two of us remained, completely on our own. Since this could give rise to suspicions, we decided to leave that place. We called my sister Marina who, along with her husband Rafael Dujarrí, took us to the other end of the city, to the home of some childhood friends. We managed to establish new contacts with the underground organization.

We revolutionaries are deeply grateful to the Cuban families who gave us their support in those days and offered their homes for our protection.

*

Around that time, one of the harshest moments of the struggle occurred. In the house where I was hiding I heard on television the terrible news that Frank País and Raúl Pujol had been murdered. It was July 30, 1957.

An extraordinary demonstration of the people of Santiago carried the remains of both combatants to Santa Ifigenia Cemetery.

Since I was not in Santiago, I prefer to present Vilma Espín's account of this event:

> Ten days before his death . . . Frank asked me to take over coordination of the province so that he could dedicate himself to actions on a nationwide basis and devote some time to writing and studying.
>
> Following that I had contact with Frank only by phone. After he left the house where I last saw him, he had moved to another; but a pregnant woman lived there, and she became very nervous out of concern he might be caught. He worried about this very much, and he went to a house that he himself had once rejected because there had already been an attempt to capture a compañero there. The compañero had managed to escape, but the house had no back exit. It belonged to a very trustworthy person—Pujol—but the house itself was a mousetrap. Frank phoned me two days before, asking me to make an important contact for an operation to send a compañero abroad to obtain weapons. When I called him later, he was no longer at home and he did not call me. Nor did he call the following day—much to my surprise because he used to call as soon as he changed houses so that we could be in contact with him. On July 30 I was hiding in a house near the zoo. Around four o'clock I got a call; they told me there was a big stir in the area where Pujol lived, but I didn't know that Frank was there. He had just phoned me twice. I had immediately started asking him why he hadn't called, and telling him the result of the tasks he had given me, but I talked very fast. Perhaps he was going to tell me something but I spoke first. He let me tell him everything, and hung up. About ten minutes later he called again, but I can't remember what he said to me—I think it was about the same mission he had given me.

At that moment he was about to leave, and he did not tell me anything about what was happening there, either.

After that, contacts we had at the Telephone Company called me; they told me there was shooting—I even heard the shots in the distance—and that someone was being chased on the roofs. I told them to inform everybody so that they would go there and see if they could help. . . .

They called me and asked if I wanted to listen in on Salas Cañizares's call to Tabernilla, if I remember correctly. I listened, and heard them say: "Hey, chief, I'm going to put on the guy who won ————." I don't remember exactly what he said, some dirty word. "Here's Sariol," and the latter said: "Are the three thousand mine, chief? We just killed Frank País." And right then the compañeros hung up on me. Amat cut me off from the call when he realized what they were saying, out of fear that I might speak and they could hear.[2]

It was terrible. We started to call around and found out the details. René Ramos Latour *(Daniel)* had been there shortly before to coordinate a task. He found Frank very depressed, because it was one month since they had killed Josué [Frank's brother]. He then left. Later came commander Villa—Demetrio Montseny—with a pickup truck. He wanted to take Frank with him, because they were already being surrounded. But Frank had already spoken with Pujol and Pujol was coming with a taxi to pick him up at the corner. So Frank said, "No, I'd better go with Pujol who is already on his way here. You go first." Pujol was not living in clandestinity. Then, when Pujol arrived he went up to the house to look for Frank. That cost him time, and as they were coming out of the house they were caught.

We have since more or less reconstructed what happened next, from Ñeña—Pujol's wife—and from Raulito, who was thirteen years old at the time. They were there and saw it all. They say that when Frank and Pujol came out, they were beaten

2. For information on the July 26 Movement's monitoring of telephone lines in Santiago de Cuba, see page 268, "Swift Action that Saved Armando Hart's Life."

and put into a car. Ñeña started running after the car, and the whole neighborhood came out too. The police realized that if they did not kill them quickly, they would not be able to kill them later—the same thing had already happened to them the last time. When they reached the alley, two and a half blocks down, the cops took them out and killed them right there.

That same afternoon we learned that it had been a woman who had fingered them—a mistress of Laureano Ibarra, who had seen Frank enter Pujol's place. They immediately got this woman out of the house and sent her to the home of a girl we knew from the university, the daughter of one of Laureano Ibarra's henchmen known as Black Martínez. It was all very fast. From there she was put on a ship that was in port and sent directly to Santo Domingo.

As part of the operation, [the police] had even brought the guy who had identified Frank once before at the garrison, someone named Randich. They had been classmates at the Teachers College. This Randich was brought to identify Frank after the woman said she had seen him. They brought Randich there and he was the one who identified Frank. So the police immediately surrounded the place. We later brought Randich to justice. But that was a terrible afternoon for all of us.

We immediately phoned Frank's mother and his fiancée, América Domitro, so they could go right away to claim the body.

Frank was lying in the middle of the street and all the people were gathering there. The area was cordoned off. The popular response was tremendous. Frank was dead and Santiago de Cuba was boiling. That same afternoon, the owners of establishments and people from the Civic Resistance began calling me to say that the people wanted to shut things down and go out on strike—bosses and workers, everybody. And indeed everyone came to agreement and began shutting things down.

At last I got [Frank's mother] Rosario on the phone. I told her: "You have to go down and fight any way you can, with your teeth—anyway you can—so that they hand over Frank's body to you." So then Rosario, who was a woman of great courage, went down there with enormous forcefulness.

He had already been taken to the coroner's when she arrived, because at first the people wanted to get close to the body and there was pushing and shoving with the cops. The popular response was spontaneous, very powerful, and from that moment on the city stopped—the people just flocked to Frank's body. Then the body was handed over. The police acted intelligently at that moment; what they did was to withdraw all the public forces to their barracks while the people crowded together around América's house, where the body was laid out in state.

There they dressed him in his uniform, because Frank had two well-defined callings, but I would say that the first one was that of a soldier, and the second that of a teacher. I insisted that they dress him in uniform with his beret on his chest—because he liked the beret very much and had used it for some time—and that a white rose be placed on top of the beret and the July 26 armband. In addition, the three-star rank corresponding to the new plan of ranks that he was preparing to send to Fidel.

The funeral procession was a demonstration by the entire people. Workplaces closed. There were no police anywhere; the whole city was taken over by the people. Those who were not going to the burial threw flowers as he passed by. There was the case of the men who belonged to the navy who waited for the funeral procession and stood at attention as it went by. These were the ones who, less than two months later, participated in the action at Cienfuegos (this I learned afterwards). . . .

The next morning [the day after the murder of País] U.S. Ambassador [Earl] Smith arrived, I don't know for what reason. I think the visit by him and his wife was meant to give an appearance of normality on the island, or something like that.

We immediately organized a demonstration of women in mourning who were to march to Céspedes Park facing City Hall, and make a lot of noise. Everybody dressed in black and went there. They clashed with the police. Gloria Cuadras bit Salas

Cañizares on his finger—almost tore it off. They were all attacked with water hoses. Nuria García was roughed up. Most
of these people could not go to the burial because they were arrested, but they managed to make a huge scandal.

The ambassador's wife, who was "unaccustomed" to watching such things so close up, was upset to see the police beating
the women, who were shouting, "Murderers!" Later in the afternoon women went to the funeral. There was a situation of
very great emotion and indignation. It was genuine. Frank had
enormous prestige. He was head of the underground action
movement of the entire island, not just in Oriente.[3]

Beginning on that day, a powerful strike movement broke
out in Santiago and throughout Oriente. Faustino, other compañeros, and I started taking steps to support it from Havana,
but it was not possible to extend the strike to the capital.

In those days I wrote an article in honor of Frank's memory,[4]
and also a letter to René Ramos Latour *(Daniel)* on August 5.
"Those of us who had the opportunity to work by his side have
an immense responsibility," I wrote to Daniel:

> . . . Underground work had become so deeply rooted in the
> consciousness of our generation and of the people of Santiago
> that his death caused a series of uncontrollable forces to erupt
> like a volcano.
>
> He had three things that are hard to come by: skill, a demand-
> ing attitude, and the capacity for action. This, together with his
> spiritual refinement, made him one of the great figures in our
> history. . . .
>
> Frank possessed a military spirit combined with a revolu-
> tionary education and a revolutionary vocation. These are just
> what Cuba needed to turn that great impulse into something
> directed and defined. . . .

3. From the magazine *Santiago,* June-September 1975.
4. See page 199, "Who was Frank País?"

Cuba is paying too high a price to overthrow this gang of butchers. . . .

And I ended, saying to Daniel:

We must go on, and we will go on. We have gone on. May destiny allow all of us—his friends—to together fill a little bit of the great void he left.

*

Beginning in August, I lived at 1606 First Avenue in Miramar, at the home of Luis Buch and his wife Conchita. From there I maintained close contact with almost all the provincial and municipal leaderships of the July 26 Movement, and I had relations with a variety of people. Nevertheless, the police did not manage to discover us.

During my stay in Havana I worked, together with Faustino, to begin reorganizing the Movement nationwide. The Civic Resistance became more combative.

Faustino and I were involved with what would become the September 5 uprising in the city of Cienfuegos. Months before, Haydée had maintained ties to the process that was incubating at the naval base in the Pearl of the South [Cienfuegos]. It had always been said that there was revolutionary influence in the navy—particularly in that city—going back to the days of Guiteras. This part of the armed forces was the one that came the closest to the July 26 Movement. In fact some of its messengers had been in contact with Frank País for months.

Julio Camacho Aguilera was entrusted with representing the Movement in Cienfuegos, since he was the coordinator for Las Villas province.

In Havana we were awaiting similar actions by the navy. On that historic day of September 5, 1957, the sailors in Cienfuegos closed ranks with the people, at the head of which was the July 26 Movement. As is known, that heroic action failed to have the hoped-for repercussions in the navy high command. In a September 15 letter to Fidel, Daniel described the actions:

> ... At a meeting held in Havana at the end of August, the plans to be implemented were worked out in detail. The navy would initiate the action at four points: Havana, Cienfuegos, Santiago, and Mariel. Once the action had begun simultaneously, our men were to take over a radio station (the National Network) and read a statement in which the people of Cuba would be informed of the uprising by the armed forces. In the name of the armed forces and of the Movement, the people and all our cadres would be requested to launch a general strike to support the action and carry out sabotage and armed struggle that would inevitably bring about the end of the regime. As a condition for making that public appeal, we asserted that the action must already have been started in Havana—that is, the statement would not be read until the first cannon shots were heard from the frigates.
>
> We had previously spoken to all the responsible people in the provinces, explaining to them what action we should carry out and when. There was a lack of coordination on the date picked by the navy, which was initially the 5th and later the 6th (it depended on the number of frigates in port), and because those responsible in the navy had not informed Cienfuegos of the change of date. Due to this lack of coordination, a disaster occurred whose consequences were suffered directly by the city's population.
>
> The uprising took place in Cienfuegos twenty-four hours before the agreed-upon date. They took over the district and gave weapons to militants of the Movement and to the people more broadly. By 10:00 a.m. on September 5, they completely dominated the city.
>
> The government sent reinforcements from Santa Clara (several tanks) and from Havana. Since the forces in revolt and armed civilians spread through the whole city taking up positions, the planes coming from Havana machine-gunned the

population indiscriminately and bombed several places, among them an offshore island used by the rebels as a refuge, where nothing was left standing.

Once the unit had been retaken by the regime at a cost of numerous dead—mostly on their side—they began to exterminate every sailor, policeman or civilian they thought had participated in the action.

The accounts of those who were there are gruesome, to the point of seeming exaggerated or made up. But the bitter reality is that these villains have shown clearly that they will stop at nothing to keep themselves in power. They have tried to take advantage of ironclad press censorship and the suppression of legal guarantees to cover up the uprising by the navy (to make it appear that it was civilians dressed as sailors) and the indiscriminate strafing and bombing of the population—unheard of in the history of the Americas. However, the truth has made its way throughout the nation, which looks with horror on this barbaric and monstrous deed.

Naturally, the conspiracy that had been discovered and had failed spread panic inside the government clique, and provided evidence of innumerable similar movements that were developing within the armed forces. . . .

Around ninety officers are under arrest, and there is great confusion within the armed forces.

Along with these events various actions were carried out by our cadres, mainly in Havana, Santa Clara, and Santiago. . . .

Warm regards,
Daniel

✳

Faustino continued working to open the Escambray front. After my escape one might have thought that the wisest thing for me would be to join our forces in the Sierra; undoubtedly, for me the danger was greater in the Llano, but I had agreed earlier with Frank to move to Santiago to help organize the

Movement there. Now, after his death, there was even more reason for me to go to Oriente.

In September 1957 I traveled by car from Havana to Santiago de Cuba with Luis Buch, his wife, and Yeyé. During the trip there were a number of routine stops at checkpoints, but I did not get out and we managed to reach the capital of Oriente without being recognized.

On arrival in the city I joined again in the work of the organization and in making contacts with the Sierra. At a meeting where Faustino, Daniel, Vilma, Haydée and I were present, it was decided that I take over national coordination of the Llano. The work would be based out of Santiago de Cuba, because that was the city where direct contact could be established with the Sierra, and from the point of view of internal organization it was the best place.

We were building on the work of the previous months, which, as is known, had been carried out under the direct leadership of Frank País.

In that period I wrote several letters to Fidel. On October 16 I sent one to explain to him all the decisions taken at the meeting mentioned above. On November 8 I sent him material with information on what we were doing and planning. I recall there was a document that evaluated the political situation as viewed by officials of the U.S. embassy. On November 22 I wrote to him about the execution of Fermín Cowley, as follows:

> The action in which he was brought to justice was meticulously prepared for months. . . . The action's success has caused such great commotion and happiness that the people toasted the event in bars and restaurants. How wretched must a country be to have the right to toast the death of a military chief. . . .

When Fidel left for Mexico in July 1955 I thought we were the group in the country with the best intentions, the most active, and with the greatest unity of purpose. But in the end we were only that: one group. I now realized that thanks to the heroism of the Sierra, and to the sabotage, agitation, and other work in the Llano, we had become much more than one of the groups; in reality we now represented the revolution.

In order to survive as an organized instrument in the Llano we had to maintain a firm and strict discipline. A sense of order and organization is not antagonistic to the terms *democracy* and *freedom.* "Discipline or severe sanction" was the alternative we posed.[5]

The sabotage and the burning of sugarcane fields, under the slogan "No sugar harvest with Batista," spread throughout Oriente in particular, but elsewhere throughout the country as well. These were forms of struggle against the tyranny employed by us, combatants of the July 26 Movement, without arms to defend ourselves from the actions of the regime's agents.

Around the end of November 1957, the Movement had planned to carry out intense agitation among students throughout the country,[6] in addition to the "Week of Resistance" from November 30 through December 7. We sent someone to the United States to ensure that, in commemorating the *Granma* landing, all the crimes committed by the tyranny since March 10 would be publicly denounced in a document signed on behalf of the July 26 Movement by mothers of a number of Cubans who had been murdered.

In order to guarantee the fulfillment of our first duty—acting as the Sierra's rearguard—those of us who were the organization's leadership had to organize the workers, the Civic Resistance, and we had to make sure that the provincial and municipal bodies were composed of true revolutionaries who, together with the Rebel Army, could guarantee the fulfillment of our program.

*

One morning, in the headquarters of the Catholic Association of Santiago de Cuba, we were meeting with trade union

5. See page 202, "To Members of the July 26 Movement."
6. See page 207, "To the Students of Cuba."

leaders of the July 26 Movement and the Civic Resistance when the sound of doors slamming was heard from the house next door. The repressive forces had arrived there, with Salas Cañizares at their head. One of the persons in charge of the association came up to us and said: "Stay calm, we'll say this is one of the meetings we usually have here." Our friend, who knew me, did not recognize me. Only when he became aware of my presence there a minute later, did he realize that audacity was the only possible escape. To flee, I had to hurl myself over a wall several meters high. When I fell in that "blessed" courtyard, my leg was injured so badly I could barely walk for several weeks. I spotted compañero Octavio Louit *(Cabrera)*, who helped me into a car. I had managed to escape once more.

*

In those days, Haydée and I lived and had our underground headquarters at the home of Dr. Ortega and his wife Eva Magi. I was immersed in my work of organizing and guiding the Movement when one afternoon in October Luis Buch arrived with some complicated information for us.

In short, the news was that a so-called Cuban Liberation Council—also known as the Miami Pact—had been created in the United States. It was composed of representatives of the Authentic Party, the Orthodox Party, the Revolutionary Directorate, students, and supposedly the July 26 Movement, and based upon an alleged unity of those organizations.

The members of the council claimed that it had been created to coordinate the opposition forces and to form a government once the tyranny had been defeated. But the truth is that it was organized without the participation of the July 26 Movement in Cuba. In the Llano we learned about this affair through the same channels as the people of Cuba—by public information—and specifically, through a mimeographed copy brought by Luis Buch.

The unity document was published by the foreign press before we knew of it or made a decision on its provisions. There was no reason or justification why members of the leadership in Cuba should have learned of this deplorable matter through the press, as a fait acompli.

On October 26 we sent a letter of reply, on behalf of the National Directorate, to those who had signed the pact representing the Movement, because—as is known—they had done so without consulting us.[7]

We made it clear to them that no member of the Committee in Exile could consider himself empowered to adopt important agreements without prior consultation with the members of the National Directorate in Cuba. Anyone who acted in this way risked being stripped of his authority.

In the letter we were conveying not our personal indignation—which of course existed—but the Movement's disagreement and intransigence, expressed objectively.

The compañeros from Santiago immediately instructed Buch to travel to Miami to repudiate the council. Faustino and the compañeros from Havana, who were also indignant about this situation, had acted similarly. Compañeros Mario Llerena and Raúl Chibás were designated by us to continue participating solely as observers; their presence implied no commitment. We thought that the public formulation of our repudiation should be made by Fidel.

In order to reject the alleged unity put forward in Miami, it was necessary to choose a president to take office after the overthrow of the tyranny. It was essential to select a person representative of the opposition to Batista, who would guarantee the fulfillment of the July 26 Movement program. However, all the figures—without exception—were committed to some political tendency of the past.

We met with the leadership of the July 26 Movement in Santiago de Cuba and pointed out the need to propose a provi-

---

7. The document was signed by Léster Rodríguez for the July 26 Movement; and Felipe Pazos, claiming to represent the signers of the Sierra Manifesto.

sional president of the republic. That would be our reply. Manuel Urrutia Lleó, the judge of the Oriente Court who had voted to acquit the November 30 combatants, seemed a good choice. We had to consult him to see if he would agree, and would be willing to have us submit the proposal to Fidel.

At the home of the noted Santiago physician Jesús Buch Portuondo, Luis Buch and I met with Manuel Urrutia. The latter told us he was willing to accept, and that he would do whatever the Movement indicated.[8] I asked Urrutia if he wanted to first go over this with someone he trusted, or with his family, and he answered that this was not necessary. I informed him then that we would submit the proposal to the Sierra and that when it became public, he would have to be outside Cuba.

For that reason, in mid-November 1957 I again went up to the mountains in the company of Tony Buch, who worked with me. This time our guide was a peasant named Eulalio Vallejo.

We reached the foothills of the Sierra, where we spent the night, and then we marched into the mountains for several hours on horse and by foot. After a long journey I found Fidel and the group of combatants. Raúl, Celia, Almeida, Ramiro, Guillermo, and Ciro Frías were there, among other compañeros; Che was not there because he had been assigned to operations in another zone. I stayed over a month with the guerrilla troops. During this time we analyzed all the details of the Miami Pact and dealt with various important matters. Fidel drafted a document in reply[9] in which he set down with radical firmness, our position in response to those events. A meeting was held in the Sierra with all the combatants and the document was read out to the unit. We later sent it to the Llano with Tony Buch to be pub-

8. Manuel Urrutia Lleó took office as president of the republic when the revolution triumphed and immediately showed himself incapable of exercising this high responsibility, hindering the implementation of revolutionary measures. In mid-1959, faced with popular repudiation, he resigned and later left the country. [AH]

9. See page 209, "Manifesto to the Nation: Response to the Miami Pact."

lished. This document had unquestionable historic significance in the struggle.

Attached to Fidel's declaration I sent this letter to Luis Buch:

DECEMBER 19, 1957

My dear Mejías:

Here goes the depth charge. Fidel agreed fully with the most radical point of view. Nevertheless, he agreed with naming Urrutia, and with a number of proposals that tend to lead us to a nonpartisan government.

We want you to speak with Urrutia and explain everything to him. Tell him on our behalf that Fidel and the Movement want him to accept, even though the rest of the organizations may be opposed. In any case he should remain always as our candidate for the provisional presidency of the republic. This document will be made public on December 26. It is therefore necessary that Urrutia leave Cuba before then. I think he already left, didn't he?

Everything is going well here. We have won great battles and there are zones entirely under the leadership of our forces in every sense.

Hoping to talk to you again soon . . .

My appreciation,
Alfredo[10]

I also sent a letter to Manuel Urrutia going over the decisions adopted in the Sierra.

I spent Christmas of 1957 and awaited 1958 in the mountains of Oriente. A few days before departing, Fidel described to me how victory would take place. He said that approximately a year would be required to overthrow Batista. And so it happened.

10. A pseudonym I began to use around then. [AH]

Who was Frank País?

Armando Hart
August 1957

This tribute, published clandestinely in *Revolución,* appeared following the assassination of Frank País by Batista's police on July 30, 1957.

> *"Freedom costs dearly, and one has to decide whether to pay the price or resign oneself to living without it."*
>
> —JOSÉ MARTÍ

That was the first thing that came to my mind when I received the news. Cuba is paying dearly for its freedom. Men of his kind are not born every day. Seldom does nature bestow such human beings on the people. His death gives him a place in Cuba's heart. But his life would have made him much greater. For anyone who knows how difficult it is to find such people, it is sad to say this.

Our revolutionary generation knows this well because we felt the direct influence of his personality. Oriente, and Santiago de Cuba in particular, will also agree with this because they knew Frank País's leadership. But all Cuba needs to know what it has lost! *On July 30, 1957, a Cuban of the stature of Mella, Martínez Villena, and Antonio Guiteras was murdered in Santiago de Cuba.* He was no less than they were, and like them he was unable to become even greater. It's the Cuban tragedy repeated once again.

Only seen in this perspective is it possible to understand that a death could lead to the most beautiful movement of civic protest that has been seen over these five years.

Frank once said to us: "For me there is nothing like preparing to teach a course on Cuban history and then explaining it until my fourth grade pupils are filled with enthusiasm." (He was a teacher at the El Salvador School.) One day he had to stop teaching history because the time had come to make history. . . .

I don't know whether he was a political man with a military vocation or a military man with a political vocation. I do know that to him the words *discipline, organization, civic virtue,* and *liberty* had a sacred value. These words came together in his mind and in his actions, with a magnificent equilibrium. This young man of 23 completely synthesized all revolutionary virtues.

He possessed a morale and a purity like few others I have known. He had at the same time an open and sincere calling as a leader. Whoever spoke to him twice knew he had been born to command. And he commanded with a Spartan morale and a noble spirit of justice. . . . He was, as Fidel himself stated, "the most unblemished and capable of all our combatants."

It was his capacity for action that most revealed his temperament and character. In the midst of events, this Cuban who liked to write poetry and play the piano always thoroughly analyzed the consequences of his acts and the best way to react to events. . . .

I felt his indisputable greatness months before November 30. One day we will publish his letters, reports, and circulars that today are jealously kept in the Movement's archives. That will allow a better appreciation of his personality.

I came to know who Frank País was even better on that desolate Sunday, December 2 [1956], when we did not know if Fidel Castro and dozens of compañeros had sunk in the sea or been machine-gunned by planes in the middle of the gulf. I remember Frank came to interrupt my anguish and despair with the following words: "Look at what I've written for the provincial and municipal leaderships," and he read it to me. In that internal circular, the order was given for large-scale sabotage and the burning of sugarcane fields. He knew how to command and what orders to give at that dramatic moment. For this reason, Frank País energetically assumed the revolutionary leadership.

Later, when it became possible to begin organizing for a general strike and centralization of the Movement, Frank País became the born leader of our action group and the leader of a revolutionary movement. Due to his abilities, he began to link this movement more organically to the masses in order to mobilize them appropriately for the struggle. Operating completely clandestinely, he was the directing center of the powerful subversive movement that brought the tyranny to the verge of collapse. Anonymously, known only in his province and among revolutionary circles, with a well-drawn battle strategy, he was capable of being a determining factor in the fight against the tyranny. Frank País, from the underground in Santiago, commanded in Cuba. From his hiding place came the sabotage, the agitation, the pennants held high, the underground press, the Civic Resistance Movement, and more.

The insurrectionary uprising of November 30, the discipline and organization of the July 26 Movement outside the Sierra—that was his work, as was the whole organizational base of the Movement. His posthumous work was the general work stoppage occasioned by his death. It is easy to say that Oriente stopped work out of emotion. But without a strategy developed many months before and an organization strengthened by tenacity and intelligence, that emotional outburst could not have been channeled. The one who forged that strategy and created that organization was Frank País.

Whatever contingency fate puts before our generation, I am sure that as we face each great obstacle we will remember Frank. He is already a part of our vital reality as a group of human beings seeking to end a historical cycle. He demands, more than ever, that we not only knock over the obstacle of Batista, but that we continue imposing upon ourselves the civic discipline and democratic conscience that characterized this exemplary life. "Death provides leaders," said José Martí. And Frank País orders us to continue preparing ourselves so that in Cuba a democracy prevails that is based on the highest revolutionary virtues, on the organization of the people, and on the public morals of its rulers.

Only when we've succeeded in organizing the people of Cuba from top to bottom into a permanent collective body will the July 26 Movement have overcome and defeated all obstacles. Today we have already come a long way thanks to the effort and blood of Frank País and so many others. The moral commitment of turning the emotion aroused by the call to action of July 26, 1953, into an organization suitable for combat has begun to be fulfilled. The obligation of bringing this task to culmination is our duty today.

That was his ideal. He died for it. In a private letter written when his brother Josué was murdered a month before, he said: "We must get there in order to bring about justice."

Only by bringing about justice will we fulfill our duty.

To members of the July 26 Movement

Circular no. 1 to the membership
1957

This internal circular was prepared by the July 26 Movement's national leadership in Havana in late 1957 for study by the organization's members.

Compañero:

This circular is addressed to you, as one who is giving all your efforts to the redemption of Cuba. Read it over several times. Analyze carefully all the matters raised in it. The success of the Movement depends to a great degree on how well each of us interprets and complies with it.

1. Member and sympathizer

The first thing to be settled is what defines membership in the July 26 Movement. This is necessary because the enormous sympathy for the Movement has at times caused us to lose sight of the dividing line between member and sympathizer. We must learn to situate ourselves with regard to everyone around us, in order to better take advantage of our energies and most effectively channel the sympathy that exists for the July 26 Movement.

A member is one who abides by the discipline of the organization, belongs to one of its bodies, and is willing to make the greatest sacrifices to achieve the revolutionary objectives, i.e., who feels deeply the revolutionary ideals for which he's sworn "Freedom or death" to achieve. A sympathizer is one who generally does what's right, but for one reason or another does not belong to a unit of the Movement and has not sworn "Freedom or death." Nevertheless he collaborates with the revolution through the July 26 Movement, without being tied to its discipline. This circular is addressed to the Movement's members.

2. Your responsibility

The July 26 Movement already has an enormous responsibility toward the people. For that reason the responsibility of each member has increased enormously and will increase even more to the degree that our strength grows. It will increase in the coming months when the tyranny is overthrown by the weight of our actions.

The responsibility of the national, provincial, and municipal leaders is therefore also immense. Precisely for that reason we are addressing you, a member of the July 26 Movement, to jointly face the situation and confront the events. We will be able to lead these events to Cuba's benefit only if we are successful in creating a revolutionary membership firmly disciplined in democratic ideals. That is our first concern. This should therefore be the framework with which you analyze this letter, and we would like it to be the primary guideline you keep in mind.

3. Relations with other organizations

All of us confront daily the much discussed question of the unity of the opposition. The Movement has always been willing to agree to any formula of unity that starts with the people as the basic element of a strategy of struggle. But a more concrete answer must be given as to what formula of unity we wish to see. Nobody has analyzed this with such precision as the July 26 Movement, and in this regard each member should refer to the [June 1957] Manifesto of the Sierra Maestra, published in newspapers and magazines, and to the article "Our Formula for Unity" that appeared in *Revolución*. These documents go over the Movement's definitive stance regarding other opposition organizations. Our position is summarized as follows:

a) We will respect any formula for unity that takes the civic institutions as its axis. These must assume the main responsibility for such unity and for the future provisional government.

b) We are willing to work jointly with any revolutionary sector on the basis of a specific action considered useful to the process. We are willing to cooperate with any effort, but always based on the specific actions to be carried out.

c) We call on workers belonging to all parties, as well as those belonging to none, to create strike committees in their workplaces or industrial sectors with a specific objective: to prepare the strike. We call on shopkeepers, industrialists, professionals, etc., belonging to all parties or none to work in the Civic Resistance Movement. Workers who are members of the Movement should await specific instructions in order to form strike committees.

4. The great question asked of us

Every member of the July 26 Movement is obliged today to answer the following question: What is the Movement aiming for? Two years ago this question was discussed by only a relatively small number of Cubans. Now it has become a national issue. Even internationally, quite a few commentators on the Cuban situation have posed this question.

It would be absurd for us to answer this in detail in an internal circular, but it is essential to have a common idea of how to respond to this question. Besides, as with every basic theoretical question, it takes us directly to the question of what each one of us should do. Plus things are done better when we know why we are doing them. We will come to that, but we have to start from an analysis of what we have done and achieved. Only by doing this will we be able to know what the July 26 Movement is really aiming at.

a) Prior to November 30 and the landing of the *Granma,* we were a sector made up of a goodly number of Cubans who set for themselves the task of initiating the revolution *in order to help bring about the fall* of Batista and penetrate all layers *of the population in an organized way.* Although we always enjoyed general sympathy, it was not until the Sierra Maestra, as well as the sabotage and agitation, that cadres of an organization began to emerge on the national scene capable of channeling all the disparate efforts, beginning to create the necessary conditions for the complete development of the revolution. After eight months we constitute the opposition to the regime. The power of the July 26 Movement's actions has been such that today it appears on the Cuban scene as the only instrument capable of conquering freedom. It's not that we consider ourselves the only organization, but we have the enormous historical responsibility of guiding revolutionary action with an appropriate strategy to channel all sincere impulses and efforts.

Would we have fulfilled our objective had our actions and the amount of blood spilled served only to turn us into an anti-Batista movement? No, the moment demands of us something more than agitation and sabotage. We are committed to bringing about the fall of the tyranny.

Such a thing can be achieved only with a more and more firmly disciplined organization in terms of its final aims, and with an appropriate strategy for the immediate objective of a general work stoppage and armed insurrection.

And what does the revolutionary organization known as the July 26 Movement seek after the fall of the tyrant? It seeks to set the Cuban people in motion behind a program of political cleansing, economic demands, and social justice to make democracy possible. To make the Cuban people an organized and disciplined force capable of assuring its own rights and its own democracy. In short, to consolidate the Cuban nation's revolutionary instrument, which is what the July 26 Movement is and aspires to continue being.

b) The only reason for Cuba's grave historical crisis is precisely that we always lacked a revolutionary instrument capable of facing up to events decisively once the immediate obstacle—first the existence of Cuba as a colony and then the Machado tyranny— had been eliminated. . . .

In summary, the July 26 Movement has two immediate objectives:

a) To overthrow Batista through popular action. This is not the same as just overthrowing him.

b) To consolidate the revolutionary instrument to ensure the fulfillment of the revolution's program, also through popular action. This is not the same as simply creating a new party.

construction of rev. party.

5. Our practical work with a view to that noble immediate objective

a) To achieve the first objective we must put into practice a plan that, under current conditions, leads us to a *general work stoppage*. Every member, through the responsible persons and committees, will receive instructions on their particular tasks.

b) To achieve the second objective we must act as follows:

1st. Determine precisely the general aspects of our program, which have already been put forward several times.

2nd. Ensure the discipline of all cadres and leaders of the organization.

3rd. Study beforehand how we are going to react to each and every development.

Every member must remain firmly disciplined in fulfilling their functions. Today more than ever, members must carefully follow instructions. Each body must plan what it should do with regard to them.

The signs of the regime's final collapse are already visible. Its death sentence has already been dictated. We will know how to take advantage, for the benefit of Cuba, of the formidable popular movement born of the rebelliousness of our youth. Once more the country is faced with a great opportunity. All the merits of the old politics are gone. Will we be capable of fulfilling the role destiny is placing in our hands? In order to do so we require organization and discipline.

The members of the July 26 Movement will understand this truth. The municipal, provincial, and national leaders must understand it even better. We are all marching toward victory, which will be nothing other than completing the cycle begun by Agramonte and Martí in colonial times: to create the great nation we all have dreamed of.

Freedom or death!

National Directorate

No sugar harvest with Batista!

To the students of Cuba

July 26 Movement
November 1957

This appeal was circulated by July 26 Movement cadres in response to the dictatorship's attempts to reopen the universities, which had been closed by the repressive forces more than a year earlier.

The regime's appeals and guarantees to Cuban students are motivated by its urgent need to present a facade of normalcy. This is a desperate effort by the government to recover from the discredit into which it has sunk as a result of the terror and abuses it has carried out across the country. Students are summoned to class at a time when the dictator—petulant, ostentatious, and arrogant as always— refuses to abolish censorship and dares to scold the Cuban press corps, with utterly no shame. It is none other than the colonels who invaded what has traditionally been the civilian sector of education and began issuing orders. The class schedules have been decided in the garrisons. Under the pressure of threats, the teaching staff, humiliated and with its functions trampled on, issues unfortunate calls to class that lack only the title "Military Order Number X." Unscrupulous politicians have gotten their relatives and their kowtowing supporters to take admission exams in an attempt to artificially create a student body.

But constitutional guarantees remain suspended, and there is no reduction in the terror's viciousness. The calls to class are made energetically, as an ultimatum, exposing their origin. An attempt is being made to bring youth into the classrooms through the common denominator of military vigilance and regulation. The troops are quartered and have erected barricades at the very doors of the campus. The idea seems to be to create docile students, in accordance with official interests. . . .

The hangmen smile "broadly and cordially." They lie! Their smile is the hissing of serpents. How can an educational climate be created without guarantees? How can Cuban students, forged in the purest traditions of sacrifice and rebellion, as a firm army of freedom, lend themselves to the fraud of a nonexistent normalcy? In the event that young people do go to school, what will happen when the students, in a demonstration of civic consciousness, wish to comply with the sacred duty of rendering tribute to their dead? It is not necessary to answer these questions. Every Cuban knows the answers. Consequently, a satisfactory climate to attend classes does not exist.

Throughout all the eras of our history, Cuban students have proved to be the most sincere and selfless advanced contingent of our society. Their struggle against tyranny, their condemnation of and opposition to the governments of thieves we have endured, their daring and bold conduct in face of the official criminals and licensed barbarians—all this has meant that the pantheon of their martyrs and heroes has grown: Rubén Batista, the martyrs of 7 Humboldt Street, José A. Echeverría and other students killed on March 13, René Fraga, Josué País, José Tey, Raúl Cervantes, and so many others. They are the newly dead, with gravesites fertilized by example, by the inflamed soil of Mt. Turquino, by the bloodstained streets of Havana, Cienfuegos, and Santiago de Cuba. Is it possible a single student forgets this? The youth of Cuba have sworn a commitment to sacrifice for the homeland. And those who gave up promising lives, even perhaps a happy future, who exchanged the book for extreme action with integrity and bravery, call out from the graves or from the lines of combat—in the Sierra or in the city—mandating us to close ranks in the crusade against the tyrant.

We should answer the garrisons' summons to class with a resounding "NO!" That is our simple answer to the despots.

With Batista there will be no classes!
Freedom or death!

July 26 Revolutionary Movement

Manifesto to the nation: Response to the Miami Pact

Fidel Castro
December 14, 1957

The following open letter on behalf of the National Leadership of the July 26 Movement was broadly circulated within Cuba through clandestine channels. When press censorship was briefly lifted, it was printed in its entirety in the February 2, 1958, issue of *Bohemia*, in a special run of 500,000 copies.

To the leaders of:
The Cuban Revolutionary Party
The Cuban People's Party
The Authentic Organization
The Federation of University Students
The Revolutionary Directorate
The Revolutionary Workers Directorate

A moral, patriotic, and even historic duty compels me to address this letter to you, motivated by events and circumstances that have concerned us deeply these last few weeks, which have also been the busiest and most difficult ones since our arrival in Cuba. For it was on Wednesday, November 20, a day when our forces sustained three battles in the space of only six hours (suggesting the sacrifices and efforts that our men here have made, without the slightest aid from other organizations), that we received in our zone of operations the surprising news and the document containing the public and secret terms of the Unity Pact, said to have been signed in Miami by the July 26 Movement and the organizations I am now addressing. Perhaps it was through an irony of fate that the arrival of this document—at a time when arms are what we need—coincided with the strongest offensive the dictatorship has launched against us.

Under the conditions of struggle we face, communications are difficult. Nevertheless, in the very midst of operations, it was necessary to convene the leaders of our organization to discuss this matter, in which not only the prestige but even the historical justification of the July 26 Movement is at stake.

Our men are fighting an enemy incomparably superior in numbers and in weapons. For an entire year they have sustained themselves with nothing but the dignity with which one fights for a cause he truly loves and the conviction that it is a cause worth dying for. They have tasted the bitterness of being forgotten by other compatriots who, possessing all the means to assist them, have systematically—if not criminally—refused to do so. They have seen, at close range, daily sacrifice in its purest and most selfless form. They have experienced the pain of seeing the best among them fall, not knowing who beside them will perish in new and inevitable holocausts to come, fated not to see the day of triumph they so tenaciously worked for, with no other hope or aspiration than that their sacrifice not be in vain. It is not difficult to understand why the news of a widely and deliberately publicized pact, which commits the Movement to a future course without even the courtesy—not to speak of the elementary obligation—of consulting its leaders and combatants, would provoke the ire and indignation of us all.

Acting in an improper fashion always leads to the worst consequences. This must be borne in mind by those who consider themselves capable of an undertaking as arduous as the overthrow of a tyranny, and the even harder task of successfully reorganizing the country following a revolutionary process.

The July 26 Movement has neither designated nor authorized anyone to enter into such negotiations. Nonetheless, it would not have been opposed to selecting a representative had it been consulted on such an initiative. In that event, it would have given very concrete instructions to its representatives when discussing a matter with such serious consequences to the present and future activities of our organization.

Instead, our information concerning relations with some of these groups was limited to a report by Mr. Léster Rodríguez, our delegate for military matters abroad, with powers limited strictly to such matters. He wrote us the following:

"With respect to Prío and the Directorate, I can report to you that I have held a series of discussions with them for the *sole and exclusive* purpose of coordinating military plans, up to the formation of a provisional government guaranteed and respected by the three groups. I of course proposed that they accept the Sierra Letter, which specifies that this government should be formed in accordance with the will of the country's civic forces. That led to the first difficulty.

"When the commotion around the general strike occurred,[1] we held an emergency meeting. I proposed that we utilize all the forces at hand right away in an effort to resolve the problem of Cuba once and for all. Prío answered that he lacked sufficient forces to undertake any action with assurance of victory, and that it would be madness to accept my proposal. I answered that he should please let me know when he had everything ready to set sail; then we would be able to discuss possible pacts. In the meantime, he should do me the favor of letting me do my work and carry out my assignment representing the July 26 Movement, with complete independence. In short, we came to no agreement with these gentlemen, nor do I believe it advisable to do so in the future. For at the moment when Cuba needed it most, they denied having the weapons that have since been seized—and in such amounts that it moves one to indignation."[2]

This report, which speaks for itself, confirmed our suspicion that the rebels could expect no outside help whatsoever.

If the organizations that you represent had deemed it worthwhile to discuss the articles of unity with any members of our Movement, these articles could not have been announced publicly, under any circumstances, as a signed agreement without the knowledge and approval of the National Directorate of the Movement—and even less so when they fundamentally differed from the points we agreed to in the Manifesto of the Sierra Maestra. To function in any other way is simply to make pacts for public relations purposes and to fraudulently invoke the name of our organization.

The National Directorate of our Movement, which functions clandestinely inside Cuba, confronted an unheard-of situation. Af-

1. A reference to the spontaneous strikes that began in Santiago de Cuba following the murder of Frank País on July 30, 1957.
2. Prío spent an estimated $5 million accumulating weapons for the Authentic Party's military organization and other anti-Batista organizations. Almost all of these were seized by Batista's police.

ter receiving the text of the pact, they had decided to reject its public and secret provisions. No sooner had they done so than they learned through underground flyers, and through the foreign press, that the pact had been announced publicly as a signed agreement. They were thus confronted by a fait accompli and were faced with the alternatives of repudiating it as a lie, with all the confusion that would bring, or accepting it, without even being able to express their point of view.

As one can easily imagine, by the time the provisions of the document reached us in the Sierra, it had already been circulating publicly for many days.

Faced with this dilemma, the National Directorate, before proceeding to publicly repudiate the agreements, raised with you the need for the Cuban Liberation Council to incorporate a series of points from the Manifesto of the Sierra Maestra. Meanwhile they convened a meeting in rebel territory in which the views of all its members were weighed and a unanimous decision was adopted, forming the basis of this letter.

Naturally enough, any unity agreement will inevitably be welcomed by national and international public opinion. There are several reasons for this. For one thing, those abroad do not know the real situation of the political and revolutionary forces opposing Batista. Within Cuba, on the other hand, the word "unity" was draped with a certain aura, based on a former relationship of forces that has clearly changed considerably since then. An additional reason is that, in general, it is always a positive thing to unite the efforts of everyone, from the most enthusiastic to the most timid.

But what is important for the revolution is not unity in itself, but the principles on which it is based, how it is achieved, and the patriotic intentions motivating it.

Agreeing to a unity whose provisions we have not even discussed; having it signed by persons with no authority to do so; and announcing it publicly without further ado from the comfort of a foreign city, thereby putting the Movement in the situation of facing a public deceived by a fraudulent pact—this is a trick of the lowest sort, which a truly revolutionary organization can have no part in. It is an act of deception to the country and to the world.

Moreover, such a trick is possible only because of the simple fact that the leaders of the other organizations that signed this pact are living in exile, making an imaginary revolution, while the leaders of the July 26 Movement are in Cuba, making a real revolution.

Our letter, however, might not have been necessary, regardless of the very bitter and humiliating procedure attempting to tie the Movement to this pact. Differences over form must never overshadow essentials. We might still have accepted it, despite everything, because of how positive unity is, because of the usefulness of some of the ideas raised by the council, and because of the help being offered us, which we genuinely need. The simple fact, however, is that we disagree with a number of its essential points.

No matter how desperate our situation in face of thousands of the dictatorship's troops mobilized to annihilate us, and perhaps with more determination because of it (since nothing is more humiliating than to accept an onerous condition under trying circumstances), we would never accept the sacrifice of certain principles that are fundamental to our conception of the Cuban Revolution. These principles are contained in the Manifesto of the Sierra Maestra.

To omit from the unity document the explicit declaration that we reject every form of foreign intervention in the internal affairs of Cuba is a sign of lukewarm patriotism and of cowardice, which must be condemned in and of itself.

Declaring that we are opposed to intervention is not simply asking that there be no intervention in support of the revolution, which would undercut our sovereignty and undermine a principle that affects all the peoples of the Americas. It also means opposing all intervention on the side of the dictatorship by supplying the planes, bombs, tanks, and modern weapons that maintain it in power. No one knows this better than we do, not to mention the peasants of the Sierra, who have suffered it in their own flesh and blood.

In short, ending such intervention means achieving the overthrow of the dictatorship. Are we such cowards that we won't even demand no intervention on the side of Batista? Are we so insincere that we ask in an underhanded way for someone else to pull our chestnuts out of the fire? Are we so halfhearted that we dare not utter a single word on the issue? How then can we call ourselves revolutionaries and subscribe to a unity document with historical pretensions?

The unity document omits the explicit rejection of any kind of military junta as a provisional government of the republic.

The worst thing that could happen to Cuba at the present time would be the replacement of Batista by a military junta, as this would be accompanied by the deceptive illusion that the nation's problems had been resolved by the dictator's absence. There are some politicians of the worst stripe, including accomplices of the March 10 coup now estranged from it (perhaps for being even more *tanquista* and ambitious), who are considering solutions that only enemies of the country's progress would look kindly on.

Experience in Latin America has shown that all military juntas tend toward autocracy. The worst of all evils that has gripped this continent is the implantation of military castes in countries with fewer wars than Switzerland and more generals than Prussia. One of our people's most legitimate aspirations at this crucial hour, when the fate of democracy and the republic will either be saved or ruined for many years to come, is to guard the most precious legacy of our country's liberators: the tradition of civilian rule. This tradition dates back to the emancipation struggle and was broken the day a uniformed junta first took control of the republic—something never attempted by even the most glorious generals of our independence struggle, either in wartime or in peace.

Are we willing to renounce everything we believe in? Are we to omit such an important declaration of principles out of fear of wounding sensibilities? (This is a fear more imagined than real with regard to honest officers who could support us.) Is it so hard to understand that a timely definition of principles might forestall in time the danger of a military junta that would serve no other purpose than perpetuating the civil war?

We do not hesitate to declare that if a military junta replaces Batista, the July 26 Movement will resolutely continue its struggle for liberation. It is preferable to do battle today than to fall into a new and insurmountable abyss tomorrow. Neither military junta nor a puppet government that would be the toy of the military. The slogan should be: "Civilians, govern with decency and honor. Soldiers, go to your barracks." And each and everyone, do your duty!

Or are we to wait for the generals of the March 10 coup, to whom Batista will gladly cede power whenever he considers it unsustainable as the best way to guarantee a transition that does the least damage to his interests and those of his cronies? It is astounding how lack of vision, absence of high ideals, and lack of a genuine desire to struggle can blind Cuban politicians!

If one lacks faith in the people, if one lacks confidence in their great reserves of energy and struggle, then one has no right to interfere with their destiny, distorting and misdirecting it during the most heroic and promising moments of the republic's life. Keep the revolutionary process free of all dirty politicking, all childish ambitions, all lust for personal gain, all attempts to divide up the spoils beforehand. Men are dying in Cuba for something better. Let the politicians become revolutionaries, if that is what they so desire; but don't turn the revolution into bastard politics. Our people have shed too much blood and made too many sacrifices to deserve such bitter frustration in the future!

Apart from these two fundamental principles omitted in the unity document, we are in total disagreement with other aspects of it.

Even if we were to accept clause (b) of article 2 of the secret part, regarding the powers of the Cuban Liberation Council, which states: "To name the president of the republic who will assume this office in the provisional government," we cannot accept clause (c) of the same article, which includes among such powers "to approve or disapprove the cabinet as a whole named by the president of the republic, as well as any changes in its composition in the event of total or partial crisis."

How can one conceive that the president's powers to appoint and replace his collaborators is to be subject to the approval of a body that has no relationship to the powers of state? Inasmuch as this council is to be composed of representatives of different parties and sectors, and therefore of different interests, is it not clear that such a procedure would convert the naming of the cabinet into divvying up posts as the only way to reach agreement in each case? Is it possible to agree to a stipulation that implies the establishment of two executive powers within the government? There is only one guarantee that all sectors of the country should demand of the provisional government: to limit its mission to a specific minimum program and to display absolute impartiality in presiding over the period of transition to complete constitutional normalcy.

To seek to involve itself in appointing each minister implies an aspiration to control public administration, putting it at the service of political interests. Such an attempt is possible only among parties and organizations lacking mass support, which can survive only within the confines of traditional politicking. Such an approach is sharply counterposed to the high revolutionary and political aims that the July 26 Movement has for the republic.

The very presence of secret agreements that do not deal with matters of organizing the struggle or plans for action, but instead take up questions of keen interest for the nation, such as the structure of the future government—something that must be proclaimed publicly—is in itself unacceptable. Martí said that in a revolution the methods are secret but the goals must always be public.

Another point that is equally unacceptable to the July 26 Movement is secret provision number 8, which states: "The revolutionary forces are to be incorporated, with their weapons, into the regular armed bodies of the republic."

In the first place, what is meant by "revolutionary forces"? Are we to grant a badge of membership to every policeman, sailor, soldier, and everyone else who at the final hour comes forward with a weapon in his hand? Are we to give a uniform and invest authority to those who today have weapons kept in hiding, in order to take them out on the day of triumph? To those who are standing aside while a handful of compatriots battle the entire forces of the tyranny? Are we to include, in a revolutionary document, the very seed of gangsterism and anarchy, which not very long ago were the shame of the republic?

Our experience in the territory dominated by our forces has taught us that the maintenance of public order is a key question for the country. Events have shown us that as soon as the prevailing order is eliminated, a series of problems are unleashed and crime, if left unchecked, sprouts up all over. It was the timely application of severe measures, with full public blessing, that put an end to the outbreak of banditry. The local residents, accustomed in the past to viewing agents of authority as enemies of the people, used to offer protection and shelter to those fleeing from justice. Now, when they see our soldiers as defenders of their interests, the most complete order prevails; and the best guardians of it are the citizens themselves.

Anarchy is the worst enemy of a revolutionary process. To combat it from now on is a fundamental need. Whoever does not understand this has no concern for the fate of the revolution, and those who have not sacrificed for the revolution, logically enough, do not share this concern. The country needs to know that there will be justice, but under the strictest order. Crime will be punished no matter where it comes from.

The July 26 Movement claims for itself the role of maintaining public order and reorganizing the armed forces of the republic.

1. Because it is the only organization that possesses organized and disciplined militias throughout the country, as well as an army in the field, with twenty victories over the enemy.

2. Because our combatants have demonstrated a spirit of chivalry free of all hatred toward the military, invariably respecting the lives of prisoners, tending their wounded, never torturing an adversary, even when they are known to possess important information. And they have maintained this conduct with an unprecedented equanimity.

3. Because the armed forces must be imbued with the spirit of justice and nobility that the July 26 Movement has instilled in its own soldiers.

4. Because the calmness with which we have acted in this struggle is the best guarantee that honorable military men have nothing to fear from the revolution. They will not be held accountable for those whose deeds and crimes have disgraced the military uniform.

There still remain certain aspects of the unity document that are difficult to understand. How is it possible to come to an agreement without a clearly defined strategy of struggle? Do the Authentic Party leaders still envision a putsch in the capital? Will they continue to accumulate weapons and more weapons that sooner or later will fall into the hands of the police, instead of giving them to those who are fighting? Have they finally accepted the thesis of the general strike held by the July 26 Movement?

As we see it, there has also been a regrettable underestimation of the military importance of the struggle in Oriente. What is being waged at present in the Sierra Maestra is not guerrilla warfare but a war of columns. Our forces, which are inferior in numbers and weaponry, take maximum advantage of the terrain, always keep a watchful eye on the enemy, and have greater speed of movement. It need hardly be said that the moral factor has been of decisive importance to the struggle. The results have been astounding, and some day these will be known in all their details.

The entire population has risen up. If there were enough weapons, our detachments would not have to guard a single zone. The peasants would not allow a single enemy soldier to pass. The defeats of the dictatorship, which obstinately sends large forces, could be disastrous. Anything I could tell you about the courage of the people here would be too little. The dictatorship takes barbaric reprisals. Its mass murder of peasants compares with the massacres perpetrated by the Nazis in any country of Europe. Each defeat it suffers is paid for by the defenseless population. The communiqués issued by the general staff announcing rebel losses are always preceded by a massacre. This has led the people to a state of absolute rebellion. But what is most painful, what makes one's heart bleed, is to think that no one has sent a single rifle to these people. While peasants here see their homes burned and their families murdered, desperately begging for rifles, there are arms hidden away in Cuba that are not being used, not even to eliminate a single miserable henchman. It seems they are waiting for these weapons to be captured by the police, or for the tyranny to fall, or for the rebels to be exterminated.

There is nothing less noble than the actions of many compatriots. Even now there is still time to correct this and help those who are fighting. As far as we are concerned, from a personal point of view, this is unimportant. No one should worry that we are motivated by self-interest or pride.

Our fate is sealed; no uncertainty torments us. Either we die here to the last rebel, and a whole generation of Cuban youth will perish in the cities; or we triumph against the most incredible obstacles. For us defeat is impossible. The year of sacrifice and heroism that our men have withstood can no longer be erased. Our victories are there, and they too cannot be easily erased. Our men, firmer than ever, will fight to the last drop of blood.

The defeat will be for those who denied us all assistance; those who made initial commitments but left us on our own. It will be for those, lacking faith in dignity and ideas, who wasted their time and their prestige in shameful dealings with the despot Trujillo. The defeat will be for those having weapons but who cowardly hid them at the hour of battle. It is they, not we, who deceive themselves.

There is one thing we can state with certainty: had we seen other Cubans battling for freedom, pursued and facing extermination; had we seen them not surrender or back down day after day, we would not have hesitated one minute to join them and die together, if that were necessary. For we are Cubans, and Cubans do not remain passive even when it is to fight for the freedom of any other country of the Americas. Are there Dominicans gathering on a little island to liberate their nation? For each Dominican, ten Cubans arrive. Are Somoza's henchmen invading Costa Rica? Cubans rush there to fight.[3] How is it now that when our own country is waging the fiercest battle for its freedom, there are Cubans in exile, expelled from their homeland by the tyranny, who refuse assistance to Cubans who fight?

To obtain aid, must we bow to onerous demands? Must we offer up the republic as war booty? Must we forsake our ideals and turn this war into a new art of killing fellow human beings, into a useless shedding of blood that does not promise the country any benefit from so much sacrifice?

The leadership of the struggle against the tyranny is, and will continue to be, in Cuba and in the hands of revolutionary fighters. Whoever wants to be considered a leader of the revolution, either now or in the future, must be inside the country directly confronting the responsibilities, risks, and sacrifices that Cuba now demands.

The exile community must assist this struggle, but it would be absurd for it to try to tell us from abroad which mountaintop we should take; which canefield we can burn; which acts of sabotage should be done; or the time, place, or manner to carry out the general strike. That is not just absurd, but ridiculous. Assist us from abroad; raise money among Cuban exiles and émigrés; wage a campaign for the Cuban cause in the press and before public opinion; denounce from over there the crimes we here are suffering. But do not pretend, from Miami, to lead a revolution that is being waged throughout the cities and the countryside of Cuba, amid battles, agitation, sabotage, strikes, and a thousand and one other forms of revolutionary action that are part of the July 26 Movement's strategy of struggle.

As it has stated on more than one occasion, the National Directorate is prepared to hold discussions inside Cuba with the leaders of any opposition organization, to coordinate specific plans, and to

3. In 1947 Castro and hundreds of others participated in an aborted expedition that was being prepared in Cuba against the dictatorship of Rafael Trujillo in the Dominican Republic. In January 1955 a number of Cuban revolutionaries went to Costa Rica following an attack on that country by the Somoza dictatorship in Nicaragua; among them were José Antonio Echeverría and other leaders of the Federation of University Students.

carry out concrete deeds deemed useful in overthrowing the tyranny.

The general strike will be carried out through the practical coordination of efforts by the Civic Resistance Movement, the National Workers Front, and any other sector free from political partisanship, and in intimate contact with the July 26 Movement, as the only opposition organization that is waging battle throughout the entire country at the present time.

The workers section of the July 26 Movement is involved in organizing strike committees in every work center and every sector of industry, together with opposition elements from all organizations that are prepared to join the strike and offer moral guarantees that they are going to carry it out. These strike committees will form the National Workers Front, which will be the only representative of the proletariat that the July 26 Movement will recognize as legitimate.

The overthrow of the dictator will bring with it the ouster of the spurious congress; of the leadership of the Confederation of Cuban Workers; and of all the mayors, governors, and other officials who, directly or indirectly, owe their positions to the so-called elections of November 1, 1954, or to the military coup of March 10, 1952. It also involves the immediate release of all political, civil, and military prisoners and detainees, as well as the prosecution of all those complicit with the crimes, the arbitrary acts, and the tyranny itself.

The new government will be guided by the constitution of 1940, will guarantee all rights recognized therein, and will be free of all political partisanship.

The executive branch will assume the legislative functions that the constitution grants to the congress of the republic. It will have as its principal duty to lead the country toward general elections in accordance with the electoral code of 1943 and the constitution of 1940 and to carry out the ten-point minimum program put forward in the Manifesto of the Sierra Maestra.

The Supreme Court will be declared dissolved as a result of its incapacity to resolve the situation of lawlessness created by the coup. This does not preclude that some of its current members may be named to the new body, provided they defended constitutional principles or maintained a firm attitude against crime, arbitrary behavior, and abuse during these years of tyranny.

The president of the republic will decide on the manner of constituting the new Supreme Court, which in turn will proceed to reorganize all the courts and autonomous institutions, removing all those whom it considers to have been clearly complicit with the tyranny. Acting impartially it will remand such individuals to trial when appropriate. In each case new officials will be named in accordance with the law.

Political parties will have only one right during the life of the provisional government: the freedom to defend their program before the people, to mobilize and organize citizens within the broad framework of our constitution, and to participate in the general elections that are called.

The Manifesto of the Sierra Maestra raised the need to designate the person called upon to serve as president of the republic. Our Movement expressed its view that this person should be selected by the civic institutions as a whole. Nevertheless, five months have passed and this procedure has still not been carried out. Inasmuch as the question of who will replace the dictator is more urgent than ever, and it is not possible to wait one more day with this question unanswered, the July 26 Movement is giving its own answer. We present to the people the only formula possible to guarantee legality and the fulfillment of the previously agreed-upon articles of unity and of the provisional government itself. That individual should be the distinguished magistrate of the Provincial Court of Oriente, Dr. Manuel Urrutia Lleó. It is not we but his conduct itself that singles him out, and we hope he will not refuse this service to the republic.

The reasons pointing to him are the following:

1. He is the judicial official who most upheld the constitution, when he declared from the bench, during the trial of the *Granma* expeditionaries, that organizing an armed force against the regime was not a crime but was perfectly legal under both the letter and

spirit of the constitution and the law. This gesture by a magistrate has no precedent in the history of our struggles for freedom.

2. His lifelong dedication to the honest administration of justice guarantees that he has sufficient training and character to serve with fairness all legitimate interests at the moment that the tyranny is overthrown by the people's action.

3. No one other than Dr. Manuel Urrutia is as free from all partisanship, since, owing to his judicial responsibilities, he does not belong to any political grouping. There is no other citizen of his stature, free of all political alignments, who has identified himself so much with the revolutionary cause.

Moreover, owing to his position as magistrate, this formula is the one closest to constitutional procedures.

These are our conditions, the disinterested conditions of an organization whose sacrifices exceed all others but was not even consulted when its name was put on a unity manifesto it does not subscribe to. If they are rejected, then we will continue the struggle on our own, as we have done up to now, with no weapons other than those we take from the enemy in each battle, with no aid other than that given by the suffering people, with no source of sustenance other than our ideas.

For when all is said and done, it is the July 26 Movement alone that has been carrying out actions throughout the entire country. It is the members of the July 26 Movement alone who have spread rebellion from the wild mountains of Oriente to the western provinces of the country. It is the members of the July 26 Movement alone who are carrying out sabotage, the execution of assassins, the burning of cane fields, and other revolutionary acts. It is the July 26 Movement alone that has been able to organize workers in revolutionary action throughout the nation. It is also the July 26 Movement alone that today can carry out the strategy of strike committees. And it is the July 26 Movement alone that has helped organize the Civic Resistance Movement, which today groups together the civic sectors in almost all the localities of Cuba.

Some may interpret these words as arrogance. However, it is also the July 26 Movement alone that has declared it does not want to participate in the provisional government, and it is the one organization that has put all its moral and material power at the service of the ideal citizen to preside over the necessary provisional period.

Let it be understood that we have renounced any quest for bureaucratic posts or participation in the government. But let it also be known once and for all that the membership of the July 26 Movement does not renounce—and will never renounce—orienting and leading the people from clandestinity, from the Sierra Maestra, or from the graves of our dead. And we do not renounce this, because it is not we but an entire generation that has the moral commitment toward the people of Cuba to fundamentally resolve its great problems.

We are prepared, even if alone, to triumph or die. The struggle will never be as difficult as it was when we were only twelve men; when we did not have a people organized and tempered by war throughout the Sierra; when we did not have, as today, a powerful and disciplined organization throughout the country; when we did not possess the formidable mass support demonstrated at the time of the death of our unforgettable Frank País.

To die with dignity does not require company.

Fidel Castro Ruz

FOR THE NATIONAL DIRECTORATE OF THE JULY 26 MOVEMENT,
SIERRA MAESTRA, DECEMBER 14, 1957

Chapter 8

1958: From prison

*The Sierra Maestra
to the Príncipe Castle massacre*

In early January, full of plans to continue the struggle, I headed down the legendary mountains toward my combat post together with Javier Pazos, Tony Buch (who had returned to the Sierra), and the peasant Eulalio Vallejo.

We traveled on horseback until we reached the foot of the mountain range, and then took a jeep down the Bayamo-Manzanillo highway. There we ran into serious mechanical problems, and we went to a peasant's house to ask for help. We made it to the city of Bayamo, where we took a train on the Manzanillo-to-Santiago route. But halfway there, near the old and by-then idle Oriente sugar mill, as the train stopped near Palma Soriano, an army corporal came into the passenger car and arrested us for looking suspicious.

They took us straight to a nearby garrison and from there to Palma Soriano. It was nighttime, and the four of us had only a few guards. It seemed to me that it was possible, albeit risky, to get away through the fields. So I gestured my intentions to the rest of the group: to seize the guards' weapons and escape.

But the others did not feel it was reasonable. I can't be sure of what would have happened, but the possibility that the operation might have been successful cannot be ruled out. From the Palma garrison we were taken to the jail in an old fort on the outskirts of Santiago de Cuba.

They did not recognize me when I was arrested. At that time I was using the name Alfredo and had an identification card under that name from the Teachers Association in Santiago. After a few days I decided it would be safer to say who I was. Either way I would be taking a risk, but the risk might be greater if they thought I was an unknown. Even though I was beaten, the fact that they did not hit me in the face or any place visible made me think they were not going to kill me.

We were in jail for several days. I know for sure I was in that cell on January 23 because from a distant radio I heard the news that the Venezuelan dictator Pérez Jiménez had been overthrown. The news made me so happy that it gave me encouragement for the struggle we ourselves were waging. I hated him as much as I did Fulgencio Batista.[1]

René Ramos Latour *(Daniel)*, sent a letter to Fidel telling him about the capture:

Fidel,

I am taking advantage of the unexpected opportunity to send this letter to let you know some of what happened. At 8:00 p.m. on January 10, the driver who had accompanied Darío[2] and Tony on both occasions showed up here [in Santiago].

He said that around noon that day, when he got to Bueycito, the jeep stalled with a broken part.

The five of them got out and went to a nearby house, where

1. On January 21, 1958, a general strike and popular uprising in Caracas, Venezuela, took place against the military dictatorship of Marcos Pérez Jiménez. In face of the movement's power, the top military officials withdrew support for Pérez Jiménez, and the dictator fled on January 23. He was replaced by a military junta that organized general elections.
2. Another pseudonym I used while underground. [AH]

they were treated courteously by the peasants. He went on to say that Tony then approached him, issuing orders to go to Bueycito or Bayamo to get the part, and that once the car had been repaired he should continue on to Santiago. They would return by train and probably arrive here before the driver himself. That was what he did, and when he got back to the house he was told that the others had got on a passing truck and left for Bayamo. The peasants had recommended that they not stay at the house, since five members of that family were in jail.

When the trains arrived that night without Darío and the others, we became alarmed. We got in touch with Bayamo so they could start investigating. We also sent the driver with two people who knew our contacts in Bayamo, Yara, and Manzanillo, and alerted all those who keep us informed of the internal activities of the regime. We got reports from everywhere that all was normal, but despite the intense search they did not appear. At 1:00 a.m. (on the 12th) we learned that Javier Pazos—along with another important person—had been arrested and that documents had been seized from them. Right then we began mobilizing all the people who could prevent the worst from happening. Havana was notified and from there the news was sent abroad. At 8:00 a.m. on the 12th there was a call from Felipe Pazos asking for guarantees for his son's life. At around 2:00 p.m. the order came in, given to Chaviano by Batista himself, to spare the life of Pazos's son, but that Armando Hart was to be killed like a dog; they were to make it look like a battle on the edge of the Sierra. I need not tell you what that horrible sentence meant to all of us. For me in particular, it took a tremendous effort to calm down and not do anything foolish.

At the same time that we were getting out the facts and publicizing the order so as to exert pressure on the institutions, consular offices, and citizenry, our people succeeded in taking over a local radio station that was broadcasting a Liberal Party rally. Interrupting the program, they informed the people that

Armando was in jail and that Batista had ordered him killed by faking a battle. They also urged the population to prepare for the struggle.

Given this barrage of resistance by the people and civic institutions, the general faced a serious dilemma. It was impossible for them to carry out the despicable action they intended.

This morning, a radio station in Havana reported the news that three outstanding revolutionary leaders had been arrested in Santiago de Cuba. I imagine this is because I asked Fausto to find a national network that would disclose the facts.

They now tell me the order has been revoked, and that Chaviano will transfer the prisoners to Havana. Someone close to him who has conducted himself very well was able to talk with the pompous little general this morning, and Chaviano said that he had the three of them and if anyone interceded on their behalf he would deny they were prisoners. He even said that U.S. Ambassador Smith had sent several telegrams inquiring about the location where the detainees were being held, which he answered by saying he did not have them, that it had all been made up. He also admitted that he had beaten Armando badly, saying that Hart had been insolent.

So in broad strokes that's what has happened during these bitter hours we've been through.

It was our goal and still is, if the circumstances or Armando's situation gets worse, or if the worst happens, to fan the flames of any reaction that occurs, which would probably be similar to the one caused by Frank's death. If this happens we will go out and fight, because we cannot stand idly by while they murder all our people and destroy the precious reserves of our country's future.

If they do commit the crime and the circumstances are favorable, we will decide the question of this epoch once and for all.

Chaviano claims he knows of our future plans. He says that war will be waged in the cities and towns. He says they do not have a big enough army now to stop those actions since their soldiers are posted in the sugar mills until the 19th. After that, he says, they will confront us in the Llano, which it seems they would like very much to do.

I anxiously await your reply. Did you mention in any of your letters the total war I proposed we carry out? I hope you all will be able to recreate all the documents that were lost.

They claim to have addresses, especially in Havana. They ordered the Sorí Marín brothers arrested and a clinic on 19th Street in Vedado searched.

From all this we can draw only one conclusion: If we succeed in preventing the death of Armando and the other compañeros, we will have scored a triumph thanks to our information network, our ability to mobilize the citizenry, and our penetration into all sectors of the country. We will have blocked a sentence of the Dictator from being carried out. . . .

Daniel

Later on in his letter, Daniel explained to Fidel the huge national and international impact of the manifesto in reply to the Miami Pact, as well as the favorable response to it by members of the July 26 Movement.

The solidarity of our combatants in the Llano and the mobilization of public opinion saved my life.[3] Daniel did such an excellent job in seeing the tasks through to completion that he achieved the goal and scored a victory over the tyranny.

I am writing these lines forty years later with eternal gratitude to all those who got involved, made an effort, and succeeded in preventing the crime. I am especially grateful to the unforgettable compañeros of the July 26 Movement exemplified by Daniel, as well as the friends from Civic Resistance.

Daniel was killed in battle in the Sierra Maestra several months later.[4] His revolutionary life reminds me of the observation by journalist Herbert Matthews that Batista did not

3. See page 268, "Swift Action that Saved Armando Hart's Life."
4. See page 274, "The Death of Daniel."

understand the type of men he was facing. Without such men, no revolution is possible.

✳

Although security principles advised that any document that might be compromising should be sent through channels other than the combatants, we were carrying a very valuable load of papers and photos, which were seized by the tyranny's army and taken advantage of by the regime. Among them was the draft of a letter I was writing to Che. I had read it to Fidel, who had told me not to send it. But I was careless enough to keep it with those papers. I have never stopped reproaching myself for carrying it with me and causing trouble for Fidel and Raúl as a result.

In those pages I discussed my opinions with regard to Che's views about the leaders of the Llano. The debate revolved around the socialist ideas that had already crystallized for Che. For many of us from the Llano, however, these ideas were in the process of formation and not without contradictions and doubts.

There is another factor that could not have failed to have an influence then: at the time, socialist ideas internationally were heavily influenced by concepts that did not fit the reality and history of our countries. That fact must be kept in mind when evaluating a revolution of national liberation, as well as the background and position of its leading cadres. Thanks to the genius of Fidel, the Cuban Revolution—with Che as one of its great architects—was in practice already transcending those disagreements. That was the heart of the matter. As we debated the revolutionary process that together we were advancing, the roots of these differences were being left behind.[5]

A few months after the January 1959 triumph, Che, with his exceptional talent, came to understand more deeply than any of us the sources of the problems that the international com-

5. For Che Guevara's account of this, see *Episodes of the Cuban Revolutionary War*, (New York: Pathfinder, 1996), p. 295.

munist movement was experiencing. He also grasped the ways of dealing with this movement and enriching it theoretically with the Third World and Latin American experience.

After 1959, Che's most important collaborators included compañeros who had shouldered great responsibilities in the Llano. At no time did these nuances color the respect that each of us felt for Che. To the contrary, his reputation grew over the years until he became one of the greatest symbols of revolutionary struggle in the world.

✳

I recall that when an official from the U.S. Consulate in Santiago de Cuba with whom the July 26 Movement had some relationship read the paragraphs of the letter I referred to above, which was published by the army, he said to Haydée, "María, how could Jacinto write this?" To calm him down, she answered, "But he's attacking Stalin." The American then told her, "That's not the main thing it's saying. Read carefully."

✳

With me in jail, Marcelo Fernández became national coordinator of the Movement.[6]

From the prison in the old fort on the outskirts of Santiago de Cuba, I was transferred to the Moncada garrison and came before Alberto Río Chaviano, the murderer of the Moncadistas. Incredibly, he did not greet me with violence. In fact, he said that if I wanted, I could meet with my wife. I asked him ironically, "And do you know who my wife is?"

A few days later I was transferred to the provincial prison in Oriente, also known as the Boniato jail due to its proximity to the town of that name. I was there from the end of January until

6. Amid the complexities of the struggle, he skillfully carried out this responsibility until after the triumph of the revolution. [AH]

July 1958, together with a large group of revolutionary prisoners.

At the beginning of February, during a time of intense and widespread unrest in the country, they brought me to the courthouse in Oriente with full police protection, going to the extreme of having a huge tank guard me. I felt greatly honored by such "security," since it showed how afraid they were of the Movement's strength. I was again convicted and sentenced. The police and court records show how greatly Batista's army lacked the capacity for analysis. They had evidence of my participation in the struggle in the Sierra. Yet they based the charges against me on the fact that the rebels had supposedly murdered a teacher named Alfredo. The clumsiness and inefficiency of those bodies of repression "aided" the revolution.

I prepared the following response to that farce of a legal proceeding:

I dedicate this document to the lawyers of my homeland, to my professors at the university, and to the honorable judicial officials, who have always inspired the respect worthy of men of law.

Defense arguments before the Urgency Court of Santiago de Cuba. . . .

Gentlemen:

. . . There are two ways to assert rights: discussion and force. The former is unique to humans; the latter is a method of beasts. But if one's goal is to keep men from resorting to arms, one must treat them as men. Discussion versus force. Understanding versus imposed will. Right versus physical might. Man versus beast. There, gentlemen, you have the two great giants of history who today, like so often in our political revolution, fight for supremacy in our country and, one could say, in all of Latin America. There you have the protagonists of the great battle to which we are committed, whose main setting is the eastern part of the country. There you have the essence of the entire political struggle in Cuba.

This court proceeding, like all court proceedings, is a simple episode, an unimportant accident in the battle that will decide whether Cuba can live in liberty and justice. You have taken one position, and we have taken the opposite one. Nothing unites us any longer from a legal standpoint, because those remnants of legality that several months ago made it possible in certain cases to apply the written law have completely disappeared with the increase of governmental terror, with the so-called National Emergency Law, and the reorganization of the Urgency Courts. I cannot speak to you in the name of the law or in the name of justice because law and justice mean very different things to you and to us. I cannot perform the farce of a legal defense while our compañeros are dying in the fields and cities for pointing out that there is no law or justice in Cuba.

I do not come here to demand justice, since I am striving to achieve it through the constitutional and viable channel of rebellion. Nor are you actually capable of granting it to me. This is not a court of justice, but rather a bureaucratic organ of the tyranny. You are not judges, but agents of repression and crime. You are not career officials, but personal delegates of the tyrant. It is you and not we who will have to answer before the courts of the republic.

You and those like you, who, as lawyers or as false men of culture, attempt to dress up the illegitimate regime in legal garb, bear more responsibility than those in uniform who sustain the government. Because many soldiers and officers might have the excuse of a false notion of discipline and order. But you, who studied civics in high school and law at the university, have no excuse or defense. In fact, you are more wretched than murderers, because crime has psychological, cultural, social, and economic causes that should be examined by the fields of legal medicine and criminology. But you, who are all fully aware that you're breaking the law, are not moved by passion for a cause, insanity, or any other extenuating circumstances. You are assaulting the law and the people in full knowledge of all the harm you are causing and the seriousness of the crime you are committing, with the sole end of earning a few bucks.

I only wish to say aloud—as loud as possible so I'm heard—that we will continue fighting until we win or we die. Because serving the cause of dignity is an honor not to be refused and it's a duty not to be neglected. Condemn me, for I already know you cannot do otherwise.

Condemn me, for it will be an honor to bear this latest illegal act against me.

Condemn me, for I will continue fighting with all my strength to see that the principles of law and freedom prevail. I hereby conclude my legal defense.

Viva Cuba libre!

During those weeks, the prisoners in Havana and the Isle of Pines staged a hunger strike against the arbitrary measures dictated by the jailers. In solidarity we staged our own hunger strike at the Boniato jail and went several days without eating a bite. We declared our support for the strike in the following words:

To the political, civilian, and military prisoners throughout the country. To the people of Cuba:

We announce to the people that as of today, Sunday, February 16, at 6:00 p.m., we have gone on a hunger strike in solidarity with the just demand of the political prisoners at Príncipe Castle.

On behalf of the July 26 Movement, we hereby call on all political, civilian, and military prisoners to go on a hunger strike as well, in support of this movement of civic protest.

We also urge the Cuban people—their civic, cultural, religious, and political institutions; the press; professional associations; workers, students, and others—to mobilize publicly in defense of the sacred right of habeas corpus, a conquest of the peoples of the world in their struggle against despotism and tyranny.

The government has used violent means to block a resolution of the Supreme Court. The fact is, just as in the era of absolute monarchy, this regime keeps its citizens imprisoned for more than a year without trial.

This is a clear, flagrant violation of the legal framework we uphold. A broad national mobilization is therefore needed, headed by the political prisoners of Príncipe Castle and those in all the prisons of the republic who, like ourselves, join this strike movement in solidarity with them.

Defend a right that has cost centuries of struggle and sacrifice! Support the political prisoners of the Havana jail!

Political prisoners of the Boniato jail

Unrest against the regime was growing day by day. "Constitutional guarantees" were then in effect, and over the radio came news of the long list of sabotage actions that were taking place, as well as news of the active presence of the combatants in the Sierra.

In jail I read many books on Cuban history, accounts of the French Revolution, and always Martí. I talked a great deal with Javier Pazos, who had studied Marxism, and I formed a strong friendship with Julio Camacho Aguilera, who had been transferred there from the prison in Santa Clara. Together with other compañeros, we organized the revolutionary prisoners.

Outside the country, a tale has been woven about how our whole struggle could have moved toward a bourgeois revolution. I invite anyone who believes this to consider the consequences of the implementation of our entire program. The enactment and strict enforcement of laws implementing the constitution of 1940 alone signified radical opposition to the interests of the domestic oligarchy and imperialism. Suffice it to say that this constitution provided for the abolition of the large landed estates.

The social composition of the most representative leadership cadres and rank-and-file combatants was not bourgeois; they came from the working masses, the middle layers (mostly of modest means), the poor peasants, and the unemployed.

By reviewing the circulars, letters, and decrees we had prepared to be issued beginning November 30, it is possible to gain
insight into the ideas and feelings of the July 26 combatants in
the 1950s.[7] These documents are proof that we were marching
toward a confrontation with imperialism, and that the idea of
social revolution had taken root among the combatants of the
July 26 Movement.

❋

While in the Boniato jail, I lived through a momentous event
for our struggle: the April 1958 strike.[8] That was the most significant date in the revolutionary struggle of the July 26 Movement in the Llano. By analyzing it, we can assess the role and
the impact of the underground movement on the war of liberation, and clarify historically what the terms Sierra and Llano
meant.

The strike was not simply an action by one group or a number of them. It turned out to be the attempt of an entire people
to bring down the tyranny and establish revolutionary power.
Several measures were taken to ensure its success. One was to
strengthen the July 26 Movement's worker cadres, so they could
take responsibility for forming strike committees, with very
precise instructions.

Between the strike committees on the one hand and the Civic
Resistance Movement on the other, everything involved in the
general work stoppage was to be organized. Propaganda for the
action was to make clear its character: we were striving not only
to stage a strike by workers but to bring the country to a complete standstill. An action plan to precipitate the general work
stoppage would be drawn up.

7. See page 277, "Revolutionary Proclamation of Santiago de Cuba and the Sierra Maestra."
8. See glossary, April 9 strike.

I will not elaborate on the many events that took place around that time. I will say only that in the first few months of 1958 and up until the very moment of the strike, the level of popular unrest was growing. The mass movement and the acts of sabotage gained tremendous strength from one end of the country to the other. On the very day of the strike, rebel actions took place in many different parts of the country.

The increase in civic protest was such that the dictatorship had to once again suspend the constitutional guarantees and freedom of the press with which it had hypocritically tried to disguise itself. From my prison cell, I was convinced the moment had come to call the strike.

In order to place April 9 in proper perspective, it is essential to emphasize, as I have stated previously, that there were two different scenes of activity for the revolutionary struggle during 1957 and 1958, both of which showed, in different ways, the nature of the process that was unfolding.

These differences must be analyzed in light of the practical shifts and adjustments in the outlook of revolutionaries looking for the best way to fight the enemy. In the Sierra, the outlook of the guerrilla fighters developed in a way that led to victory. In the cities, the urban cadres and combatants over time arrived at a perspective that led us to the events of April 9.

This was the historical result of a strategy developed in the Llano based on a general strike in the cities, which, combined with the decisive blow against the regime's armed forces in the mountains, would bring down the tyranny. This strategy did not prove valid for reaching the stated goal; in fact, things happened the other way around. The regime crumbled as the rebel troops advanced, and after this the general strike consolidated the popular victory.

Whatever the differing emphases given in each of these areas of activity to the actions necessary for victory, it was clear to all that the revolution's foundation was armed insurrection of the masses, the revolutionary general strike, the July 26 Movement program, and Fidel's undisputed leadership.

"At this very moment the revolution is starting in Cuba."

FRANK PAÍS, NOVEMBER 30, 1956

MIL FOTOS CUBA

On November 25, 1956, 82 revolutionaries set sail for southeastern Cuba from Tuxpan, Mexico, aboard the yacht *Granma* **(below)**. On November 30, the July 26 Movement launched an uprising in Santiago de Cuba, organized to coincide with expected landing. **Bottom:** main police station was attacked and burned to ground. **Left:** Otto Parellada (top) and Pepito Tey (bottom), two young combatants killed in the battle.

MIL FOTOS CUBA

MIL FOTOS CUBA

BOHEMIA ARCHIVES

"For us in the cities, it was vital to maintain the Rebel Army in the Sierra. That was our first and fundamental obligation. The triumph of the revolution depended on the success and maintenance of the guerrilla nucleus in the mountains."

A few days after the *Granma* landed on Dec. 2, 1956, the 82 expeditionaries were ambushed and dispersed, with a quarter killed and many taken prisoner. Some two dozen regrouped and formed the nucleus of the Rebel Army whose base of operations was in the Sierra Maestra mountains. The Batista regime reported that Castro, together with all the rebels, was dead.

In February 1957 the *New York Times* published an interview with Castro **(above)** obtained by correspondent Herbert Matthews. It alerted millions in Cuba that the rebels were not only alive but preparing for combat. **Facing page, top:** simultaneously the first meeting of the July 26 Movement leadership was held in the Sierra. From left, Frank País, Faustino Pérez, Raúl Castro, Fidel Castro, Armando Hart, and Universo Sánchez.

Several weeks later, a reinforcement detachment of some 50 fighters arrived in the Sierra. Consisting largely of veterans of the November 30 Santiago uprising, it included three U.S. youth living at the naval base in Guantánamo Bay. **Facing page, bottom:** Armando Hart (right) with the three American volunteers.

More and more, the guerrilla struggle in the mountains merged with growing resistance in the cities. **Below:** a demonstration organized by women in Santiago de Cuba protests Jan. 1, 1957, cop murder of 15-year-old William Soler. The sign reads: "Stop the murder of our children. Cuban mothers." The woman at far left is Vilma Espín.

"**Insurrectional activity was growing all over the country. From our prison cells we heard the explosions of bombs that the July 26 Movement set off as a popular response to the vicious tyranny.**"

In early 1957 Armando Hart was helping to organize July 26 Movement cells throughout Cuba and establish links to organizations of workers, peasants, students, and professionals. In April 1957 he was arrested and jailed in Havana. **Above:** Hart (in dark prison clothes) is shown in court together with fellow July 26 Movement leader Faustino Pérez.

Facing page, top: on March 13, 1957, members of the Revolutionary Directorate attacked the Presidential Palace. Several weeks later, four of the leading participants who survived were murdered in cold blood in an apartment at 7 Humboldt St. **Right:** to protest the murders, Hart (front left) and other prisoners sing the Cuban national anthem as they are led into court. Shortly after this, Hart escaped from the courthouse, shedding his prison clothes.

"The burial of Frank País was a demonstration by the entire population. The whole city was taken over by the people."

VILMA ESPÍN

The seething revolutionary resistance found expression in two events in the summer of 1957. On July 30 Frank País **(above)**, central organizer of the July 26 Movement urban underground, was murdered in the streets of Santiago de Cuba. In response, a general strike erupted throughout the province, and a funeral march in Santiago drew 60,000 **(top)**.

On September 5 an uprising took place in Cienfuegos, led by anti-Batista forces within the navy. **Facing page:** members of the July 26 Movement and others took up arms to support the uprising, which was crushed by the regime.

"Organizers of the military uprising in Cienfuegos on September 5 gave weapons to militants of the July 26 Movement as well as to the people more broadly."

RENÉ RAMOS LATOUR, 1957

"We were marching toward a confrontation with imperialism. The idea of social revolution had taken hold deeply among the combatants."

Below: Batista (left) is presented with a solid gold telephone by executives of the U.S.-owned Cuban Telephone Company, as a token of appreciation for a March 1957 rate increase he had imposed. **Bottom:** U.S. ambassador Arthur Gardner is saluted by Gen. Francisco Tabernilla, head of the Cuban army. Gardner served from May 1953 until June 1957.

CORBIS-BETTMAN

Washington's support for Batista became an object of protest within the United States. **This page, top:** members of the July 26 Club in Tampa, Florida, organize a picket line on July 26, 1957.

Sympathy for the anti-Batista struggle was fueled by a slowly growing radicalization underpinned by the mass movement in the U.S. South against racist segregation of Blacks. **Bottom:** a mass meeting in Montgomery, Alabama, February 1956, to support the 1955–56 bus boycott in that city demanding an end to "Jim Crow" segregation laws.

"In the first few months of 1958 the level of popular unrest grew. The mass movement gained unprecedented strength throughout the country."

In mid-November 1957 Armando Hart, July 26 Movement national coordinator, went to Sierra Maestra for leadership meetings on recently announced Miami Pact and clandestine work in the cities. **Top,** from left: Fidel Castro, Armando Hart, Celia Sánchez, Raúl Castro, Javier Pazos. The day after this photo was taken, Hart, Pazos, and Tony Buch were captured as they came down from the mountains. **Bottom:** brought to the Moncada garrison, Hart (in striped shirt) and Pazos are shown with Gen. Alberto del Río Chaviano (at right), butcher of Moncada combatants. Hart's life was saved when the July 26 Movement quickly made known throughout the country Batista's orders to murder him. Throughout 1958 he was held in different prisons. **Facing page, bottom left:** in Boniato jail, Oriente province.

JUANITO MARTÍNEZ POZUETA / ANDRÉS MATA FOUNDATION

While in jail, the imprisoned revolutionaries learned of the failed attempt by the July 26 Movement to launch a general strike on April 9 **(top right)**. Shortly thereafter, Hart also learned of the death on April 21 of his brother, July 26 Movement cadre Enrique **(top left)**, who died when a bomb he was making exploded.

Bottom right: The Cuban Revolution was part of a broader revolutionary ferment throughout Latin America. In January 1958 a popular rebellion in Venezuela toppled the military dictatorship of Marcos Pérez Jiménez. That action in turn gave fresh impetus to the struggle in Cuba.

"In face of the Rebel Army's westward advance, an imprisoned officer told us, 'It's not possible; it's not feasible militarily.' A compañero answered him: 'Colonel, they didn't know it was impossible.'"

In July 1958, the Rebel Army defeated an offensive by the Batista troops in the Sierra Maestra. The rebels then sent columns westward to other provinces and advanced on the cities in Oriente. By November–December 1958, the revolutionary momentum generated by the rebels' victories was accelerating.

Facing page, bottom: In a last-ditch effort to create a democratic facade, the dictatorship organized fraudulent elections on November 3, 1958. The July 26 Movement organized a boycott, and the elections were turned into a debacle for the dictatorship throughout the country. **Facing page, top:** Rebel commander Camilo Cienfuegos (left) with members of his column during the battle of Yaguajay in northern Las Villas province, late December 1958.

This page, top: Raúl Castro addresses the Congress of Peasants in Arms, September 21, 1958. Seated behind him is Vilma Espín. **Bottom:** members of the Rebel Army column led by Che Guevara celebrate the liberation of a town in Las Villas province, late December 1958.

"Popular insurrection plus general strike was the revolution's final formula for eradicating the ignominious regime born on March 10, 1952."

This page, top: On January 1, 1959, Batista (right) hurriedly fled Cuba in face of the rebels' advance and a spreading popular insurrection. In the photo is General Eulogio Cantillo. **Bottom:** In a move backed by Washington, Cantillo (left) attempted to forestall the Rebel Army victory by replacing Batista with a military junta.

Meanwhile, working people took to the streets to finish off the dictatorship. **Facing page, top:** When Cantillo's treachery became known, Fidel Castro issued a call for a nationwide general strike, and the junta collapsed within hours. **Center:** Havana citizens take over the offices of a pro-Batista political party. **Bottom:** a mass celebration in Havana's Central Park, January 2.

"On January 8, 1959, the commander in chief and his victorious guerrilla fighters triumphantly entered Havana. Fidel was coming back four and a half years after his departure from Cuba, as he had promised, with 'the tyranny beheaded at our feet.'"

Top: Fidel Castro (left) as the Liberty Caravan arrived in Havana January 8, greeted by hundreds of thousands of Cubans. **Bottom,** Armando Hart (left), minister of education, with Rebel Army commanders Raúl Castro (center) and Camilo Cienfuegos at a September 14, 1959, ceremony turning over the Camp Columbia military base in Havana to the Ministry of Education, which transformed it into the "school city," Ciudad Libertad.

Months after the failure of the April 9 strike, on October 3, 1958, Faustino wrote me this letter from the Sierra Maestra:

Compañero and brother:

Today I want to shake the laziness out of my pen and write you the letter I've owed you for such a long time. Ever since the ill-fated days when you were taken prisoner I have wanted to convey to you all the concern and anguish that came over us and the entire Movement as to what would happen to you in the clutches of the henchmen and as to what your capture meant to us. The Movement was entering a stage of revolutionary consolidation, it continued to enjoy growing public support, its military strength was multiplying, and on the organizational side its cadres were definitively taking on a more militant character. We were still lacking a completely integrated leadership, a more systematic guidance of our action, and a more complete and precise doctrine and program.

Your visit and stay in the Free Territory made us feel assured that we would be able to give a strong boost to those goals upon your return. Analyzing and discussing all the questions relating to the revolution and the Movement together with those like yourself—who, in addition to extraordinary abilities, have the conscious impatience and will to raise, define, and solve these questions—could not fail to be fruitful. It's no wonder that out of those conditions a document of such revolutionary character and historical scope as [Fidel's December 14] letter to the so-called Cuban Liberation Council could emerge.

We also knew of the vitality with which you conducted yourself as the Movement's coordinator, where in a very short time you left a brilliant and productive mark. But at the best moment the worst happened. Once again we were left with a poverty of leadership. Although the Movement demonstrated its strength by preventing your murder—and this was yet another victory that provided fresh encouragement to go forward—after that things could not be the same as they would have been with your guiding presence invigorated by the trip. But the effort had to go on and we gave Zoilo [Marcelo Fernández] the responsibility that you'd had, since he was the one who would make your absence felt the least.

I was still convinced of the need to give Havana special attention. By going back there, and with the decisive help of all the compañeros, I believe we led the Movement into its "golden age" in the capital, whose high point was the time between the kidnapping of Fangio and the issuing of the twenty-one point manifesto that came out of a meeting in the Sierra.[9] It was a time of great revolutionary upsurge in the Llano. We all agreed that the degree of organization that had been achieved and the prevailing climate made it advisable to encourage the general strike. A total student strike had spontaneously occurred. We set about working toward the decisive dates of April 1 and 5 set forth in the manifesto. At the time there seemed to be a prolonging of the death agony of a regime already in convulsions. We felt that the best date would be Monday, March 31, but in raising this with the compañeros from Santiago they thought it would be better to wait a few more days, and that was how we came up with the date of April 9. It was one of the first mistakes that led to a needless failure. The other mistakes, which were even more serious, consisted of inadequate and counterproductive tactics that we employed in order to call and stage the strike. Thus, we later saw very clearly how an organization that had reached an acceptable degree of effectiveness nonetheless failed to function because we did not give it a chance.

We kept the agreed-upon date a secret, supposedly for the sake of the militias' action, and we made a fleeting announcement on several radio stations at a time—11:00 a.m.—when only a few housewives were listening to the radio, and on a date

9. To publicize their cause, a July 26 Movement commando squad kidnapped Argentine auto racer Juan Manuel Fangio in Havana on February 23, 1958. He was released unharmed a day later. On March 12 the National Directorate of the July 26 Movement issued a twenty-one point manifesto, proclaiming the final stage of the struggle against Batista and mandating stepped-up preparations for a general strike.

when the "climatic wave" was decidedly on the downswing. We caught our own cadres of the organization by surprise (workers, members of the Civic Resistance, students, and even members of the action cells) as well as the people as a whole, who began to find out unevenly, through various channels, about a [general strike] call whose source they were not completely sure of. Had it been issued as a slogan forty-eight hours earlier, mobilizing the entire organization, it would have served as a formidable and necessary element of prior agitation and saturation. All of this, combined with only the partial success of the sabotage of public utilities and other less-visible and immediate causes, destroyed a real possibility that should have been decisive.

So the strike in Havana "evaporated" and its tragic consequences have been incalculable. For not only had we wasted yet another opportunity to overthrow the tyranny, and not only were the streets of Havana and all of Cuban soil soaked in generous blood. But it gave the general public and even many revolutionary leaders the false impression that the strategy upheld until then of the general strike and armed insurrection was not correct. This in turn gave way, even among our militants, to clamors for unity and the thesis of the war of opposing armies. I personally felt heavily responsible for all that, and it was a gut-wrenching experience, more so than any other difficult situation I had surmounted.

My feelings were not unmoved by the loss of so many brave combatants. We lost both their potential growth for the creative tasks of the future, as well as for the very real necessity of struggle in the present. To mention only those nearest to us, in just a few days we lost Fontán, Alcides Pérez, Mingolo, Sergio, Marcelo, Pepe, Alemancito, Lucero, and, to top it all off, your brother—our brother—Enrique, who, as you said, was killed by his own dynamism. Full to the brim with restless vitality, he always kept the cord of action taut. Nothing around him could be static or dead. He was like the "strong water" used to test pure gold and cast aside the fake stuff. The revolution will feel his absence and we, along with the pain of not having him, will feel the spur of his example and his fiber.

The failure of April 9 with its tragic consequences, and the consciousness of the errors committed, as well as my personal faults and weaknesses, left a deep mark on my spirit. My soul shattered, I left for the heroic Sierra with my convictions somewhat adrift. I had thought I was stronger, and that belief made me weaker. But this Sierra is a savior. It has saved the revolution from being annihilated, and it saves sick spirits from death. Breathing the free, oxygenated air of the mountains, living surrounded by nature, exercising muscles and willpower with the exertion of hard living and all-out sacrifice, stirring once again with the emotion of fighting for freedom in a setting where one dies illuminated by the sun's rays and the grateful earth welcomes one into its bosom—this detoxifies, encourages, heals, restores, revitalizes.

Stubbornly pursuing me, like my own shadow, was the thought—perhaps with a little self-pride—that Havana, slandered and troubled, was capable of responding, and that I could and should achieve that. But the proposal for the changes and the Executive Committee in the Sierra prevailed, and I returned here with Daniel, Mario, and Franqui, who together with Fidel would make up the Executive Committee. It took me almost a month of arduous travel to reach the General Command at a crucial time for the revolution. The dictatorship, emboldened by the failure of the strike, thought the moment had come to finish off the stronghold of the Sierra. They concentrated their forces on that objective, unleashing an offensive of fantastic proportions. They penetrated deeply into the mountains, and every day the line of siege by the "helmets" drew closer. The situation grew quite critical.

The fact that we are right and our cause is just operates as a moral yeast; it increases one's fighting spirit and multiplies the invisible forces. It affected the men in the Rebel Army—sometimes consciously but more often intuitively and contagiously. With the help of Fidel's strategic genius, it produced the miracle—or, rather, the extraordinary feat—of turning an extremely difficult situation for us into a resounding victory, and turning an easy victory for them into an embarrassing military debacle.

I don't know if the wall of bars and silence that separates you from the outside world allowed you and the other prisoners to learn of the successive military dispatches issued by the general command during the offensive. These dispatches—in their accuracy, force, informative elegance, and political orientation—reveal Fidel's great ability, revolutionary sincerity, and mature leadership, . . . his extraordinary ability to work and his powerful intuition.

The results of the offensive may be summed up as follows: more than 500 weapons seized, including .81- and .60-caliber mortars, bazookas, heavy machine guns, a large amount of ammunition; more than 400 prisoners and wounded soldiers, whom we turned over to the International Red Cross, an event of incalculable military, political, and human consequence. Several hundred enemy dead. On our side there were 27 dead and 50 wounded, without a single one falling prisoner. The remaining forces of the tyranny fled hastily from the entire Sierra and the adjacent towns. The Free Territory was consolidated and extended, with an immediate offensive by multiple rebel columns already invading the western provinces. Batista's army was increasingly demoralized, with massive insubordination in some locations. The fighting spirit in the cities has increasingly returned.

In truth, I never believed in the possibility of what I have seen, and that has been one of our greatest errors in appreciation: to consider the Sierra a great nucleus of rebellion with extraordinary symbolic importance, but discounting its military possibilities. I still remember telling Fidel when I came with [*New York Times* reporter Herbert] Matthews that the important thing was that they not be destroyed, that they should go to the bottom of a cave, since it was enough to know he was there for us to do the rest in the Llano. Today I am glad he ignored me. . . .

On a day of tragic significance for the Movement, we lost Daniel. It was July 30, the one-year anniversary of Frank's death. He was our only casualty in the next-to-last major battle during the offensive, on the verge of the victory he had helped forge on the front line. It was yet another loss that Cuba, I am sure, has mourned in silence. Because it is inconceivable that a man of integrity, a true revolutionary, a generous son could sacrifice his life for his mother and she could then suffer without shedding tears. We lost another brother and we feel our heart getting smaller and smaller.

My role in this entire offensive was more that of an active spectator than a direct protagonist. Now I'm beginning to exercise my limited capacities as head of the Civil Administration of the Free Territory (ACTL). I think it will set an extremely positive and symbolic example for the Movement to show that, even in the heat of battle, it is serious about organizing collective life in the territory under its control in a revolutionary manner, serious about defending and furthering the legitimate interests and concerns of the people, about promoting and bringing to the people the possibilities for creation and enrichment permitted by circumstance and provided by nature and work. About offering demonstrations of the responsibilities and aims that drive us, demonstrations of what can be done in Cuba with all the resources of power in the hands of the revolution. During the offensive, activities not directly related to war were suspended, but as the fighting moved on, various needs among the peasant population were attended to. We already have numerous schools, hospitals, and courts spread all over the territory. There's a jail (Puerto Malanga) with a penal system in which the level of humanity, hygiene, and public utility could not be surpassed. There's a School for Recruits headed by Aldo [Santamaría], the worthy sibling of his brother and sister, with some four hundred students at the present time. Citizen-soldiers are forged there, and attention is given not only to military development, but to education and health care as well.

The peasants are being organized and, in short, any project or endeavor that seeks to benefit or improve the life of the peasants is being encouraged. If on top of the natural difficulties and scarce resources, amid the majestic, eloquent silence of these mountains, we succeed in turning our desires into tangible facts, I would be satisfied. As the indomitable rebel columns penetrate into the heart of the provinces to shake the scaffolding and damaged foundation of the tyranny, many valuable compañeros are coming deep into these mountains to find refuge for their capacities to create and work.

You cannot imagine how much we miss you when we discuss topics of revolutionary, political, and human interest. I am encouraged by the thought that in the end we will have the contribution that Cuba and its revolution expect from the creative power of your restless, hard-working mind. . . .

This letter is already too long. Just one bit of family news. The only thing I've heard about your family is that some of them are in Caracas and others are in Miami, and everyone is well. As for mine, I can tell you that I am the father of another beautiful baby girl (according to her mother) named Nélida. I am told that the other two little cubs are doing well and miss Daddy very much. I hide my homesickness in the crannies of this rugged terrain, fertilized by so much blood, shaken by so much struggle, pulsating with so many aspirations, and supported by hope.

Warmly,

Fausto

On December 24, 1958, from the Isle of Pines prison, deeply moved, I answered him:

Dear Fausto,

I have jealously guarded your letter because in it you synthesize—with the clarity, simplicity, and elegance in which you are capable of expressing the most profound ideas—something that is a piece of our history, a piece of ourselves. I consider your

observations to be uncommonly valuable in terms of experience and knowledge of our strengths and errors with regard to
this event, in these times that are so full of great events.

I don't want to talk to you about that, about the entire process before and after April. My letter would go on forever because for me the month of April 1958 signifies doctrine, ideas,
strategy, political tactics, and above all injustice and cruelty. Let
me say only that in my opinion you yourself came out of that
process bigger and stronger than ever. There were mistakes, and
those cannot be placed on any one individual in particular. It
would be necessary to analyze and delve into the entire strategy and significance of the July 26 Movement to understand
why things happened as they did. Whatever happened or failed
to happen there—the events of February, March, and April—
the errors and great accomplishments are not attributable to any
one individual. They are mistakes and great accomplishments
of our very essence, and they reflect the very nature of our revolutionary generation. A generation that wants all or nothing.
A generation that today, with growing strength, power, and confidence in victory, for its most legitimate happiness because it
is responding to a historical necessity, puts forward individuals
like yourself, who have the privilege—so envied from here—
of enjoying the events of these months of pain—a pain that is
balanced only by the unparalleled grandeur of the pages you
are writing.

As for me—and I can tell you this with the conviction of one
who ponders everything—I don't think there could be a better
historical possibility for achieving what we want. And above all
because I sincerely believe that Fidel's greatness grows each day
and because I'm sure that Cuba will owe much of its future
happiness to the Movement's soundest decision: uniting and
assembling the leadership in the Sierra, and the close collaboration of you all. Because revolutionary unity is the only thing
that can save Cuba, and allow us to justify and explain ourselves
to those who now live only in our memory and in the work we
are creating.

Through you I am sending to all the compañeros in the leadership some digressions on certain fundamental questions for our Movement. These lines, the letter I wrote to the National Directorate after April, and other papers they seized from me in Boniato, are the main things I have been thinking about this year. . . . You all will see, of course, that some of these ideas are nothing more than the written expression of what I have always put forward, at times not so skillfully but always with firmness—and what I will still maintain when I leave here because, in my opinion, they hold the key to our triumph and are the justification for our conduct. There are also other ideas to which I had not yet given a name: When analyzing what I think and feel that I am, Fausto, I have seen what I didn't believe I was. I have also changed in a fundamental way: in a certain sense we need to define ourselves. This is how we will gain respect even from those we most hurt with our definitions, if we know how to raise issues and develop our ideas in step with our political and tactical requirements.

I have arrived at a conclusion that I had already mentioned to you at the municipal jail: maturity means understanding the immaturity of others in order to be able to expound the most mature and demanding ideas. But maturity cannot consist in ignoring what we are and should be, nor in saying it so coarsely or hastily that it provokes a violent reaction in many immature people. And in Cuba, Fausto, there are too many immature people. I have not seen any people outside the Movement who are truly mature. At times, judging from afar, I have thought that there were some here or there, but when I have bumped into those people who I had assumed to be very mature and experienced, I have found weak-mindedness, a lack of rigor in every sense. . . .

It is our generation that has to make the next twenty-five years. I only want to emphasize to you that all these ideas are not as refined or clarified as they should be. I would have liked to revise them and round them out, but I'm afraid I'll be searched; in recent days I have been searched several times, just to speak of myself. Besides, even though these ideas are not sufficiently polished, you will understand me because we always speak the same language. For my part, I will continue trying to make progress on this document, which is composed of this general introduction and something on point 5 (the mass instrument) and which should continue on with a detailed analysis of all ten points.

There are very many compañeros here of great revolutionary value, some of whom you know, and others whom you will know. . . .

We also have Quintín [Pino Machado], who is first rate, and all these compañeros, the majority of whom have spent more than a year in jail, and have made good use of the time. Rest assured that they will turn out to be extraordinarily useful when they channel the indignation resulting from helplessness into the great vehicle of our generation. I am in permanent session with Mario [Hidalgo], who for your personal information, has progressed and matured as a revolutionary to an extraordinary degree in these two years. In addition to Quintín, Carlos, and Aldo Santamaría, we owe Mario a lot for the formidable organization and discipline that has been maintained here. Many of the ideas in the document I am sending you come from conversations and discussions with him. He sends you his greetings.

I want to tell you that our Ideological School bears Enrique's name and operates as he would have always liked it to: with all-out effort. This Ideological School has been a tool for forging unity, and we have seen this work in practice whenever problems have come up such as those that always appear in every human organization, but which are overcome when you act in a revolutionary manner.

I don't want to make this letter any longer; the only thing I have left to say is that I owe you special congratulations for the birth of Nelidita. I often hear about Nélida through Aurora. As for my family, you probably already know that all of them are out of circulation. The revolution has dragged them into the whirlwind. Even though this is just and correct from a historical standpoint, it's nonetheless cruel and hurts me on a personal level. To everyone there and to Aldo, who should consider this letter as also addressed to him, I send warm regards and memories from the one who, I repeat, envies you all.

Your brother,
Armando

P.S. Very special regards to Celia.

This indelible memory of what the April 9 strike was shows the close unity that had been attained among all revolutionaries of the Sierra and the Llano.[10]

*

Both letters refer to the fact that my brother Enrique died on April 21. The Movement had put him in charge of action and sabotage in Matanzas province. On that tragic day he was at a house on Yara Street, in the Cumbre neighborhood of Cárdenas, preparing some bombs for general use during the insurrection. The devices exploded, taking his life and those of the young combatants Carlos García Gil and Juan A. González Bayona.

My brother was the image of a revolutionary combatant of the insurrectional period. I could see the same features in many other compañeros during those years. From March 10 on, we shared the same politics. We began immediately to establish relations with the most active groups based upon two conditions: that they held firm positions in favor of insurrectional action against the tyranny, and that they not have held responsibilities in the ousted government or in the traditional opposition parties.

10. For more on the July 26 Movement leadership's evaluation of the April 9 strike at a May meeting held in the Sierra at Altos de Mompié, see "A Decisive Meeting" in Ernesto Che Guevara, *Episodes of the Cuban Revolutionary War, 1956–58*, pp. 316–22.

The barracks coup brought him suddenly, without a moment's hesitation, into the fighting vanguard. He was on vacation that day, at the home of an uncle in Trinidad. As soon as he heard the news on the radio he packed his suitcase, returned to Havana, and began to actively involve himself in the fight against the tyranny.

He explained this to me in his own words. Prior to the coup he saw no solution for Cuba's problems, he told me, but the action by the military had opened the road of revolution for the country. I recalled at the time that months earlier he had ridiculed the top Orthodox leaders for not having turned Chibás's funeral into a movement aimed at the revolutionary seizure of power.

Enrique was one of the young people who went to the university in those memorable days following the coup. It should be said nevertheless that his strongest ties were not at the university. He developed closer relations with bank workers and later with people in the Movement.

To Enrique, an insurrectional position against the government was a matter of principle. The political dividing line had become popular insurrection and political independence.

Like all of us, he joined Fidel and the July 26 Movement, to channel his rebelliousness and thirst for social justice. With the possibilities opened up by Fidel's political leadership and with the yearning for action that existed among the mass of youth and working people, Enrique became one of the most intrepid and boldest members of the underground movement.

In 1956 he spent several months traveling in the United States. During that time he worked in a factory, and when he returned to Cuba he was more anti-imperialist than before. These are some of my most cherished memories of a brother who died for his ideals and convictions. As I once told Faustino, he was killed by his excess of dynamism. He died fighting to advance the popular insurrection, with a deep hatred for the bourgeois political and social environment, with clear anti-imperialist sentiments, and with the very firm conviction that this was a revolution of the workers and the exploited.

In those sad days of April 1958, from the Boniato jail, I wrote a letter to my family:

Dear everyone:

Nothing, nothing provides justification. It can be explained only by the cruelty and disequilibrium with which, by the strange design of fate, nature shows men the existence of a love and an equilibrium that escape us. In our limited comprehension, we have the absurd spectacle of so many mediocrities, so many worms living in darkness, only half-alive—which is not living at all—while those filled with life die precisely for wanting to live.

He died because he was born to live in the full breadth of our world. He died because his breadth was greater than the world's. He died because he felt, he thought, and, above all, because he acted. A lover of greatness, impassioned, he was one of those who, as Martí said, are the firstborn in a society bound by shackles and full of evil. He therefore had to be heroic in order to live.

Woe to a people that in 150 years has needed thousands and thousands of corpses to advance slowly and painfully forward! The greatest figures throughout Cuban history have died on the battlefield. Other, more fortunate peoples have been governed by their own greatest figures.

It is no longer the corpses that make us sad now, but the fact that Cuba needs them. The sacrifice of thousands of Cubans has been necessary in order to show that in this latter half of the century Martí's homeland is not made up of vulgar materialistic people. We have needed their blood to tell all the peoples of the world that the cowards and mediocrities who so often drew Enrique's ire do not represent us. The worst part is not even so many deaths; the really terrifying thing is so many pseudo-lives.

The people are with us. But unless the vast majority, those who truly feel the cause of freedom, find ways to make the mediocrities obey; unless we are capable of unleashing the latent rage of the masses; unless we oust them from all power (notice I said power, not government); unless, after so many sacrifices, we succeed in having justice prevail, and in steering and channeling Cuban life according to dignity, honor, and law—principles that we must have either learned as children or picked up through the heroic lives of those who have given everything for Cuba's historical destiny; unless our generation—Enrique's generation—is able to achieve all this after so much sacrifice, then our only honor will be to die.

And, even more seriously, we cannot go astray because, as he correctly said, this is Cuba's last chance to save itself. The first chance was in 1902, the second in 1933, and the third in 1944.[11] Our generation has the last chance.

To avenge Enrique's death will be difficult. What a tremendous commitment we have taken on! I always recall something Frank said when his brother died: "We have to get there in order to bring about justice." How difficult it will be without them!

Justice is not barren hatred. It is not the tyranny of our ideas. It is not absurd bias. Our idea is precisely the negation of absolutism! The only absolute thing is freedom and that which spontaneously derives from its daily practice. Our idea is the predominance of right, of warm understanding among the real components of Cuban society. Justice means elevating homo sapiens to the category of man. It is giving everyone their material goods and their rights. It is having every Cuban fully enjoy the cultural and material heritage of our times. . . .

This is the marvelous century of the atom and flights to outer space, with all the power of science at the service of knowledge to better mankind, which in truth is its only god! It is the high point of our aspirations and thoughts. . . .

If in spite of all the accumulated experience in sociology and history, we do not succeed in mobilizing every Cuban in definitive action against the tyranny, or if after its overthrow we cannot keep them moving toward emancipation from all their

11. See chronology.

chains—if we cannot do these things, then we will have failed to avenge Enrique. If we do not adopt appropriate methods of political, social, and economic reform capable of assuring the continuous movement of the Cuban people toward freedom, then we will have failed to avenge Enrique. If now or later Cuba remains in the hands of the worst elements, of the scum of the people, then those of us still here had best exit this world in grand style.

If, through our inability, craziness, or ignorance, we fail to channel or appreciate such greatness burning in this huge fire started by others, then those remaining should burn up as well. Such a calamity would demand an example of total sacrifice from those who are obligated to save the future of Cuba, from those who are committed to reaching a satisfactory resolution of the conflict, and from us, the new Cuban generation. For many this example of total sacrifice is no sacrifice at all. In that event we will have to shout out—as loudly as such disgrace demands—that this generation does not accept the alternative: ". . . or not to be."

If, with public opinion on our side, with the masses of youth, and with our decisive influence, we are not capable of fulfilling the assigned mission, then we will have to be capable of joining in the tragedy once and for all, inasmuch as we cannot join in the glory of saving the historical legacy of the founders. Rage is what I felt when they gave me the news, and you all know that injustice and wrong always provoke a spontaneous outburst of rage in me. But rage is caused by helplessness. And if those who feel enough dignity, so that it determines all their actions are not strong or intelligent enough to impose it, then I should like to die of rage. In that case I think it would be our right. Our only right and our final duty.

Let no one say that Enrique and so many others did not think! Let no one reduce his life to feelings! I probably knew him better than anyone. Twenty-six years sleeping in the same room! Whatever demanding and radical ideas I may hold, I definitely owe to him. He was a formidable critic. Sometimes it seemed to me that in his passion for analysis he destroyed everything and ended up nowhere. Then we would argue until it reached the point of passion. But his passion was for logic, for reason. He had absolute faith in those values.

I, who thought life was much broader, now understand where the disagreement was. Deception and lies (for him the greatest enemy) are useless in life and politics when both are essentially revolutionary. Therein lay the entire essence and basis of his attitude toward life and all his greatness.

He hated whoever told the first lie; he felt that the first lie gave rise to the second, and that it created all criminal deceit that makes the art of governing and creating so difficult. He felt that all this deceit would have to be destroyed by science and technology, a more powerful destructive agent than human relations. Perhaps what we have yet to fully understand is that human relations also have their own science and their technology.

He knew, though, that the basic point of everything was the will to create ("urges," according to Gustavo). And the impulse for action that he gave to his life was the clearest example of this conviction. He knew about the usefulness of sacrifice; he felt the need to *do*, and when he was *doing* chances are he was not sacrificing.

He was tireless. When he was finished with one thing, he immediately would go on to another. He was a whirlwind of action and work. When men find a way to make themselves effective, they become tireless. He found such a way and thereby found his glorious and immense destiny.

I think that the six of us remaining . . . have come of age with this event. To me Enrique is everywhere. The world seems more serious to me. What was yesterday a duty to Cuba and my conscience, a desire of my temperament and a love for glory that comes only from serving the cause of humanity, is today all of that, but it's something even deeper. It is a duty to him.

I must live to either avenge him or subject myself to an identical fate. I used to think of the latter as a right that I might not

be strong enough or brave enough to exercise. Today, that choice
is my primary duty in life. A duty you cannot avoid without
dishonor. I used to feel that I had a certain right to withdraw
out of fatigue, which I wished would never arrive. Today I feel
only the right to avenge him or follow him. Hopefully I will
have the strength and courage. Otherwise I would be a despicable being. All of us have a very special duty as well. He left
behind those who must be educated like he was. I know Mercy
will do so. It is her commitment to Enrique. Those children must
be taught to become calm, strict judges of the entire revolutionary process of the next twenty-five years. They must be taught
to be relentless toward error and falsehood, and passionate ad-
mirers of the most complete revolutionary triumph. Therein
will lie the answer to a question they will have to ask themselves: Did he die in vain?

It will be our duty to educate them as we were educated. Not
so much with words, which were never lacking, but with an ever-
present example. Honor, integrity of character, good manners,
a passion for knowledge, the view that society's first asset is the
law—all these forged in Enrique an ideal that gained strength
and took shape in his independent, sovereign spirit. These teachings must be passed on to his children, as our great duty toward him.

The cowards are accusing Dad of inciting us. Cowards know
they're lying when they accuse him of insurrectional activity
and imaginary inciting, but that's because cowardice cannot
tolerate a spirit of integrity and decency that, as the cornerstone
of an impeccable thirty-three-year career as a public official,
served us as a model for confronting those who violate the law.
Cowards cannot stand the dignity and courage with which Dad,
along with others, demanded an end to illegal persecutions.

I think that under the current circumstances, for someone
who has devoted his life to the administration of justice, this
accusation from the cowards is the greatest of rewards.

Wretched are those who have cowardly helped spread it. I
can forgive cowardice, but when it causes or supports crime, the

republic cannot forgive it.

Vile tricks by people with a certain educational level is, in my opinion, the most serious of crimes. . . .

And these are the ones truly responsible for the situation, the perpetual upholders of injustice. It was their fault that the civilian and republican unity needed to confront an illegitimate power was lacking at the time of the coup or afterwards. And we have had to search for that civil unity through rivers of blood and destruction. The onus is on them.

When this letter—which was more the explosion of my feelings in the initial moments—was almost finished, Mom arrived with letters from Marinita, Martha, Gustavo, and Fermín. They all blur together and call for a thousand answers and comments. Some of these might be contained in what I've written above. Feelings, Gustavo, make ideas appear in all their clarity. When I read and reread the above lines, I see how they show, more clearly than I have ever seen, basic concepts of my life, as well as Enrique's. Indeed, Gustavo, decency and morality are a strong and powerful root of all things revolutionary. That's how he was. And morality is based on truth. That was his passion. It is through the accurate interpretation of the truth and its practical workings that the ideas derived from that moral root take on a life and intellectual character of their own. Here begins the influence you have had on me. The tragic part of our debates is that there was no room for differences. I say tragic because today and tomorrow, when we put together the ideological jigsaw puzzle, he will be missing.

I would like to talk to everyone. I started to write a letter to Martha and was unable to continue. When I read her letter, life becomes too concrete and the events too specific to be able to face them. There are now six of us . . . you have summed up the entire question in a single sentence. I was going to write to you all here about unimportant details that unfortunately now have importance. But just because I was unable to continue writing along those lines doesn't mean I have a right to try, making you suffer as a result. . . .

My entire life I have taken refuge in the world of ideas and a passion for the abstract. . . . But it must be that way, because when one feels passion for a general cause, for an abstract value such as justice, every honest man must give himself over to it, since it's through revolutionary action that those abstract values translate into very concrete and vital things for the vast majority of men. Defending the cause of mankind is an honor not to be refused and a duty not to be surrendered. Those abstract values (the ideas) arise from the interpretation of concrete events. . . .

I was not happy until, in running away from myself, I found myself. . . . This life has not been a sacrifice for me. The sacrifice has been for you.

That is as it must be, because wretched is he who, possessing a rebel passion and rage against injustice and abuse, finds nothing to resort to, no compensation mechanism to protect himself from the pain and anguish.

Today, running away once again, I do not speak of the Enrique that makes me cry, but of the one who makes me indignant at the injustice of fate.

Mother, the letter of Marinita and Martha, and Jorge's shout at the wake[12] take me back to the Enrique who is indeed dead. The one I once traded punches with and fought with in our childhood quarrels. I cannot speak of him, although I wanted to at this time. It seems that Gustavo did not want to mention him, either.

Think of how his life was certainly not a sacrifice for him either. . . .

Everyday life can be delicious if one does not have a tragic temperament. . . . Gustavo, if life were, as you say, "a sickness," then he died of life.

At this point now, amid solitude and dejection, and finding in Yeyé both simplicity and turbulence in a single person, I have again found another part of my life. The one that has made me love all of you more and more. That part of life that I have never

___

12. "Down with Batista!" [AH]

abandoned, but was hidden from the outside deep within my innermost self; it was as if unseen, unexpressed, since love for the cause of human dignity, passion for the glory of serving history as modestly as I can, kept it from showing. But it could not be killed; that was impossible.

And today, as I reel from this merciless blow, it is overflowing its banks and compels me to tell you that I love you with all my soul, that I need you with all my soul, and that not for a single instant in my life have you all ceased to be at my side.

We should all feel equally proud. Each of us has taken or will take for our own lives a certain line in accordance with the principles of dignity and sincerity. Some have felt the historical passion more strongly than others. But if one analyzes this more deeply, this passion is not a sacrifice, because when one follows the line of destiny man encounters no sacrifice. How great and happy he must have felt to be able to resist! . . .

I repeat, you are the ones who have truly and legitimately made sacrifices, and perhaps you will find consolation in the increase of your historical passion. This is unequivocal proof that my life up until now has not been a sacrifice but a mandate. Not all of us are born with the same faith or identical passion, nor must all of us carry out identical work. But the seven of us have been faithful to the teachings that only in creative work can life's legitimacy be found.

None of us, it must be said proudly, has lived a pseudolife. Now, added to the examples received from Mom and Dad, to Dad's true sacrifice (because his career was his priesthood), is the greatest sacrifice of all, Enrique's, the one that cannot be equaled. We have once again confirmed in our consciences the ideas of honesty and character that we have been breathing in our family ever since we were old enough to understand. That is what has truly angered the cowards and mediocrities who don't know the value of virtue and the grandeur of character. Poor wretches!

> With all my soul, yours,
> *Armando*

P.S. Write me. All of you, write me and write a lot. That is what I most need today. You can do it by mail, within the obvious limitations of censorship. Do it.

After four decades my ethical, political and philosophical conceptions have not changed. I always remember what I read as a teenager: *Las fuerzas morales* [Moral forces] and *El hombre mediocre* [The mediocre man], by José Ingenieros. The latter contains unforgettable paragraphs, in which he recommends to those who have the "mysterious" mechanism of an ideal working inside of them, "to care for it like a sacred ember," because if it disappears we become "cold human refuse."

In order to confront arbitrary acts and strengthen our own spirit we have to nurture solidarity, love, and the fight for justice. The best way for men to put up resistance against those who "hate and destroy" is to exalt in our hearts those who "love and build."

*

The strike had failed, and there was talk about the extermination of the compañeros in the Sierra. Although I did not believe this, many of our hopes were cut short.

I was visited in prison by a janissary of the tyranny who fancied himself a lawyer and had obtained his degree from a university certified by the regime, without ever having studied law. I was transferred to a nearby office for the interview with the henchman. A large group of political prisoners gathered behind the bars, thinking the regime was about to kill me; all of them were fighting to save me. The henchman and I got into a debate in which he called me an idealist and a romantic, and said we had no future. We held a long debate on these topics. In the end he took me back to my compañeros. They were anxious and concerned about my fate. As I was walking toward the cellblock, I thought of my dead brother, the failure of the April strike, and the fallen compañeros. Then I turned to the henchman and said to him, "I am happier than you are."

In March 1958 an important group of judicial functionaries with long and solid professional careers submitted a complaint to the Supreme Court demanding an end to the crimes being committed by the authorities.

To my father, compliance with the law was a moral principle and an essential link in the organization of social life. Because of his integrity, which had no place in a corrupt society like that one, he was branded "naive" and "stupid," and he was even called these things on a personal level. Men who maintain ethical principles are often branded as "idiots."

At the time of Batista's coup, my father suffered greatly because of the break this signified for the nation's constitutional rhythm. Although he would not have wanted his children to run the risks involved in the insurrectional struggle, he considered our conduct ethical and legitimate. His legal training made him adopt a stance of solidarity toward the activities of Enrique and me. It was the scandalous increase of crimes committed in full public daylight in the months prior to the strike of April 9 that led a group of officials to decide to submit the above-mentioned complaint to the Supreme Court. In response, they were removed from their posts and barred from exercising their profession.[13]

✱

The main compañeros from the Llano went off to the Sierra after the April strike. On May 3, at Altos de Mompié, a meeting that had strategic importance for the struggle was held.[14]

13. My sister Martha and her husband Fermín Portilla went off to the Sierra in November and joined the Third Eastern Front until the end of the conflict. My father, mother and other brothers and sisters had to leave the country until the triumph of the revolution. Upon their return, my father was named a Supreme Court justice; he would later become chief justice. Toward the end of his career, on Fidel's proposal, he was awarded the José Martí National Order. [AH]

14. See page 282, "The Meeting at Altos de Mompié," by Luis Buch.

Following that meeting, Haydée came down to Santiago to implement the decision that she leave the country. While there she learned that with the failure of the strike and the death of Enrique I was feeling pretty low. Ramona Ruiz Bravo visited me frequently and told her that I was insistent on a possible escape, despite how closely they were watching me.

With great audacity, Haydée decided to go and see me, and she showed up at the jail to explain everything to me. She had made this decision without consulting Daniel. When she arrived at the prison, she said she was my sister Martha, and they let her through. I was shocked when I saw her arrive: she had been a prisoner at that very same place, she was underground, she had come down from the Sierra to go abroad on a mission, and yet she went to the prison to tell me all this and say goodbye. Only her immense courage made it possible for her to carry out that action.

Haydée agreed to go abroad because Fidel had requested she do so. All she asked was that she be allowed to choose her own way of carrying out the mission. She spoke to Daniel and obtained the authorization. She herself told the magazine *Santiago* how she managed to leave the country:

. . . I traveled with Marcia, the wife of Léster Rodríguez. . . . I was to arrive at the airport first, and she would come later. If something happened to me, she would not get on the plane and would report what had happened; otherwise, she would board as normal after me and we would continue on together. There too the people were in solidarity with us. When I got to the airport and handed over my passport, which bore an assumed name and someone else's photo, the young man looked at me, looked at the name, the photo, looked back at me and said, "Stay here."

Then I approached Marcia furtively and said to her, "Look, I think they're onto me. Go to the end of the line, so that if something happens to me you can leave."

I hesitated as to whether or not I should leave, but as the line was moving the man appeared again on one side: "Excuse me, come this way." I protested: "But everyone's already on the plane." And he answered, "Yes, yes, but there were no seats left, and we just found one." He grabbed me and took me through another area toward the plane, going around the other checkpoints. Marcia, who saw what was happening but could not hear what he was telling me, ran up and yelled at the guy: "Listen, they told me I can't get on, but now I see this woman behind me getting on, so I should get on too." She said defiantly: "So there were no seats, huh?" This was a lie; there were plenty. . . . But the young man said to her, "Okay, you can get on too, come on." And still she was saying to him, "Such unprofessionalism!" Then, when I was about to climb up the stairs onto the plane, he shook my hand, got a little embarrassed, and said to me, "Good luck!"

✳

In early July 1958, one year after my escape from the Havana courthouse, I was transferred from the Boniato jail to Príncipe Castle in Havana. I was taken under heavy guard on a military plane. The guards took me by mistake to the detention cells on the top floors of the Príncipe—the Vivac—where the prisoners who had not been sentenced were held. Even though I did not call attention to the mistake, right away the military officers there said that I should be taken downstairs to the area where cells for those who had already been sentenced were located.

One of the first people I ran into there was Quintín Pino Machado, who had been imprisoned on the Isle of Pines and had also been transferred to Príncipe Castle for some hearings. As soon as he saw me, Quintín asked, "Armando, are we communists?" I stood there thinking, caught off guard and not knowing exactly how to answer him. Quintín had been influenced by socialist ideas in Santa Clara, where his mother, Margot Machado, ran a school where very advanced ideas predominated. He was a communist within the ranks of the July 26 Movement.

In going back over the various letters and documents I wrote at that time, reviewing the strategic ideas I had about the seizure of power and many other subjects, I can confirm that by then I clearly had a socialist world view, as did other compañeros in the July 26 Movement.

Around that time, revolutionary literature from the Frank País Second Eastern Front, commanded by Raúl Castro, arrived at the jail. We learned that Raúl had consolidated his forces throughout that entire vast region and they were carrying out important cultural, social, and ideological work in one of the poorest territories in the country. One of the documents we received had a very big impact on me because of its social and anti-imperialist content: a June 27 message to the youth from Raúl. This document confirmed the beliefs I already had, and it was a moral and political reaffirmation of the convictions held by many of the revolutionary prisoners at Príncipe Castle.[15]

We were transferred to a much more uncomfortable cellblock where we were overcrowded, fostering an increase in tension among the members of the action groups. It was harder to develop an organization like the one we'd had there the previous year. More restrictive prison policies had been ordered regarding visits and meals, and a number of abuses had been committed. At 3:00 p.m. on August 1, 1958, tension reached a high point. On that day the guards had kicked our relatives out of the prison and mistreated them. The truth is that they didn't want any witnesses to the approaching massacre.

The perpetrators of this heinous crime against the political prisoners were the well-known killers Conrado Carratalá Ugalde and Esteban Ventura Novo, escorted by more than twenty henchmen who were members of the National Police and the Military Intelligence Service (SIM).

Those who died in that massacre at Príncipe prison, all of whom were in the detention cell block, were political prisoners

15. See page 285, "To Cuban Youth, to All Latin American Youth, to the Youth of the World," by Raúl Castro.

Vicente Ponce Carrasco, Reinaldo Gutiérrez Otaño, and Roberto de la Rosa Valdés. Another twenty were seriously wounded.

We put up valiant resistance in that unequal encounter. Cornered behind bars, we fought with beds, with bottles, with anything we could get our hands on.

In the detention cell area, the compañeros who were near the wounded assisted them, until finally, little by little, the beasts began to get control of themselves. In spite of the uncertainty we managed to stay calm. Later we had to stand for two hours with our hands in the air, under close watch. The wounded went three hours without any medical attention.

The criminals had the gall to inform the public that the incident had been instigated by the political prisoners themselves, who had been carrying firearms and resisted, setting off the "battle" because they refused to peacefully hand over these weapons to the police. On August 2 we learned that there had been eight more victims of the sinister massacre.

We managed to send out an account of what had really happened, and I explained the details in a denunciation that we were hoping to publish both nationally and internationally.[16] We were also able to send out several letters describing the events, such as the following excerpts from a message I sent Yeyé on August 4, 1958:

> . . . I cannot write you a very long letter because several documents must go out with this letter and conditions are obviously tight. I don't mean to alarm you, but I have never had or been through a more difficult situation. We were protesting the suspension of visits and the fact that compañeros who had been arrested and then released later turn up murdered. . . .
>
> We were protesting in a heroic and rather forceful manner, so the chiefs of all the repressive bodies assembled here—in-

16. See page 291, "Make the Events of August 1 the Focal Point of Our Agitation and Propaganda," and page 292, "Letter to Radio Rumbos, Caracas, on the Príncipe Prison Massacre," by Armando Hart.

cluding the "flower" of the regime under the command of Pilar García. They spent three hours machine-gunning the cellblock. Since we had made barricades out of burning iron beds, it was hard for them to get in. Carratalá was wounded and that saved us, as he had the worst intentions. Those in the detention cells were not so lucky, because it was easy to get in and they had no chance to buy time. We have heard that their plan was to take advantage of the occasion and murder Aldo Vera, Odón [Álvarez], Carlos Iglesias, and me. But after three hours of murder at the jail, three ministers (Interior, Justice, and Finances) had turned up, and they apparently held back the massacre. Also, Pilar García (his son accomplished the "heroic feat" in the detention cells) gave orders to stop.

About a hundred men in our area were holed up amid the flames and weapons, and then all of us were put up against the wall. At our backs were Irenaldo, Pilar García and all the chiefs of the repressive forces, the greatest murderers of this regime. . . .

The courage and integrity exhibited by everyone was unsurpassed. There was no vacillation or weakness, not even when someone posed the question "where to start.". . . I remembered the tremendous blow Mom and Dad had suffered, and I thought that they might not be able to withstand this second blow. . . . But we all held firm.

Later we were transferred to the cellblock and forced to clean it. Someone told Martín Pérez who I was and he said to me, "I thought you were taller and heavier! How we've looked for you on the street! Now get sweeping." . . .

I answered him: "I know how to sweep and I take pride in doing any kind of work." He said, "Yes, I know. Set the broom down," and he went on speaking in a diplomatic and reflective tone, saying that I should have been among the dead, but that the people in the detention cells had saved us. What a tragedy!

The worst of it is they now know the way to do this.

Here we have risen up and that's how it must be, since revolutionary morale demands it. We are, as you said, sitting on top

of a powder keg. . . . What intuition you have. I think you fig-
ured everything out from over there. . . .

Eight bombs exploded that night in Havana. We have raised
the fighting spirit in the capital, which had been affected by so
many setbacks. . . .

We will take the protests to the trials, and we will direct our
slogans toward the outside. We will make Havana tremble if we
get help from outside. And we will try not to use any violence.
We will only resist. . . .

Perhaps the most significant thing would be if they transferred us to the Isle [of Pines], where I also have a lot of work
to do. I think that by the time they take me there, this will have
already progressed. . . .

I had a long report on that for the leadership, but I burned it
when the events took place. . . .

The events of August 1 constitute an example of the violence
systematically used by the regime against the political prisoners. The hatred they unleashed on us strengthened the combatants' morale. Not even with death could they intimidate us or
break our spirit.

I wrote the following note to the Movement during those
days. It illustrates our true concerns:

The latest issue of *Revolución* has pleased everyone here
very much. In the revolutionary study groups that meet every
night, we read what we're being sent from the outside. Send me
any of the Movement's propaganda, since there are eighty in-
mates in the prison and four hundred in the detention cells who
we have to keep informed and give guidance to. At the Isle of
Pines we have four hundred prisoners. Information for the prisoners is vital and must be carefully attended to.

What I most liked about *Revolución* is that we read the previous issue only ten or fifteen days ago. Regularity of publication is extremely important and has always proven difficult to
achieve.

Greetings to all the compañeros and special congratulations to those responsible for the propaganda and to those who are working on the issues of *Revolución* and *Vanguardia Obrera* that I have read.

Yours in revolution,
Hart
PRÍNCIPE PRISON

Swift action that saved Armando Hart's life

Carlos Amat, Rosita Casán, and Luis Buch

Carlos Amat and Rosita Casán, members of the July 26 Movement underground in Santiago de Cuba, were both working at the Cuban Telephone Company in January 1958, when Armando Hart was arrested near Bayamo in eastern Cuba. They were interviewed for the June–September 1975 issue of the magazine *Santiago*, from which these excerpts are taken. The account by Luis Buch, head of public relations for the July 26 Movement in Havana at the time, was prepared specially for *Aldabonazo*.

Carlos Amat
. . . I was still in high school when I went to work at the company. I worked in what was called the Transmission Department. Given the technique used in splitting the incoming lines on their way to the operator switchboards, all lines passed through our department first. We had our own switchboard through which, whenever a call came through, we were able to listen in on the operators and on the people talking without them noticing. This was done by the company as a measure of supervision and control. But it would later be of great use to us. . . .

Rosita Casán

Generally speaking, I had to remain on guard continuously. If I was off work, I'd be at home or easily findable. But I spent most of my time at the phone company, because we also had to keep an eye on the local phones in Santiago. We knew where the compañeros in hiding were, so whenever the military would monitor the phones, we had to warn them immediately. For this we devised a system of passwords and countersigns.

"Hey, how's Aunt Dora?" someone would ask.

"Aunt Dora couldn't be better," we'd answer. That meant they could speak freely.

But sometimes the response was: "Aunt Dora's seriously ill, and today she's terrible. We had to admit her to the hospital." By that, the compañero knew the military was listening in.

Another aspect of our work was that Rogelio [Soto] would listen in to Chaviano's phone at the Moncada garrison and to the offices of the Military Intelligence Service (SIM), to find out everything they were talking about. Often we intercepted orders to arrest or search people, and we'd warn them. . . . These cops were very clumsy in their repressive work, and they committed real indiscretions over the phone.

In this way, the telephone jobs made it possible for the Movement to have a secure means of communication locally and nationally both for directing our clandestine effort and as a source of first-hand information on the enemy's communications. . . .

There's a concrete case where the telephones fulfilled a fundamental mission. It was in January 1958. One night around 10:00 p.m., I got a call from Vilma [Espín]. "They've seized a number of people," she said, "and we need to find out who they are. Make inquiries in Bayamo."

A little later Daniel [René Ramos Latour] phoned me and told me the same thing, but he referred to some farmland attached to the Palma sugar mill, located between Palma Soriano and Bayamo, where they had arrested Jacinto Pérez (Armando), Tony Buch, and Javier Pazos. Carlos Amat called me, too, with the news and I phoned Haydée. Meanwhile, I called an operator in Bayamo who worked with us, and told her to investigate the lines to the Bayamo garrison. She called back around midnight.

She confirmed that the prisoners were indeed being held, that they would be transferred to Santiago the next morning, and that they were "three big shots." I immediately passed this all on to Déborah (Vilma) and Daniel.

Later when we were at work, Carlos [Amat] and I listened in on a call where Tabernilla ordered Chaviano to kill Hart and the doctor (Buch). Tabernilla reminded him that Hart had escaped from the courtroom once before.

"Get moving and do it fast!" I recall Tabernilla saying. "These degenerates mobilize quickly and they mustn't learn of this. The father of one of them (Felipe Pazos) is appealing to the president. Don't dally. Carry out the order!"

Carlos Amat phoned Haydée and I called Déborah (Vilma). I was simultaneously speaking with Daniel, because in those days the phone in my house had a secret connection to what we called the Cave, the basement of an apartment building that had virtually been converted into our headquarters.

The mobilization was immediate. From the Cave, a number of compañeros took off by car: Eduardito Mesa, Belarmino Castilla (Aníbal), Miguel Ángel Manals, Carlos Chaín, and Gloria Casañas. The latter was carrying two hidden revolvers for the emergency operation they were leaving to undertake: seizing a radio station over which they would announce the news so that the population would remain on alert.

Arriving at the station—located on the second floor of the Lido social club in the Terrazas neighborhood of Vista Alegre—the compañeros pointed a gun at the announcer and the operator on duty. Meanwhile, Carlos Chaín took the microphone and warned the population what was happening, urging them to remain on alert and to remember the strike around [the murder of] Frank [País].

Carlos Amat

. . . Tabernilla phoned Chaviano again to tell him not to kill Javier Pazos, because the latter's father had spoken with Batista and was pulling strings, but that the others should be killed right away.

"Kill Armando like a dog!" Tabernilla said. "Hurry up, since the news is spreading, and afterwards you won't be able to."

Chaviano answered that the news was already out, since a radio station had just been seized. "What should I do?" he asked.

"Imbecile! You've wasted a lot of time! Now there's nothing you can do."

A few days later the prisoners were transferred to the Boniato jail. Their lives had been saved.

Luis Buch

Captured on Hart's person were some compromising documents, and he was savagely beaten. In a second telephone call— this time from Tabernilla to Chaviano—the order was given to stage an alleged skirmish between the army and rebels, with three rebel dead—that is, the three prisoners. . . .

From what we know, the order was not carried out immediately due to the opposition of Laureano Ibarra Pérez. This would not help the government at all, Ibarra Pérez raised, since Hart was the son of a respected magistrate, Pazos was the son of a noted professional who had been president of the National Bank of Cuba and was very well known among economists in Latin America, and Tony Buch was the son of a distinguished doctor with a high scientific reputation, who exercised his profession in Santiago itself and was highly regarded by the entire population. It was easy to order the death of the three prisoners from afar, he said, but those who ordered the execution would confront the indignation and rebellion of an entire city that could become transformed into a national protest, as had happened when Frank País was killed.

These contradictions within the tyranny's high command caused a delay that was decisive for gaining time for the efforts that were carried out in Havana and Santiago de Cuba.

A little before 6:00 a.m., through the July 26 Movement's clandestine phone line at my home in Miramar, my wife Conchita got a call from Haydée Santamaría. "My child is gravely ill," Haydée said tersely. "You must send the medicine as urgently as possible.

There's no hope of saving him."

We had absolutely no doubt that she was referring to Armando Hart, that he had been arrested and was in an extremely precarious situation. . . .

Rushing into action, we headed to the official residence of the Papal Nuncio, where we were greeted by a nun. We explained to her the reason for our presence at such an early hour, which was to urgently meet with Monsignor Luigi Centoz. The nun told us to wait in a reception room. She came back to say that the Nuncio could not be bothered at the moment, because he was saying mass.

In face of our insistence that she pass on to him our life-and-death message, however, she agreed. A few minutes later we were in the presence of Monsignor Luigi Centoz, ambassador of the Holy See and dean of the Diplomatic Corps accredited in Cuba, who asked us into his office. We apologized for the unscheduled visit, explaining that we were there to ask for help from his good offices to save the life of Armando Hart, who had been arrested by the police, and that we had learned through totally reliable channels that the order had been given to physically eliminate him. Such a deed could possibly be averted through his swift and valuable intercession with Cuban authorities.

Monsignor Centoz stammered out a few reasons why such efforts could not be made, given the position he held as dean of the Diplomatic Corps. By virtue of that position, he said, he would have to speak with the other ambassadors, which would take some time.

We insisted on the urgent need for him to carry out the efforts, and proposed that these be made not in his capacity as dean, but simply as ambassador. In light of his refusals, our request was losing ground and our concern was growing, since we were conscious that minutes lost could be fatal.

Facing what seemed a lost cause, Conchita then addressed the monsignor, who was seated behind his desk. In back of him on the wall was an enormous portrait of the Pope. She told him that this improvised meeting was symbolically presided over by the Holy Father. She was convinced, she said, that if a human life depended on his efforts, he would surely make them without hesitation.

Those words seemed to move Centoz, and from then on he began to change his stance. He told us that it was 6:30, too early to call Gonzalo Güell, Batista's minister of state. He would do so at 8:00.

Despite his initial reluctance, in face of our insistence, he eventually decided to telephone him at that early hour.

We didn't know who he spoke with or the content of the conversation, but on returning to his office, he informed us that at 8:00 a.m. he would be received at the Ministry of State, that he was optimistic, and that we should come back at 9:00 a.m.

We showed up again at the Nuncio's residence half an hour before the scheduled time to find out the response.

Monsignor entered the room, somewhat discombobulated, which put us all on tenterhooks. Addressing us, he said he had made the efforts and had been promised that the lives of the three prisoners would be spared. He was very unhappy, however, since he had not been received by Minister of State Gonzalo Güell—whom he had requested the interview with—but rather with Undersecretary Cortina. And he was going to send a vigorous diplomatic note to the Cuban government protesting the disrespectful attitude shown to him by the minister. . . .

We left the Nuncio's office. Although our concern had been lessened a bit, it had not disappeared entirely, since it was not possible to trust the promises of Batista's henchmen.

Utilizing the telephone again, Haydée Santamaría called Armando's parents, but this time she was more direct, since the conversation was done clearly and openly: "Armando has been arrested together with Buch and Pazos. Their lives are in danger, so you must make every effort to prevent them from being killed."

The family mobilized. They spoke with José Miró Cardona, to arouse the interest of the Lawyers Guild. Through that organization, efforts were made with the U.S. embassy. The embassy was slow to react. When those concerned met with the official attending them, he showed them a newspaper that already had information on the arrest of Hart, Tony Buch, and Javier Pazos.

The death of Daniel

Faustino Pérez
August 12, 1958

The following document on the July 30, 1958, death in combat of René Ramos Latour—whose nom-de-guerre was Daniel—was published in the clandestine *Revolución.*

SIERRA MAESTRA, AUGUST 12, 1958

To the brave and selfless compañeros and compañeras of Santiago:

"Daniel has fallen." With him, the Movement loses one of its strongest hearts. The revolution has been deprived of a first-rank combatant, a pillar of the future Cuba. As for us, we have lost a brother. Through the pain I feel, I know the pain you feel, since it is born of the common identification, affection, and admiration we had for him.

It is exactly one year since the death of Frank País, that other giant of sacrifice and of the revolution, his "older brother," the person for whom he was the best replacement. Radio Rebelde intended to devote the program that day [July 30] to a tribute to the great leader of the revolutionary youth on the first anniversary of his death. We informed Daniel that he could not be absent at such a moment and that we would be expecting him personally. But the imperatives of the struggle brought us together at the battlefront on the afternoon of July 29.

Daniel seemed happy because of the prospects for victory, displaying this happiness with that open and clean laughter that poured out from him with the spontaneous sincerity with which he thought, expressed himself, and fought. He told me of his satisfaction with the course of the struggle and the spirit of combat and discipline of the young men he commanded. When the brave captain [Ramón] Paz fell, the latter's men were left under the orders of commander Daniel, as we all knew him here, and as he was known in the underground throughout the country, thus increasing his column up to 150 men.

We separated at dawn on the 30th. Together with the commander in chief of the Rebel Army and some 500 combatants, we had walked all night—from El Salto and Providencia, where the previous battle had ended, to Arroyón, where the next one would take place. It was the 30th, "an outstanding day in revolutionary Santiago." Frank, Josué, Pepito Tey, Otto [Parallada], Tony Alomá, Raúl Pujol—all objects of our grateful, emotional, and pained remembrance.[1] Circumstances did not allow us to pay further tribute than through our devotion to the cause for which they had fallen, wherever those circumstances placed us. . . .

The news that he was wounded began to circulate everywhere, making us move urgently, full of anxiety to find him. But the search was unsuccessful. We took the opposite direction from those tending to him in their anguished retreat. The next morning the terrible news spread; there was no further doubt or hope. Everyone spoke of it with pain: "Commander Daniel has died." Our comrade and brother fell in the midst of the battle for freedom and the revolution, at the height of his abilities, when he was most needed for future creative work and present struggle.

We had known him for a year. Frank, the extraordinary leader and National Action chief, had been murdered and the difficult task of naming a replacement lay ahead of us. The comrades of the National Directorate did not then know Daniel and had thought of me for such a difficult enterprise. The whole of Santiago and Oriente were rising up with the angry cry of "Strike!" in their throats, projecting themselves onto the entire nation that was solidarizing with the struggle and with the pain of the indomitable and tormented land of the Maceos. The directives issued by the

---

1. All these individuals were killed in action on the 30th day of different months.

compañeros from Santiago were correct; in Havana we received the first letter signed by Daniel, which impressed us very favorably. The clarity of the information, the way it was expressed, and the pertinent suggestions and guidelines for action revealed the sure organizational, strategic, and revolutionary vision of the person who was writing them. Very soon Daniel visited us in Havana and we had a wide-ranging exchange on the problems affecting the Movement and the revolution. We understood at once that he was the indicated person to replace Frank País, as the leading compañeros in Oriente already thought. He immediately devoted himself to organizing nationally the Movement's militias, based on Frank's ideas and plans, and we all know of his enthusiastic and total devotion, of his responsible and persistent work.

Throughout that year full of events and responsibilities, we saw him grow in capacity and revolutionary maturity. The whole organization received the benefits of his creative action. When it was agreed [following the failure of the April 9 strike] that we would establish an executive committee to direct the Free Territory [in the Sierra], he was among those chosen, and together we headed off to fulfill that new task assigned by duty and discipline. We arrived here at the height of the dictatorship's offensive, and repelling it was a question of life or death for the revolution.[2] It was necessary to devote all our efforts and energy. For that reason he asked to go in the front line and left at the head of his platoon. The action was intense. The fighting was without letup. Our victorious arms were repelling the offensive, and we had to crush it completely. Santo Domingo, El Jigüe, again Santo Domingo, El Salto, Providencia, Las Vegas, and lastly Joval and Arroyón in the prelude to the final battle against the offensive—all these actions felt his presence, which was simultaneously vigorous, calm, and aggressive.

To win yet another victory, the revolution paid the high price of his life . . .

---

2. From late May until late July, the Batista army mounted an offensive in the Sierra Maestra with 10,000 troops. The 300 armed rebel fighters withstood and eventually crushed this effort.

Here, in the very heart of the Heroic Sierra we have founded the René Ramos Latour *(Daniel)* Library, a very modest tribute to his memory. It symbolizes within the scene of battle the revolution of ideas and actions—of the book and the rifle—that always accompanied him as a combatant . . .

I clasp your hand,
Faustino

Revolutionary proclamation of Santiago de Cuba and the Sierra Maestra

November 1956

The following document was drafted by the July 26 Movement leadership. It was to be released following the *Granma* landing and the Santiago de Cuba uprising of November 30, 1956, to announce the formation of a revolutionary government headed by Fidel Castro and to present its program.

THE JULY 26 REVOLUTIONARY MOVEMENT, in fulfillment of its promise of Freedom or Death, is initiating the revolutionary struggle against the corrupt and criminal dictatorship of Fulgencio Batista and all the causes that produced it.

Invoking the most glorious battles of the peoples for their freedom, . . . *we are exercising, as a duty to our generation and to Cuba's history, the right of resistance to tyranny that is granted us by Article 40 of the Constitution of the Republic. . . .*

Below are the general lines of the governmental program [of the July 26 Movement]: . . .

THE REVOLUTION AND THE ARMED FORCES

Batista and a group of military leaders who have enriched themselves have put the armed forces in conflict with the nation, depriving the country of freedom and democratic life. To shake off this yoke, the blood of young Cuban revolutionaries and soldiers has had to be spilled. The shiny boots that from Camp Columbia command the soldiers to oppress the people while they receive millions from smuggling, illicit gambling, drugs, and dirty business dealings have not gone to the mountains of Turquino and Guantánamo to be with the soldiers. The revolution will embrace all officers, noncommissioned officers, and members of the armed forces in general who have not been complicit with the murders and mistreatment of citizens and who have maintained their honesty.

The revolutionary youth aspires to an *army* of the republic made up of soldiers who are brothers of the people, guardians of their liberties and rights. It will be possible to belong with pride to that army of the democratic government because it will not be a scourge to its people. On the contrary, it will be an instrument of national progress, defense of the homeland, co-executor of the government's plans to distribute lands, test soil and subsoil, harmonize water resources, draw up maps, carry out a census of agricultural resources and cattle, give technical and financial assistance to farmers and agricultural entrepreneurs, and wage campaigns for literacy, hygiene, popular culture, and reforestation.

The soldier will teach how to drill artesian wells, drive and repair tractors, vaccinate cattle and fowls, and artificially inseminate cattle.

That soldier, an agent of economic and cultural progress, will not be confused by unfulfilled, demagogic promises of wage increases. By his own merits he will earn substantial per diem expenses paid for by the farmers and entrepreneurs who benefited, by the corresponding ministries, by autonomous development banks, or by the budget of the army itself.

The revolutionary youth aspires to a *navy* that does not protect smugglers and does not promote the Via-Cuba Canal treason. Rather, it aspires to a navy whose members—respected and admired in the spirit of the *mambí* naval leaders, General Emilio Núñez, Pérez Carbó, and Castillo Duany—help foster the merchant marine, establish centers of nautical training, build dams, construct shipyards, protect the natural riches of the coastal zones, prepare nautical charts, encourage systematic scientific research of the Cuban seas, look for marine species to catch and put to industrial use, and proudly carry the Cuban flag to fish for cod and other species in the open seas, waving the banner of the solitary star across the seven seas.

The revolutionary youth aspires to a *national police* that guarantees democratic coexistence, has true training schools, scientifically researches criminality, protects the citizen, helps instruct him in his civic duties, and saves lives through systematically studying and solving traffic problems. Such a police, steadfast and respected, would not allow its chief to connive with illicit gambling, drugs, and pimping. Thus, Cuba would not again have to bear the shame of the international press exposés that the chief of the national police received $50,000 a week from organized gambling alone.

THE REVOLUTIONARY YOUTH CONFRONT
THE NATION'S BASIC PROBLEMS

We will leave analysis of our ideology and position on each concrete question for the document that the July 26 Movement will address to the country, making a calm study of each of the vital issues in front of us. Here we put forward only in general terms some of our programs.

Ours is a country with an export economy, open and subject to the uncontrollable ups and downs of the world market. The supposed economic security of six million Cubans rests on the sugar industry, which is not capable of expanding to the same degree as the rate of growth of the population and cannot offer steady, productive employment to the unemployed and underemployed and to the thousands of Cubans who each year join the ranks of potential producers. The possibilities of economic expansion through industrialization and high-productivity farming are hindered by our economic relations with the United States of America. We need to end the frightful unemployment and underemployment figures and create new industries to employ more than 40,000 young people annually. We need to change Cuba's economic structure, establishing industries to replace imports and produce for export. We need to change the nature of current U.S. imports and become less dependent on a single market. To achieve all this we must overthrow Batista and mobilize all the nation's economic sectors, so that under the auspices of a revolutionary democratic government we can move toward rational planning of our economy and establish a program of economic development under effective state intervention that supports, finances, protects, subsidizes, or complements private initiative.

In face of economic crises, sectors opposed to Cuba's economic development—sugar speculators, greedy importers, absentee corporations, and landgrabbers—have put in place overseers to wield the knife and the noose. From 1929 to 1933 Machado was kept in power at all costs. In 1935 and the following years Batista was placed in power, and this tropical Attila was utilized again in 1952. Batista is the assassin of workers and peasants, of merchants, industrialists, and small entrepreneurs in crisis, of professionals, of housewives, of unemployed youth.

To stay in power serving his masters, Batista has dangerously reduced reserves in dollars, gold, and foreign currency. He has given away the resources of the subsoil to foreign industry. He has attacked social conquests and facilitates private foreign investment in an indiscriminate way, compromising the economic and political future of generations to come. Thus, added to his political crimes against Cuban democracy is treason to the nation's economy.

We believe that true democracy can be attained only with citizens who are free, equal, educated, and have dignified and productive jobs. The revolution's educational policy will be based on the following main lines:

a) *Turning the Ministry of Education into a technical body*, taking up the old ideal of the 1940 constituent assembly of keeping this ministry free of corruption. The ministry's mission will not be confined solely to scholastic purposes. Its wider tasks comprise national education as an entire process to be carried out jointly by all state bodies and directed not just to children and youth, but to adults and citizens in general.

The minister should be assisted by permanent technical commissions with a long-term policy. These will study in a rational and overall way the financial and economic implications of educational plans, keeping in mind educational statistics. Literacy campaigns will be carried out, together with basic education for adults who already know how to read and write. These will be complemented by a policy of creating or subsidizing libraries, museums, laboratories for scientific research (either their own or in collaboration with those at universities and other centers of higher education and research), theaters, art films, choruses, dance, symphony orchestras, and popular printshops. These are to be organized or created not just in the city of Havana but throughout the republic. To achieve these ends the most modern educational methods for the masses will be used, among them films, radio, press, and television.

b) *Decentralizing the national bureaucratic apparatus*, giving provincial and regional authorities more power of decision making within established general policy. This will eliminate a colonial scourge that is endemic to the structure of the Cuban state.

c) *Restructuring our educational system*, after a review of our school curricula, and establishing an organic relationship between primary, secondary, vocational, and university education. It should be guided by knowledge of the nation's realities and adapted to the new demands of progress as well as the needs and interests of those whom educational policy is directed toward.

It goes without saying that classrooms will not be for sale at the Ministry of Education of the revolutionary government, since the organization of classroom study will be based on technical capacity and human dignity.

The nation can expect from the revolutionary youth a democratic government of honest and capable men, full of love for Cuba. The most authoritative specialists and the healthiest intellectuals in the country have already rendered their collaboration to the July 26 Movement for a calm and profound study of national issues.

Cuba possesses natural and human resources, capital, technology, and institutions that are necessary to transform us into a prosperous, democratic, and civilized nation that will shine in the constellation of peoples as a cultured and free republic, for which dictatorships and empires are anathema. We will head toward that great destiny through the revolutionary effort initiated November 30. . . .

COUNCIL OF THE CUBAN REVOLUTION

Don't hold on to this, circulate it

The meeting at Altos de Mompié

Luis Buch

This account of the historic May 1958 leadership meeting of the July 26 Movement, held in the Sierra Maestra, was written specially for *Aldabonazo*.

. . . At 9:30 a.m. I contacted Yeyé. When I told her that I had worked out the details of my departure, she asked: "Why don't you go to the Boniato jail and visit Armando?" I told her that wouldn't be possible since I had to be at the airport at 11:00.

"There's no problem," she said to me. "Everything will be taken care of. In a few minutes, there will be a car there to take you to Boniato, and afterward to the airport. It's very important that Armando know of the Mompié agreements. Since you're a lawyer, you can identify yourself as such, and you'll surely be able to see him without any difficulty."

So we went to the Boniato jail, I showed my lawyer's card and asked to see the inmate Armando Hart. Within a few minutes they brought him out accompanied by a sergeant. The interview was held standing up, with the guard moving away discreetly. I was able to explain to him in a few minutes the agreements and the other things that happened during the Altos de Mompié meeting, as well as the motives of my trip and Yeyé's.

I told Armando that the meeting began at 6:00 a.m. on May 3, 1958, in the hut of the Mompié family. Attending it were the following compañeros: Fidel *(Alejandro)*, who chaired it; Ernesto Guevara *(Ché)*; Faustino Pérez *(Ariel)*; René Ramos Latour *(Daniel)*; Vilma Espín *(Débora)*; Celia Sánchez *(Aly)*; Marcelo Fernández *(Zoilo)*; Antonio Torres *(Ñico)*; Haydée Santamaría *(María)*; David Salvador *(Mario)*; and me *(Roque)*. Enzo Infante *(Bruno)* arrived at noon.

Celia took the minutes.

We began with a critical and detailed analysis of the failure of the April strike.

The main agreements were the following:

To unify the July 26 Movement under a single leadership exercised by an executive committee to be located in the Sierra, and whose general secretary would be Fidel. All the weapons and other instruments of war and explosives would be sent to the General Command Post. From there they would be distributed in accordance with the coordinated actions projected. A united leadership of the war under the immediate leadership of Commander in Chief Fidel Castro was established.

Faustino Pérez would rejoin the Sierra with the rank of commander. Delio Ochoa was named coordinator in Havana.

Marcelo Fernández gave a detailed report on the Movement's organization and activities in each of the provinces and important municipalities. He also talked about the Civic Resistance Movement and efforts to broaden and strengthen it.

He was assigned to draft a document going over the meeting's results and agreements, so that they would become known at all levels of the Movement.

Marcelo was to continue in his post until a new assignment was made.

René Ramos Latour was to be reincorporated into the Rebel Army with the same rank of commander that he held in the militias.

Haydée was to go abroad to take charge of the organization's finances.

It was agreed that Fidel would address the exiles and émigrés to call for order and discipline in carrying out the work they were responsible for abroad. The July 26 Movement Committee in Exile was recognized as the only official body.

I was to go abroad with precise instructions for Urrutia. I would be the only one of those abroad who would have the code to decipher messages, and I would be responsible for public relations. Toward that end I was to maintain political contacts with foreign governments, and especially I was to work to expedite receipt of the armaments promised by Venezuelan president Larrazábal.

With reports coming in of movement by enemy troops with equipment of all types, which foreshadowed upcoming battles, the meeting of the National Directorate in Mompié ended.

It was Sunday, and Fidel ordered that the first ones to descend would be Haydée and me. Since we had to depart for abroad to fulfill the missions we had each been given, it was decided we should run the least risk.

To Cuban youth
To all Latin American youth
To the youth of the world

Raúl Castro
June 27, 1958

This document by the commander of the Rebel Army's Second Front in northern Oriente province circulated clandestinely, including in Príncipe Castle prison among members of the July 26 Movement.

JULY 26 REVOLUTIONARY ARMY
'FRANK PAÍS' SECOND FRONT (NORTHERN ZONE)
FREE TERRITORY OF CUBA, JUNE 27, 1958

Compañeros:

From the rebel mountains of this eastern province—Free Territory of Cuba—on behalf of youth who, sacrificing everything, have promised to win or die rather than live under such ignominious oppression at a decisive moment of our history, we issue this *urgent call to all young people in the world* to unite their efforts with ours, so as to help save the youth of a brother people from destruction and extermination. We call on them to help a defenseless people that is being cruelly subjugated by the worst gang of criminals and murderers that any nation has ever suffered. We will never abandon the fight, no matter how unequal it might be.

On March 10, 1952, eighty days before general elections in which the people were to freely choose their rulers, Mr. Fulgencio Batista assumed military control of the country through a coup d'état. With a stroke of the pen he swept away all democratic institutions, assumed control in an autocratic way, and imposed the darkest despotism on the people. The leaders of the traditional political parties betrayed the people and abandoned them to their fate, taking refuge in their comfortable positions to await better times, in order to reappear with the stupid ambitions that have always helped characterize them as vultures over a battlefield. In this situation, Batista prepared phony one-man elections, electing himself president together with a housebroken congress.

Meanwhile, a people who suffer want to fight. It was then that Cuban youth decided to take the reins of the resistance. Students, workers, peasants, and professionals prepared to fight. On July 26, 1953, a youth ready to conquer its own destiny waged a frontal attack on the second most important fortress in the country. When the attack failed, a hundred young people paid with their lives for their brave act of rebellion after suffering horrendous tortures. The students, on a struggle footing from the very first moment, saw their ranks diminished with the fall of new martyrs, including José Antonio Echeverría, the leader of the Cuban students. The sugar workers shook the country with tremendous strikes for the conquest of their just demands and the defense of violated liberties, facing the regime's repressive apparatus and the gangster machinery of the officialdom imposed on the trade unions. New losses are being added to the already long list of combatants of the Cuban proletariat.

At the end of 1956, after several years of preparation, the insurrection broke out in the countryside and the cities under the leadership of Fidel Castro and Frank País, an insurrection that continues and grows today. In mid-1957 the murder of Frank País in the streets of Santiago de Cuba produced the most formidable explosion of popular indignation ever witnessed in our country, and the general strike caused by his premature death at twenty-three years of age was drowned in blood. . . .

José Martí, our mentor and guide, whose work and ideas we are firmly determined today to carry forward, was not only concerned with the future of Cuba but of Our America—as he called the Latin

American republics. Martí proved to be one of the greatest states-
men of all time. He saw accurately, before anyone else, the threat
that the newly born empire represented to our young republics.
On the eve of his death, from the fields of Free Cuba, in a letter to
his friend Manuel Mercado, he wrote, among other things: "I have
lived inside the monster and know its entrails; my sling is the sling
of David. . . . I am daily in danger of giving my life for my country and my duty—since I understand that duty and am prepared
to carry it out—the duty of preventing the United States from
spreading across the Antilles, as Cuba obtains its independence, and
overpowering with that additional strength our lands of America."

Foreseeing his approaching death he opens his heart to his distant friend and adds: "All I have done up til now, and all I will do,
has been with that aim. I have had to work quietly and somewhat
indirectly, because there are things that must be kept under cover
in order to be achieved. Because to proclaim them openly would
raise such difficulties that the objectives could not be reached."

The events smashed to pieces Martí's dreams. The events that
he tried, with the independence of Cuba and Puerto Rico, to prevent, unfortunately came to pass.

So much fighting, bleeding, suffering and dying just to have
our island pass from one set of hands to another. . . .

With Batista in power accompanied by the worst den of thieves
and murderers ever suffered by a people anywhere, open U.S. interference continues. Mr. Gardner, their ambassador to Cuba, publicly declares his government's unwavering support to the island's
tyranny, going so far as to accuse Cuban revolutionaries of being
gangsters.

Batista has handed over great wealth to U.S. interests, but the
Yankees want more, and to obtain it they are employing the tactic
of a diplomatic shift. Now they are naming as ambassador Mr. [Earl]
Smith, who pretends to pester Batista and support the revolutionary opposition. The goal was clear, and within a few days bore fruit:
Batista, fearful of losing Yankee support, delivered scandalous concessions: the Moa cobalt mines, located in the territory of this Second Front; new concessions to the Telephone Company, to the Elec-

tric Company, to the oil companies, to the King Ranch cattle farm, and so on. We are so sure of what we say that our denunciation is being confirmed as we write these lines. This very morning, June 26, we heard on the radio that Batista has signed a decree with new and more humiliating concessions of Cuban subsoil to U.S. companies, *in perpetuity* no less. We have never seen such great monstrosities done to the economy of a nation. Undoubtedly these latest concessions come in exchange for the military aid the U.S. government is giving Batista at this precise and terrible moment.

As irrefutable proof of these charges, we point out the following facts: Colonel Tabernilla Palmero, chief of the dictatorship's air force and responsible for the merciless bombings of the cities of Cienfuegos and Sagua la Grande, was decorated by Major General Truman H. Landon, chief of staff of the U.S. Air Command of the Caribbean, on the express orders and on behalf of President Eisenhower himself. This event was recorded in photographs by several newspapers of our country. At the end of May, officers of our Department of Rebel Intelligence informed us that throughout the month, the enemy air force had been supplied by bombs of all types at the Caimanera U.S. naval base [at Guantánamo Bay]. One of these reports reads: "On May 8 the dictatorship's army received 300 rocket bombs and 300 rocket-launch tubes with a weight of 9.6 tons. The Batista planes, after bombing the Sierra Maestra and this Second Front, often fill up their gasoline tanks at the base itself." These documents will be published in official organs of our Movement, and photographs and documents obtained inside the base itself will make their way around the world, presenting irrefutable proof of the charges we are making. . . .

An infinite number of shells for 60 and 80 mm. mortars have been captured in the different battle fronts of this Second Front, as well as bazooka shells, rifle grenades, and weapons of recent manufacture coming from U.S. arsenals. Unexploded bombs of the most varied types with the invariable inscription, "Made in USA," have been seized in the towns attacked by the dictator's planes. They are being kept as evidence of what we declare here. Our troops in combat have seized from the enemy light machine guns with the following inscription: "Fábrica San Cristóbal, República Dominicana."

In the battle zones, our combatants, armed only with land mines and Molotov cocktails, have had to face tanks obtained from the Nicaraguan dictatorship. In view of the popular reaction aroused in Latin America by a few demagogic statements that no more weapons would be delivered to Batista, as well as the existing pressure everywhere, it's easy to see why the U.S. government eliminated the direct and public supplying of military aid.[3] Instead, they now do so indirectly through Dominican dictator Leónidas Trujillo and the Somoza dynasty, oppressors of the sister Nicaraguan republic. At the same time and behind the back of world public opinion, they continue their direct aid through the Caimanera U.S. naval base, as we detailed earlier.

As a consequence of these events, the Cuban people suffer the following evils:

In addition to the economic consequences already explained, the Cuban people suffer the most cruel and criminal oppression such as few nations in the world have had the misfortune of enduring. With the military aid that the U. S. government delivers to the murderers of Cubans, our people have and are continuing to suffer, on an ever greater scale, the most barbaric air raids ever seen in any republic of the American continent. With those same weapons, delivered by the U.S. government, thousands and thousands of Cuban youth, the flower of our generation, have been murdered. The beasts that are kept in power with the help of the U.S. government—many of whom were released from penal institutions by Batista—have turned our once happy cities into hell. They have tortured children of thirteen and fourteen and raped women of all ages. The most refined tortures, which make the worst Nazis look like children, have been put into practice with the diabolic cruelty of Batista's henchmen and the criminal knowledge and consent of the U.S. government. . . .

---

3. In response to the worldwide outcry against the crimes of the Batista regime, in March 1958, the U.S. government had announced it was imposing an embargo on arms shipments to Cuba.

We may fall in the struggle, but we will have done our duty by holding aloft til the end the principles of José Martí. We are the historic link between past generations and future generations—of those children now five, eight, and ten years old who look at us with admiration and who tomorrow will pick up the banner of the struggle, a banner not just for today or tomorrow, but for the future.

Cuban youth have taken a step forward. They have mounted an untamed beast in a high-speed race, and it is no longer possible to stop it or turn it around. There is thus only one outcome possible: either the beast is tamed, or it throws us off and tramples us. That depends on you, Cuban youth, Latin American youth, youth from anywhere in the world. If you maintain an indifferent silence, you will become accomplices of those who today murder us and tomorrow will murder you. It does not matter if you are North American, Soviet, Chinese, or Venezuelan; we are all brothers. Across borders, languages, political or religious beliefs, we all belong to the great family of the world's youth. We confront the same problems, suffer the same consequences, and live under the same threats. In face of that, arm in arm, with a firm footing and our heads held high, let us all sing the same hymn of hope. Let us aspire to and fight for peace and future happiness. And let us conquer the common good for the well-being of all.

Finally, Martí, whose road we follow, told us something that is part of the body of ideas we put forward on behalf of Cuban youth who await your determined support: "Every American of Our America is a Cuban. In Cuba we do not fight only for human freedom, nor for a well-being that is impossible under a government of conquest and bribes, nor for the exclusive well-being of a revered island that inspires and strengthens us with its simple name. *In Cuba we fight to assure, with our independence, the independence of Latin America.*"

Freedom or Death

Raúl Castro Ruz
COMMANDER
'FRANK PAÍS' SECOND FRONT (NORTHERN ZONE)

'Make the events of August 1 the focal point of our agitation and propaganda'

Armando Hart

August 1958

The following note on the Príncipe Castle prison massacre of August 1 was smuggled out of the Havana municipal prison and published clandestinely in *Revolución*.

We must make the events of August 1 the focal point of the July 26 Movement's agitation and propaganda in the capital. The sections coordinating propaganda, the Civic Resistance, and the workers must all inform the people of the monstrous act that has been committed. If this is known in all its aspects, it will become a highly important mobilizing factor. Secondly, it will protect the lives of almost four hundred political prisoners who are today threatened with a new massacre.

Our propaganda, therefore, must be along two lines: to say what happened here, and to warn of what may happen.

It's possible that some of us will be sent to the Isle of Pines. The compañeros who will stay here have been instructed not to create any provocation that could precipitate another massacre.

The repressive bodies have plans to return. They are even keeping a list of those they consider most committed, in order to assassinate them at some point. On August 1 they came with that intention, but those from the detention cells, as well as our prolonged resistance, made them desist.

The July 26 Movement can never demand guarantees. That would be ridiculous and absurd. But to all citizens, in a revolutionary way it should issue warnings and denunciations, and indirectly rouse other sectors of opinion to intervene and exert influence on the country's general situation.

Letter to Radio Rumbos, Caracas, on the Príncipe prison massacre

Armando Hart
August 3, 1958

The following letter describing the August 1 massacre at the Príncipe Castle prison was written to Radio Rumbos in Caracas, Venezuela.

PRÍNCIPE CASTLE, AUGUST 3, 1958

Mr. Manuel Iglesias
Caracas

Dear compañero:

First of all, a revolutionary embrace for the formidable job being done by Radio Rumbos, which we listen to here every night. I send you these greetings on behalf of all the compañeros in prison.

The main reason for this letter is to enclose a document that explains our position on how the events of August 1 took place. The document and the personal information I'm sending say it all. I cannot add much, since that would entail difficulties in getting it out of here.

You may assert that August 1 in Príncipe was one of the most terrible crimes committed by the tyranny in its long chain of murders. We were protesting arbitrary acts by the prison authorities and the repressive bodies. All the repressive forces then massed in Príncipe, machine-gunning the defenseless prison cellblocks for more than three hours. Unfortunately, the detention cells were more accessible to them than were our cellblocks, which are off toward a side in the castle. Here we were able to resist with better luck. We set fire to our mattresses, closed the cell doors, and obstructed the passage with the burning iron grating of our beds.

Eventually, by machine-gunning the cellblocks they were able to force their way in, where they were met by shouts of "Down with the tyranny!" and "Death to the murderers!"

Colonel Carratalá was wounded in the face by his own men, and it seems we owe our lives to this fact. After we surrendered, they took us to a wall, amid blows and insults, and lined us up against it. Nearly a hundred men stood firm with our arms in the air and the henchmen's guns at our backs, as we awaited the shots. At that point news arrived from the detention cells, and they abandoned their plans. Perhaps they did not want the scandal to become bigger than it already was. Or perhaps it was that a number of hours had already gone by, and the climax of the situation had passed.

The one who directed the massacre at the detention cells was Irenaldo García Báez, second in command of the Military Intelligence Service (SIM). We've also heard—although they're keeping us cut off from contact—that Esteban Ventura was there. You can state that García Báez fired on Cellblock 1, where all the dead and wounded basically were.

You should also tell the people of Cuba that the honesty and integrity of the imprisoned combatants was just as firm as when they confronted the murderous bullets of the regime in the streets or in the mountains.

Here, my friend, there's a whole legion of selfless combatants from the clandestine movement who demonstrated once again the extraordinary heroic capacity of Cuba's youth, because the stance of the compañeros on the afternoon of August 1 can be termed sheer heroism. You can confidently assert that the argument about us having weapons is false. Had we in fact possessed them, we would still be resisting today. You can also state that the story about an escape plot by us is false. It was simply a protest against the arbitrary acts of the prison system, which the tyranny, without even hearing us, responded to by machine-gunning the cellblocks.

But the most serious threat—that they will return—is weighing heavily today on the minds of all the political prisoners in Príncipe Castle. We have news that they will try to take advantage of any situation for a new act of savagery. On the afternoon of

August 1 they came with the specific aim of murdering a group of us whom they considered most committed.

For this reason, we ask you to keep public opinion in Cuba and internationally on alert, and to help the compañeros of the July 26 Movement committees with a series of instructions you've received—or will be receiving—in this regard through the organization. We don't need to stress the necessity of this, because we know you can appreciate them.

Before finishing, I want to stress that you should broadcast all the news and information without even a hint of who the informant is. Otherwise, there would be no way to continue with the work I'm involved in.

In addition, don't say that we listen to you every night, because if so, they will take away our radio.

I send a strong comradely embrace to you and special greetings for Radio Rumbos. I hope to be able soon to listen to your fiery revolutionary words over CMQ.

Warm regards,
Dr. Armando Hart Dávalos

p.s. Report that Captain Ramos was the one at the prison who telephoned the repressive bodies, and that Colonel Pérez Couset, head of the prison, gave his approval.

Chapter 9

1958: From prison

The Isle of Pines to victory

Soon after the Príncipe massacre, apparently in an effort to isolate us from the capital, or for some other reason I am unaware of, they made the decision that a group of us would be transferred to the National Prison on the Isle of Pines, which they called a "Model Prison."

Built by Gerardo Machado during his rule, it had started operating in 1931 and was later given the name National Men's Prison. In all, it consisted of five circular buildings with a capacity for five thousand prisoners. Innumerable revolutionary combatants against the tyrannies of Machado and Batista passed through there.

We were put in one of the huge cellblocks, where there were hundreds of revolutionary prisoners of every tendency, including "Los Puros," the military men who had been sentenced for the April 1956 conspiracy. Also, there were the members of the *Granma* expedition whose lives had been saved and who were arrested after the landing. The main force was the July 26 Movement.

I shared those months with a number of compañeros and personal friends such as Quintín Pino, Mario Hidalgo, Jesús Montané, Casto Amador, Joaquín Mas, José Ponce, and others. When I got to the Isle of Pines, I informed Fidel and the National Directorate of the magnificent organizational work carried out at the prison by the commission that, from the Sierra and at my suggestion, had been appointed by the commander in chief himself. It consisted of Carlos Iglesias, Quintín Pino, Mario Hidalgo, and Jesús Montané, among others.

I made contact with the group of officers of the conspiracy led by Ramón Barquín, even though we did not trust him politically. I struck up a personal friendship with Enrique Borbonet and José Ramón Fernández, and in the Movement we made a very positive evaluation of them both.

The prison authorities used to select a prisoner to be overseer of the cellblock. Enrique Borbonet had carried out this function and Fernández did so later. Fernández also served as military instructor of the battalion formed within the circular building itself, and he had taught classes for more than a year. Both of them were able to carry out this responsibility because of their capacity for leadership and organization, and because they had the collaboration of the political prisoners from the July 26 Movement.

On September 5, 1958, the first anniversary of the heroic events in Cienfuegos, we held a patriotic military march in the jail, making use of the huge space of the circular cellblock. It was organized by the July 26 Movement, and we did it in order to achieve greater discipline and pay tribute to our heroes and martyrs.

The Movement had a strong organization, with better conditions than at Príncipe. We were able to devote ourselves more to reading and to organizing study circles. We even had a lecture series.

One day, late in the afternoon, a scuffle started among combatants on one of the upper floors of the circular building. The conflict reached the point where they were threatening to throw a compañero all the way down. Some of the military men, with Fernández at the head, and a group of us from the July 26 Movement went up into the crowd to impose discipline. I remember shouting, "The July 26 Movement commands that order be restored!" and we succeeded in calming down the whole aggressive bunch. We held a trial and the compañero who was responsible for it all was placed in a small cell there in the building. He was a prisoner among the prisoners, punished for the act of indiscipline he had committed.

When the incident was over I said to Barquín, "Do you see how it's the July 26 Movement that can bring order to Cuba?"

The cellblock belonged to the July 26 Movement.

On October 12 Fidel sent us a letter and, on behalf of the guerrilla fighters, five thousand pesos to help out the revolutionaries who were locked up there. He also instructed us to elect a commission to distribute the money fairly. So an election was organized and various debates took place on the issue of who the members of the commission should be. In the end, the candidates proposed by the leadership of the Movement were elected.

In the final months of 1958, Fidel proposed to the tyranny the exchange of Colonel Carrasco, who had been captured by the Rebel Army in the Sierra, for Enrique Borbonet. This must have bothered Ramón Barquín, the highest-ranking representative of the imprisoned military men.

Once Quintín Pino asked Borbonet, "If the revolution becomes socialist, will you remain within it?" To which this honest military man replied, "If the people are with the socialist revolution, I will be there." And he kept his word. He embraced the ideas of socialism and died in his homeland.

Inside the prison we had a clandestine radio that was operated by compañero Casto Amador. It was the final weeks of December 1958. We spent the night of the 24th listening to the news about the advance of the rebel troops. We learned that the forces under Almeida's command were approaching Santiago, that Camilo and Che were marching toward the center of the island, and that various towns in that region had been captured.

Regarding the westward invasion by the columns led by Camilo and Che, Barquín said, "That's not possible; it's not feasible militarily." And a compañero answered him, "Colonel, they did it because they didn't know it was impossible." The general atmosphere in the cellblock was one of an ascending revolution.

It has been said that Ramón Barquín was promoting a coup d'état from inside the prison, based on his contacts in the army and his connections with the U.S. embassy, and that his goal was to neutralize the victory of the revolution. Given his political background, it would have been absurd for him not to try to accomplish that, since it reflected his way of thinking.

Barquín was not a member of the July 26 Movement, and although we regarded him as a military man with democratic and constitutionalist ideas, we knew he was not a man of the revolution.

＊

On the night of December 24, 1956, I'd had supper at Vilma's house. I awaited the year 1957 in rebel Santiago. I welcomed 1958 in the Sierra with Fidel. And at Christmas 1958 and New Year's Day 1959, I was in prison on the Isle of Pines along with a large group of compañeros.

In the early morning hours of that historic January 1, we heard over Casto Amador's clandestine radio the "Sensational News!" that was being broadcast. We all began getting ready to leave, but the guards would not permit it. They held us there until 2:00 or 3:00 p.m., when a group of officers came looking for Barquín and the imprisoned military men. They wanted to play this last card against the popular movement.

The officers who had arrived from Havana wanted the civilian prisoners to remain in jail. Barquín adopted a similar position.

Borbonet, Fernández, other military men, as well as the leadership of the July 26 Movement told them this was unacceptable. I went to argue with Barquín, and I demanded the release of all the political prisoners.

Barquín also wanted to leave an officer from the overthrown regime whom he trusted in charge of the Isle's garrison. I did not agree and immediately went to see Fernández at his cell. I proposed to him, on behalf of the July 26 Movement and the revolution, that he assume military command. He of course agreed. Fernández committed himself to ordering the release of all the prisoners once he had assumed command, and to respect orders only from the July 26 Movement.

The intention of leaving the compañeros of the Movement in prison was frustrated by the unity in action between Borbonet, Fernández, and the military men they headed, and the mass of militants of the July 26 Movement that we represented.

Fernández, with a great sense of ethics, explained the reasons why he had not already joined the Movement. With the stance taken both by him and Borbonet, those military men entered the ranks of our organization on January 1.[1]

Later, some July 26 Movement leaders left the prison together with several officers and headed to the garrison to inform them, and to continue putting into practice the decision we had taken.

Although Barquín told me to leave with him for the Columbia base, I decided to remain on the Isle of Pines to assume the task, together with other compañeros, of arming the prisoners and taking possession of that zone. Because we did not know what was going on at Columbia and the rest of the country, and we thought that this territory could serve as a reserve force for the Rebel Army.

Quintín Pino Machado and Mario Hidalgo accompanied Barquín. The task entrusted to them by the Movement was, as soon as they arrived, to send us news of what was happening at

---

1. See *Making History: Interviews with Four Generals of Cuba's Revolutionary Armed Forces* (Pathfinder, 1999), pp. 89–90, for an account by José Ramón Fernández of his collaboration with Hart and the July 26 Movement in the Isle of Pines prison.

Columbia. In the meantime, together with Fernández, Montané, and other compañeros, we took control of the main positions and arrested the most notorious henchmen.

Jesús Montané was named top civil authority of the Isle of Pines municipality, and on January 2, at around 10 a.m., he was inaugurated as mayor, giving a speech on the porch of city hall.

At midnight on January 1 the compañeros we had sent with Barquín phoned us and informed us that Batista's army was defeated. They advised us to leave for the capital that same night. We did so in the early morning hours of January 2. We took a plane loaded with men and weapons to the airfield at Columbia, today Ciudad Libertad.

Casto Amador was the organizer of that armed troop of freed prisoners who landed at the old Camp Columbia.

At the command post I immediately ran into Barquín, who was sitting in Tabernilla's chair. He said to me: "They haven't given me command of any army!" It was not worth responding to him. Cuba already had another army: the one commanded by Fidel!

Imperialism trusted only Batista and his regime. For that reason in April 1956 it did not have the foresight to support Barquín and therefore lost its last chance—if that ever existed.

The truth is that the fate of imperialist interests in Cuba was inseparably linked with the big chief of March 10.

From abroad Haydée phoned Columbia and spoke with me. She was amazed to find me there. I told her Columbia was already under the control of the July 26 Movement.

From Palma Soriano, Fidel had issued a call for a general strike to block any coup d'état and assure the total triumph of the revolution. When I phoned Santiago to ask for instructions, they informed me that Camilo Cienfuegos was to be at the head of the Columbia military garrison. I met with Barquín and the military men and informed them of the revolution's decision. Barquín was stunned and displeased. Immediately he said: "If you want me to, I'll hand over the garrison to you." I answered: "That won't be necessary. Camilo is about to enter Havana."

Following this conversation I traveled to Santiago de Cuba in a military plane to make contact with Fidel. At the home of the Ruiz Bravo family, where I had stayed in the underground, I met up with Raúl Castro, who was at the head of the Moncada garrison and of the city of Santiago.

Fidel was on his way to Camagüey.

Before departing for that province, I attended the inauguration of Manuel Urrutia as president of the republic. It took place at the University of Oriente, since Santiago had been proclaimed the capital of the country. In the library of that center of learning we held a ceremony that was widely publicized.

My meeting with Fidel took place at the Camagüey airport. When I talked with him and Celia, they told me the proposal was that I become minister of education.

The arrival of my father and Haydée from Miami was a source of great emotion. The following day President Urrutia, Faustino Pérez, Luis Buch, and other compañeros arrived in Camagüey province to meet with Fidel and then depart for Havana. So did I, together with the president and some members of the first cabinet of the revolution.

From Rancho Boyeros Airport we went straight to the old Presidential Palace, where the compañeros of the March 13 Revolutionary Directorate were.

On January 8, 1959, the commander in chief and his victorious guerrilla combatants triumphantly entered Havana. Fidel was coming back four and a half years after his departure from Cuba, just as he had promised, with "the tyranny beheaded at our feet."

The guerrilla force, and around it the development of an armed popular movement, was transformed into an effective form of struggle to achieve the revolutionary victory. Fidel's tactics and strategy of the guerrilla struggle were conceived, brought to life, and reached epic levels during that brief but historic time.

During the second year of the war, Raúl left the Sierra Maestra to organize the Second Front; Almeida advanced to the outskirts of Santiago and organized the Third Front. In the final months, Che and Camilo marched westward across the immense plain that begins in Bayamo and Manzanillo and extends through Las Tunas, Camagüey, and Ciego de Ávila up to the Escambray mountains, and then settled in the center of the island—a march with which they were commemorating the heroic feat of Gómez and Maceo sixty years earlier.

Fidel remained in the Sierra fighting decisive battles, directing from there the strategy of the war, and becoming the most extraordinary popular leader of Our America.

The victory of the Rebel Army crowned the feat, and the liberators entered Santiago de Cuba, conquered Moncada, "avenged" the dead, and won the right to "break the hard crust of colonial rule."

Popular insurrection plus general strike was the revolution's final formula for eradicating the ignominious regime born on March 10, 1952.

The revolution of the peasants, workers, and students—under the leadership of the one-time university student Fidel Castro—had triumphed.

A decisive stage of Cuban history was drawing to a close. In twenty-five months four and a half centuries of colonial domination were swept away forever, a synthesis of almost a hundred years of struggle for independence and freedom.

＊

The Cuban Revolution triumphed on the threshold of the 1960s, in a country then subjugated to U.S. neocolonialism, in a world divided into spheres of influence by the victors of World War II. It emerged victorious in the peculiar framework of the ideological, cultural, and political conflict between the socialist ideal and the world capitalist system, and in the midst of the accentuated anticommunist campaign of the first fifteen years of the Cold War. In contrast to that international panorama, a popular expression was heard all over the country: *"Si Fidel es*

comunista, que me pongan en la lista." [If Fidel is a communist, then put me on the list.] That saying summed up the evolution that was taking place naturally in the patriotic consciousness of the vast majority of the people. This marked for all time
the originality of our process, going back to the Cuban revolutionary tradition of the nineteenth and twentieth centuries.

From then on, education and culture were placed at the center of political and social activity and of the challenges facing a
nation located "at the crossroads" of the world,[2] which had
adopted as its own the highest values of Western culture placing itself irrevocably on the side of the poor.

In those days of January 1959 I arrived at a building in Old
Havana that had been the seat of the House of Representatives
during the initial years of the Republic and later the Ministry
of Education.[3] I was twenty-eight years old. Inspired by Martí's
idea, "To be educated is the only way to be free,"[4] I assumed the
responsibility for guiding the radical transformation of education in Cuba on the basis of these objectives:

• Extending instruction to the entire school-age population,
and eradicating illiteracy in the adult population.

• Promoting a general reform of instruction based on offering a scientific and rounded education combined with training
in ethical and patriotic values inspired by Cuban culture rooted
in Martí's ideas.

• Facilitating communication and strengthening ties between
the family, the school, and the community as a central element
of the educational process.

• Promoting and fostering the people's participation in the
tasks of the ministry. Developing close relations with social and
mass organizations.

• Having administrative and technical decentralization in

2. José Martí, "Manifiesto de Montecristi" [Montecristi manifesto], in *Obras
completas*, (Havana: Editorial Nacional de Cuba, 1963), vol. 4, p. 101.
3. One of the most important centers of corruption of the old regime. [AH]
4. José Martí, "Maestros ambulantes" [Traveling teachers], op. cit., vol. 8, p. 269.

order to achieve these purposes.

In Cuba more than a million people were illiterate; 50 percent of the school-age children had no access to education; high school and university education were far more limited. That is why one of the first measures taken by the Ministry of Education of the revolutionary government was the creation of classrooms all over the country. Five thousand classrooms for nine thousand unemployed teachers could be created just with the financial resources available in the long list of *"botellas"*[5] formerly handed out by the Ministry of Education of the old regime. When I told Fidel I was going to devote myself to creating five thousand classrooms, he pointed out that we should talk to the teachers and ask them to cut their salaries in half and thus create twice as many classrooms—ten thousand—with agreement that their salaries would then be raised gradually in a short number of years. That's what was done.

Broadening educational services was a priority from the very first moments, clearly exemplified by the creation of the ten thousand new classrooms, the conversion of garrisons into schools, and the nationalization of private schools.

I called on the specialists and educators of the country to cooperate in all these endeavors. The patriotic tradition of Cuban education inspired our policy. In fact, from my post as minister, I had the privilege of becoming a pupil of the best teachers in Cuba.

In 1960, at the United Nations General Assembly, Fidel announced that a national campaign against illiteracy was being organized, and that in 1961 Cuba would be free of that scourge that humanity suffered and still suffers today.[6]

An entire generation of young people, students, and teach-

5. Literally "bottles." A term used popularly to describe the corrupt payments to persons who were on the payroll but never did any work. [AH]

6. Fidel Castro's speech to the United Nations is contained in Fidel Castro, Ernesto Che Guevara, *To Speak the Truth: Why Washington's 'Cold War' against Cuba Doesn't End* (Pathfinder, 1992).

ers, of cadres of mass organizations, began their revolutionary lives, and their historic contributions to the country, in that literacy drive, which had its most immediate antecedents in the literacy efforts conducted by the Rebel Army during the insurrectional struggle.

During the 1961 campaign 300,000 Cubans were organized, among them more than 100,000 student brigadistas in the Conrado Benítez brigades, 121,000 popular literacy teachers, 35,000 teachers integrated as cadres and specialists, and 15,000 workers in the "Patria o muerte" brigades. To this we must add an untold number of workers in all areas, as well as administrative and service personnel, whose efforts were indispensable to assuring the material and organizational success of the campaign.

The high proportion of young people among that impressive mobilization of literacy teachers was an extremely important fact. That campaign became the first great mass undertaking by a new generation. Youth who were too young to participate in the struggle against the tyranny were given a no-less-heroic task at the triumph of the revolution: that of defending the country and the revolutionary program, one of whose points was the elimination of illiteracy. A legion of these youth went to every corner of the country—workbook, textbook, and lantern in hand—to teach reading and writing. They learned the first political lesson of their lives as literacy teachers. Our young students and teachers taught more than 700,000 Cubans, as they simultaneously learned from them that being rooted in the people as a whole is the fundamental thing in order to create and advance in a revolution.

The literacy campaign, in short, was an educational and cultural act that created revolutionary consciousness in new generations. It was part of the intense popular movement, with deep aspirations for the radical renovation the country was living through in the revolution's early years. In those beautiful days, centuries of ignorance and exploitation came crashing down.

With the noblest of passions, the people brought tumbling

down the old economic and social structures, the old customs, and the decrepit ideas that had accumulated over centuries of history but had no roots or strength in the consciousness of our nation. They were thus unable to withstand the growing momentum of the socialist revolution.

On December 22 of that same historic year—historic because in 1961 we also triumphed over imperialism at Girón—Fidel proclaimed in the Plaza of the Revolution that we had won the battle against illiteracy. The Cuban educational and cultural process took on exemplary national and international significance. That's why he was able to say: "There is no moment more solemn and thrilling, no instant of greater joy, no minute of more legitimate pride and glory than this one, in which four and a half centuries of ignorance have been toppled."

The tens of thousands of literacy brigadistas gathered in the Plaza of the Revolution chanted in unison: "Fidel, Fidel, tell us what else we need to do!" His answer was: "Now you must become teachers, artists, professors, technicians, engineers, and specialists in the most diverse disciplines of science and culture."

For the first time in our history, bringing education and culture to the masses became a problem that demanded a practical solution.

Thus, alongside the image of José Martí was born the educational, cultural, and scientific movement generated by the Cuban Revolution that for more than four decades has been its backbone. It is decisive to the country's independence, and is Cuba's calling card to the world.

Epilogue

These reflections are the recollections of someone who is grateful to the Cuban Revolution. My aim was not to investigate what was done badly, or what could have been done, or what should have been done better. I have tried to imbue these chronicles with my conviction of the need for political unity of revolutionaries. It is difficult to do that, but less complex than in reality itself.

In this book there is a large dose of my personal life that does not belong to me. As I lived through the moments described here, I dreamed in the depths of my soul about a future I could not define in its specifics, for which we had no design, no "model." Perhaps we were lucky in that respect. My brother Enrique used to say that no revolution could be preconceived in its details. Young people like us, who passed through Cuban prisons, who fought in the Llano and the Sierra, had feelings and ideas fed by aspirations of Cuba's redemption coming out of this very long, epic struggle.

The main interest of this book lies in showing some fundamental elements of a historical thread that should not be forgotten, and that can serve as an important point of reference to better understand how the fabric of the Cuban Revolution was woven and, more broadly, the second half of the twentieth century. Throwing light on these pieces of the great jigsaw puzzle of the history of the last fifty years is a duty—first and foremost to honor the many, many people who were deeply involved in that decade full of a genuine spirituality.

To arrive at this synthesis I had to strive for emotional and intellectual equilibrium, which is not easy to achieve when one is involved in this history. For that reason I did not want the contradictions underlying what was narrated to be presented too sharply. I have preferred to show them for the sake of useful reflection, both for the present and the future. It is necessary to delve into the roots. Something forgotten or overlooked signifies a gap in the historical memory. And a people that loses its memory is like a people lost in shadows.

Revolutions are not a stroll through beautiful meadows and gardens, where men march without difficulty or anguish. A process of change is filled with both, and multiplies them. History does not move in a straight line. Contradictory situations generate passions that are full of human conflict, and mark revolutionary conduct.

In the midst of problems of this kind following Fidel's departure for Mexico—months before the *Granma*—Haydée saw that I was worried and told me something I will never forget: "You like politics and working with ideas, but these types of problems come with it. If you don't want to have such problems, put politics aside and see if you can make the revolution without this type of debate." She knew that was not part of my nature.

When politics is taken seriously, one has to take on the conjunctures and rise above the minor contingencies they bring with them. Immense calmness and patience are necessary to deal with politics successfully. How hard that often is!

A few of those who were there at the beginning of these epic events ended up outside this history of glory. They missed the joy of living it together with the people of Fidel. They aspired to be more than what they could be in the revolution. They were moved by resentment.

The Cuban Revolution was the first and, up to now, the only socialist revolution to triumph in the Western Hemisphere. That feat is even greater when one considers that the forty-some years that have passed since then have been marked by the decline of socialism in Europe and in the USSR.

In November 1959, in a complex discussion taking place in the Council of Ministers, I stated my position: "To understand Fidel one has to bear in mind that he is promoting socialist revolution starting from the history of Cuba, Latin America, and the anti-imperialist and universal ideas of José Martí."

I became a Fidelista because Fidel has been capable of defending and bringing into being, with dignity and talent, the ethical and democratic principles contained in this patriotic tradition.

These more than five decades, counting since Moncada, will never be erased from the history of Cuba, the Americas, and the world.

The Cuban Revolution was an *aldabonazo*—a knock on the door of the conscience of the world.

Chronological notes, 1868–1959

1868

October 10 – Carlos Manuel de Céspedes launches fight for Cuba's independence—the Ten Years War—at his La Demajagua sugar mill in eastern Cuba. At the head of a group of patriots, he frees his slaves and calls for an end to Spanish domination.

October 11 – The first battle of the Ten Years War takes place, as Céspedes leads attack on Spanish garrison in the nearby town of Yara, in what becomes known as the Grito de Yara—the "cry of Yara."

1869

April 10 – Meeting of revolutionary constituent assembly is held at Guáimaro in Camagüey province. Cuba's first constitution is approved and the Republic of Cuba in Arms is born. Two days later Carlos Manuel de Céspedes is elected president.

1871

November 27 – Eight medical students at University of Havana are executed, falsely accused by procolonial forces of desecrating the grave of a Spanish journalist.

1878

February 10 – The Zanjón Pact is signed between the Spanish colonial government and independence forces, ending the Ten Years War. Under its terms, Cuban forces are to put down their arms in exchange for concessions from Spain, but not independence.

March 15 – In what becomes known as the Baraguá Protest, a group of independence army officers led by Antonio Maceo declare their refusal to accept the Zanjón Pact and their determination to continue the war until independence is won and slavery abolished.

1879

April 15 – The last independence forces in the Ten Years War withdraw from the field of battle without surrendering.

August 25 – A number of leaders of the independence forces launch what becomes known as the "Little War," which lasts into 1880.

1887

October 7 – Slavery in Cuba is abolished by the Spanish crown, and the last 25,000 slaves obtain their freedom.

1892

April 10 – The formation of the Cuban Revolutionary Party is announced in Tampa, Key West, and New York. José Martí is elected delegate, the party's highest position.

1895

February 24 – Under Martí's leadership, the Cuban Revolutionary Party reinitiates war for Cuba's independence in town of Baire, in what becomes known as the Grito de Baire. Simultaneous uprisings take place throughout eastern Cuba.

March 25 – A program of the Cuban revolution is issued, known as the Montecristi Manifesto. It is signed by José Martí and Máximo Gómez.

April 1 – Antonio Maceo and other revolutionary fighters land in eastern Cuba, followed on April 11 by Gómez and Martí, to help lead the independence army.

May 19 – José Martí is killed in battle in Dos Ríos, Oriente.

October 22 – At the head of an invasion column, Antonio Maceo sets out from Oriente to cross the island and extend the war to the entire country. At the end of November, his forces are joined by those of Máximo Gómez. The invasion columns reach the western province of Pinar del Río by January 1896.

1896

January 17 – Valeriano Weyler is designated by Spain as captain general of Cuba. He orders the forced resettlement of much of the rural population under concentration camp-type conditions, in what the colonial authorities call the "Reconcentration." More than 200,000 Cubans die from starvation and disease.

September 16 – Independence forces sign the constitution of Jimaguayú.

1897

October 29 – The constitution of La Yaya is approved. Bartolomé Masó becomes head of the Republic of Cuba in Arms.

1898

February 16 – The *U.S.S. Maine* blows up in Havana harbor under mysterious circumstances. The battleship had been sent three weeks earlier to "protect U.S. citizens." The incident becomes a pretext for Washington to declare war on Spain.

April 25 – With the Cuban liberation forces dominating the countryside, Washington enters the conflict. One of its goals is to prevent the independence fighters from advancing on the cities. By July the Spanish forces are defeated.

December 10 – Spain signs Treaty of Paris with Washington. Simultaneous to Spain's withdrawal from Cuba, the U.S. is to occupy the island. Cuban independence forces are treated by both powers as if they don't exist.

1899

January 1 – U.S. forces begin first military occupation of Cuba, which lasts until 1902.

1901

June 12 – The Platt Amendment—proposed originally by U.S. Senator Orville Platt and signed into law in the United States on March 2—is approved as an amendment to Cuba's constitution by a vote of 16 to 14 in the constituent assembly. Under its terms, Washington is given the "right" to intervene in Cuban affairs at any time and to establish military bases on Cuban soil. Under this provision, the U.S. naval base at Guantánamo Bay is set up in 1903. The Platt Amendment will remain in effect until 1934.

1902

May 20 – The Cuban neocolonial republic is born. Cuba declares its independence, but its economic and political system is completely subordinated to U.S. imperialist interests. Tomás Estrada Palma becomes president of the first in a string of pro-U.S. neocolonial governments that will rule the country for the next 57 years.

1906

October 13 – Charles Magoon becomes governor of Cuba in the second military occupation of Cuba, which lasts until 1909.

1922

December 20 – The Federation of Students at the University of Havana is formed, under the leadership of Julio Antonio Mella. The following month it begins a struggle for university reform.

1925

August 16 – The Communist Party of Cuba is founded by Julio Antonio Mella, Carlos Baliño, and other revolutionaries.

1927

March 30 – The University Student Directorate is formed to protest President Gerardo Machado's imposition of a constitutional change extending his term in office. Led by Antonio Guiteras, Eduardo Chibás, and Gabriel Barceló, the Directorate organizes a wave of protests around the country that is brutally suppressed.

1929

January 10 – Agents of the Machado dictatorship assassinate Julio Antonio Mella in Mexico City. *not C P ??*

1930

September 30 – A new University Student Directorate is constituted. In a demonstration it organizes that day, student leader Rafael Trejo is shot and killed by Machado's cops.

1931

August 17 – An expedition of Cuban combatants under the command of Emilio Laurent lands in Gibara, Oriente, to wage armed struggle against the Machado dictatorship.

1933

April 29 – Revolutionary combatants led by Antonio Guiteras rise up in arms in Oriente province. They attack and capture the town of San Luis and establish a guerrilla front in the region.

August 12 – Dictator Gerardo Machado is overthrown in the midst of a revolutionary general strike led by a spectrum of political currents. U.S. embassy brokers a deal that replaces Machado with Carlos Manuel de Céspedes, son of the initiator of Cuba's independence struggle in 1868.

September 4 – The Céspedes government is toppled in a coup led by noncommissioned officers, students, and civilians, sometimes referred to as the "Sergeants' Revolt." A coalition government is soon formed known as the Hundred Days Government, which includes anti-imperialist leaders such as Antonio Guiteras. The new provisional government decrees annulment of the U.S.-imposed Platt Amendment, the eight-hour day, and measures contrary to the interests of U.S. imperialist companies in Cuba, all of which earn it Washington's enmity.

1934

January 14 – With support of U.S. embassy, Fulgencio Batista, army chief of staff under the Hundred Days Government, leads a coup against it. Over next several years he buys off leaders of the anti-Machado movement, combining this with murderous repression against those refusing to buckle.

1935

May 8 – Antonio Guiteras, head of the revolutionary organization Young Cuba, is killed in battle together with another combatant while preparing to leave Cuba and return with an armed expedition against the regime.

1940

July 5 – A new constitution is signed. Reflecting deep nationalist sentiment of the Cuban people, it includes provisions for land reform and other national democratic measures. These provisions, however, remain a dead letter under successive pro-imperialist regimes, which refuse to pass laws necessary to implement them.

1944

June 1 – Ramón Grau San Martín replaces Batista when Grau is elected president of Cuba on Authentic Party ticket.

1947

May 15 – Founding of Cuban People's (Orthodox) Party led by Eduardo Chibás. The party's youth movement attracts a new generation revolted by government corruption and subservience to Washington. Fidel Castro becomes leading figure of the party's most radical wing.

1948

January 22 – Sugar workers and Popular Socialist Party leader Jesús Menéndez is murdered in Manzanillo.

April 9 – While organizing a Latin American student conference in Bogotá, Colombia, Fidel Castro participates in a popular uprising known as the *Bogotazo*, joining resistance to armed assaults by police and troops against the Colombian people.

October 10 – Authentic Party leader Carlos Prío succeeds Grau as president.

1949

March 11 – Several members of the U.S. Navy are photographed climbing atop the statue of José Martí in Havana's Central Park, and urinating on it. As word of the outrage spreads, demonstrations quickly develop. The following day a protest led by the Federation of University Students (FEU) is held in front of the U.S. embassy. One of the leading participants is Fidel Castro.

1951

August 5 – At the conclusion of radio address protesting government corruption, Eduardo Chibás issues his *"último aldabonazo"* [final knock on the door], fatally shooting himself at conclusion of speech. His funeral becomes largest demonstration yet seen in Cuban history.

Fall – Fidel Castro seeks Orthodox Party nomination for House of Representatives in elections scheduled for June 1952. At age 25, he is already a nationally known political figure in Cuba.

1952

March 10 – Fulgencio Batista carries out coup d'état and ousts government of Carlos Prío, two and a half months before scheduled presidential elections on June 1. Batista takes control of both the government and army, suspends the constitution, and cancels the elections, establishing a brutal military dictatorship that defends U.S. imperialist interests.

March 13 – Seeking openings to denounce the coup publicly and convince other forces to join the fight against it, Fidel Castro files charges against Batista in court.

April 6 – In first public demonstration against the coup, University of Havana students lead march to give symbolic burial to Cuba's 1940 constitution. It kicks off two-month Oath to Constitution campaign throughout Cuba.

April 9 – Revolutionary upsurge in Bolivia, with tin miners in the vanguard, topples military government. As byproducts of the upsurge, the largest tin mines are nationalized, the trade unions are legalized, land reform is initiated, and Bolivia's indigenous majority are enfranchised.

1953

January 15 – A bust of Julio Antonio Mella, erected five days earlier in front of the University of Havana, is splattered with paint. Students hold vigorous protest demonstration, which is fired on by cops. Demonstrator Rubén Batista is mortally wounded and dies a month later, the first student martyr in the fight against the tyranny.

January 27 – March of the Torches sets off from the University of Havana to commemorate the centennial of José Martí's birth. The majority of participants will later become part of the Centennial Generation. The young revolutionary movement-in-formation led by Fidel Castro makes its first public appearance as part of the march.

April 5 – Members of Revolutionary National Movement (MNR) are arrested for planning an anti-Batista uprising centered within the military. The subsequent trial of MNR leader and university professor Rafael García Bárcena and others becomes opportunity to denounce regime's crimes. Armando Hart is García Bárcena's defense attorney.

July 26 – Some 160 fighters led by Fidel Castro launch insurrectionary attack on Moncada army garrison in Santiago de Cuba and Carlos Manuel de Céspedes garrison in nearby Bayamo. The attacks fail, and more than 50 captured revolutionaries are murdered. Fidel Castro and other fighters are subsequently captured and put on trial.

August 22 – Washington organizes military coup in Iran to topple government of Mohammad Mossadegh, which had nationalized British oil holdings, and installs dictatorship of shah Mohammed Reza Pahlavi.

September 21 – Trial opens in Santiago de Cuba for those charged with attacking the Moncada garrison.

October 16 – Speaking in his own defense, Fidel Castro delivers what becomes *History Will Absolve Me*. Castro and 27 other jailed Moncadistas are sentenced to up to 15 years in prison.

1954

February 20 – Melba Hernández and Haydée Santamaría, the two women Moncada combatants, are released from prison.

March 3 – A Guatemala support committee is formed by the Federation of University Students (FEU) in Havana.

March 14 – The FEU declares its support for the struggle by the Nationalist Party in Puerto Rico against U.S. colonial rule.

May – A Cuba-wide campaign for amnesty of political prisoners is or-

320 / CHRONOLOGICAL NOTES

ganized. Supporting campaign over next 12 months are relatives of Moncada combatants and thousands of revolutionary-minded young people. Haydée Santamaría and Melba Hernández become leaders of campaign.

June 17 – Mercenary forces backed by CIA invade Guatemala to oust government of Jacobo Arbenz, which is carrying out land reform measures. Among those volunteering to fight the imperialist-organized attack is young Argentine doctor Ernesto Guevara. Arbenz refuses to arm the people and resigns 10 days later; mercenary forces enter Guatemala City in August.

June 22 – Cuban students organize demonstration at the University of Havana in defense of the Guatemalan people.

October 10 – Armando Hart, Faustino Pérez, and other MNR members are arrested for anti-Batista activities. When hand grenades are found at Pérez's office at 222 Salud St. in Old Havana, they are all detained. Hart is released later in the year.

October – Defenders of July 26 combatants and supporters of amnesty begin campaign to circulate *History Will Absolve Me,* Castro's courtroom speech written down by him in prison and smuggled out. Tens of thousands are distributed.

November 1 – Batista regime holds fraudulent elections to provide legal facade for dictatorship. Fulgencio Batista is "elected" president.

1955

January – Somoza dictatorship in Nicaragua organizes military attack against Costa Rica. A number of Cuban student leaders volunteer as combatants to oppose the aggression, among them José Antonio Echeverría.

May 15 – Popular pressure forces Batista to release over 200 political prisoners. Fidel Castro and the remaining Moncada prisoners are freed after 19 months in jail.

June 12 – July 26 Revolutionary Movement is organized through fusion of Moncadistas; members of the Orthodox Party, particularly its youth; and forces within the MNR including Frank País, Armando Hart, and Faustino Pérez.

July 7 – Fidel Castro arrives in Mexico to begin preparations for expedition to launch insurrectionary struggle against Batista regime.

November 19 – A mass outdoor meeting of tens of thousands is held at Muelle de Luz pier in Havana sponsored by Society of Friends of the Republic (SAR) led by Cosme de la Torriente.

December 2 – The Federation of University Students holds a demonstration calling on Cosme de la Torriente not to seek an understanding with the Batista regime. The demonstration is brutally attacked and dispersed by the police.

December 5 – Bus boycott begins in Montgomery, Alabama, announcing opening of mass civil rights movement by Blacks to bring down "Jim Crow" system of segregation throughout U.S. South. The boycott ends over a year later, with the elimination of segregation on Montgomery buses.

December – A nationwide strike by 200,000 sugar workers protests government move to cut wages. A number of towns in Las Villas, where the strike is centered, are virtually taken over by workers and their supporters, among them the leaders of the Federation of University Students.

1956

February 24 – At a public meeting at the University of Havana, José Antonio Echeverría proclaims the formation of the Revolutionary Directorate as the political vanguard of the Federation of University Students.

April 3 – The conspiracy of "Los Puros" [the pure ones], composed of anti-Batista army officers, is discovered. Twelve active-duty officers are arrested and jailed.

April 29 – Under the leadership of Reynold García, a group of revolutionaries attack the Goicuría garrison in Matanzas. Following the unsuccessful action the combatants are massacred.

June 24–July 3 – Fidel Castro and 27 other revolutionaries are arrested by Mexican police. They are released in late July.

August 30 – Fidel Castro and José Antonio Echeverría sign Mexico Pact, representing unity of the July 26 Movement and the Federation of University Students in both perspectives and action.

November 25 – Expedition led by Fidel Castro aboard the yacht *Granma* departs from Tuxpan Mexico with 82 combatants, en route to Cuba to initiate the revolutionary war.

November 30 – July 26 Movement organizes armed uprising in Santiago de Cuba led by Frank País in support of the scheduled *Granma* landing. Combatants Tony Alomá, Otto Parellada, and Pepito Tey are killed in battle. In its wake, Batista's police begin a wave of arrests and murders, especially in Santiago and throughout Oriente province.

December 2 – Delayed by storms, the expected landing of the *Granma* takes place at Las Coloradas in Belic, Oriente province.

December 5 – *Granma* expeditionaries have their first encounter with dictatorship's army at Alegría de Pío. The combatants are surprised by Batista's troops and dispersed under enemy fire; the rebels are hunted down and half are murdered or captured and imprisoned.

December 15 – Juan Manuel Márquez, second in command of the *Granma* expedition, is captured and murdered by forces of the tyranny.

December 18–21 – Several groups of dispersed fighters reunite in Sierra Maestra mountains, including Fidel Castro, Raúl Castro, Juan Almeida, Che Guevara, and Camilo Cienfuegos. At this point there are 15 combatants in Rebel Army with 7 weapons. They head higher into the Sierra.

1957

January 1 – Young revolutionaries William Soler, 15 years old, and Froilán Guerra are murdered by the police after having been arrested. The crime sparks a demonstration in Santiago de Cuba of several thousand women organized by the July 26 Movement.

January 15 – Batista suspends civil liberties throughout Cuba and imposes press censorship.

January 17 – Rebel Army obtains its first victory, 45 days after the *Granma* landing, capturing Batista army outpost at La Plata, in coastal region of Sierra Maestra.

February 17 – National Directorate of July 26 Movement meets in the Sierra Maestra.

– *New York Times* correspondent Herbert Matthews interviews and photographs Fidel Castro in the mountains. The interview is published in the *Times* several days later. After Batista officials declare interview a fake, the *Times* publishes a photograph of Matthews with Castro, providing sensational evidence that the guerrillas have not been wiped out.

February 26 – Censorship is lifted. *Bohemia* and other Cuban periodicals publish reports on Matthews interview with Fidel Castro, giving Cuba's people the first confirmation of rebels' existence. A new 45-day censorship decree is imposed on March 2.

March 13 – Armed units of Revolutionary Directorate carry out simultaneous attacks on Presidential Palace and Radio Reloj in attempt to eliminate Batista. The attack fails and a number of revolutionaries are killed, including the Directorate's leader, José Antonio Echeverría.

March 17 – Fifty reinforcements, sent by July 26 Movement in Santiago de Cuba, join rebel troops in Sierra Maestra.

April 15 – Censorship is lifted briefly following expiration of 45-day decree, then reimposed shortly after.

April 18 – Armando Hart is arrested and jailed in Havana.

April 20 – Joe Westbrook, Fructuoso Rodríguez, Juan Pedro Carbó, and José Machado, leaders of the Revolutionary Directorate, are murdered at 7 Humboldt St. apartment. All four had participated in the attack on the Presidential Palace.

April 23 – Fidel Castro is interviewed and filmed in Sierra by U.S. journalist Robert Taber; the interview is shown in May by CBS-TV.

May 10 – In a Santiago de Cuba courtroom, 22 arrested *Granma* expeditionaries are sentenced to up to nine years in prison. Judge Manuel Urrutia votes against verdict. Dozens of other political prisoners on trial, including Frank País and other participants in November 30 Santiago uprising, are acquitted.

May 18 – Over two dozen automatic weapons and 6,000 rounds of ammunition reach Rebel Army in the Sierra, sent by July 26 Movement in Santiago.

May 23 – Landing of *Corynthia* expedition in northern Oriente province, organized by military wing of Authentic Party. Victims of an informer's tip, virtually all the combatants are murdered by the dictatorship's forces. One survivor makes his way to Sierra Maestra and joins Rebel Army.

May 28 – The nascent Rebel Army wins battle against well-fortified army garrison at Uvero.

– July 26 Movement members in Havana conduct sabotage action, cutting off electricity for 57 hours.

June 4 – A United Press International dispatch announces that 800 U.S.-trained and -equipped Cuban troops will be sent to the Sierra to combat Rebel Army.

June 30 – On the streets of Santiago de Cuba, Josué País—brother of Frank—and two other revolutionaries are murdered by the tyranny's henchmen.

July 4 – Armando Hart escapes from jail in Havana.

July 12 – Manifesto of the Sierra Maestra is issued, signed by Fidel Castro, Felipe Pazos, and Raúl Chibás. It calls for broad opposition front to support Rebel Army and overthrow Batista.

July 21 – Ernesto Che Guevara is named head of the Rebel Army's second column and promoted by Fidel Castro to rank of commander.

July 30 – Frank País, head of clandestine action for the July 26 Movement's National Directorate is murdered by Batista henchmen in Santiago de Cuba, together with his comrade Raúl Pujol.

July 31 – Sixty thousand attend funeral march for Frank País in Santiago de Cuba. U.S. ambassador Earl Smith goes to Santiago that same day and is met by street protest of women demanding end to U.S. support to Batista.

July – The Rebel Army now consists of 200 fighters; Batista's armed forces number over 30,000.

August 1 – The funeral procession for Frank País gives impetus to a spontaneous strike movement that develops throughout the country. Lasting until August 6, the strike shakes the foundations of the dictatorship.

September 5 – Cienfuegos uprising. Anti-Batista forces within the naval base in Cienfuegos seize city, with support from local cadres of July

26 Movement and other civilians. Uprising is brutally suppressed by the dictatorship.

November 1 – Miami Pact is signed by Authentic Party, Orthodox Party, Revolutionary Directorate, and others; among the signers is Felipe Pazos, who falsely claims to represent signers of Sierra Manifesto, including Fidel Castro. The Pact creates the Cuban Liberation Council, dominated by bourgeois opposition forces; it does not oppose U.S. intervention and encourages military coup to replace Batista.

Mid-November – Armando Hart travels to Sierra Maestra for leadership meetings to discuss the Miami Pact and the clandestine work.

November – The July 26 Movement and Rebel Army organize to sabotage the annual sugar harvest by burning cane belonging to owners of large landed estates. On orders from Fidel Castro, cane fields belonging to Castro's own family are among the first targets.

December 14 – Fidel Castro repudiates Miami Pact in name of July 26 Movement.

1958

January 10 – As they are coming down from the Sierra Maestra, Armando Hart and two other youth are arrested by forces of the dictatorship. Quick action by July 26 Movement cadres in publicizing the arrest saves the prisoners' lives. Hart spends the next year in different prisons throughout Cuba.

January 23 – Venezuelan dictator Marcos Pérez Jiménez is overthrown by popular rebellion in Caracas. That event gives fresh impetus to revolutionary struggle in Cuba.

January 25 – The Batista regime briefly restores suspended constitutional guarantees and lifts censorship in all provinces except Oriente.

January 27 – July 26 combatants conduct a sabotage action against ESSO Standard Oil Company installations near Havana.

February 2 – *Bohemia* publishes full text of Fidel Castro's letter repudiating Miami Pact, in special run of half million copies.

February 8 – Combatants of the Revolutionary Directorate led by Faure Chomón land at Nuevitas, Camagüey, to establish a new guerrilla front in the Escambray mountains of Cuba's central region.

February 16–17 – Rebel victory at second battle of Pino del Agua marks decisive shift in military relationship of forces, opening several months of expanded operations by Rebel Army.

February 24 – Radio Rebelde begins its transmissions from Sierra Maestra.

March 1 – Rebel Army Column no. 6 led by Raúl Castro sets off for northeast Oriente province to establish the Rebel Army's Second Front. The same day commander Juan Almeida sets out to establish the Third Front northeast of Santiago de Cuba, with the aim of encircling the city.

March 12 – The July 26 Manifesto is issued by Fidel Castro. It states that the struggle against Batista has entered its final stage, and announces total war beginning April 1. Calls for stepped-up preparations for a general strike.

– The dictatorship suspends constitutional guarantees and postpones general elections from June to November 1958.

March 14 – In face of the Batista regime's growing isolation, the U.S. government officially declares an embargo on the sale of weapons, although in practice Washington continues to furnish arms through third parties, including the Trujillo dictatorship in the Dominican Republic and the Somoza dictatorship in Nicaragua.

April 9 – July 26 Movement calls general strike throughout Cuba, leading to actions in Havana, Sagua la Grande, Santa Clara, Ciego de Ávila, Santiago de Cuba, and many other places. The strike fails and the tyranny's forces step up repression.

April 21 – Cuban revolutionary Enrique Hart Dávalos and two other July 26 Movement cadres are killed when a bomb they are preparing accidentally explodes.

May 3 – Meeting of July 26 Movement National Directorate at Altos de Mompié in Sierra Maestra assesses April 9 strike failure; center of July 26 Movement national leadership is shifted from Havana and Santiago to Sierra Maestra, under the direct command of Fidel Castro.

May 24–25 – Seeking to take advantage of April 9, Batista launches "encircle and annihilate" offensive, sending 10,000 troops into the Sierra Maestra. Rebel Army, then with 300 fighters and 200 usable rifles, concentrates forces around command post of Column 1, drawing in government troops. Between May 25 and July 21, battles fought in Santo Domingo, Meriño, Las Vegas de Jibacoa, Las Mercedes, El Jigüe, and other skirmishes inflict over 1,000 casualties on Batista forces.

July 11 – Battle of El Jigüe begins. Decisive Rebel Army victory under Fidel Castro's personal command marks defeat of government offensive and constitutes turning point in the war. Rebels, now 800 strong, capture 600 weapons and 100,000 rounds of ammunition. The battle concludes on July 21 with the surrender of the army's decimated 18th Battalion. Rebel Army plans counteroffensive.

July 30 – Rebel Army commander René Ramos Latour *(Daniel)* is killed in battle.

August 1 – Batista regime assault on political prisoners held in Príncipe Castle jail in Havana leaves three revolutionaries dead after hours of fighting.

August 21 – On Fidel Castro's orders, Cmdr. Camilo Cienfuegos leaves Sierra Maestra, at the head of Antonio Maceo Column, setting out for Pinar del Río province on the western end of Cuba.

August 31 – Ciro Redondo Column, commanded by Ernesto Che Guevara, sets off from Sierra Maestra for central Cuba.

September 4 – Mariana Grajales Platoon, consisting of rebel fighters who are women, is formed in the Sierra. Women combatants have been members of Rebel columns since March 1957, starting with Celia Sánchez.

September 21 – First Congress of Peasants in Arms is held in Soledad de Mayarí Arriba, in the territory of the Second Eastern Front. Raúl Castro, gives closing remarks.

October 7 – Rebel Army forces reach Las Villas province.

October 10 – Rebel Army issues Law no. 3 of the Sierra Maestra, granting tenant farmers, squatters, and sharecroppers title to the land they work.

November 3 – Amidst repudiation by the population, Batista regime holds fraudulent elections, in attempt to give "legal" covering to the dictatorship. July 26 Movement calls for boycott, and voter abstention is massive. Batista's candidate, Andrés Rivero Agüero, is declared president-elect.

November 20 – The historic battle of Guisa in the Sierra Maestra begins. It is opening of drive by Rebel Army to surround and seize Santiago de Cuba. The battle concludes November 30 in a key rebel victory.

December 1 – July 26 Movement and Revolutionary Directorate issue Pedrero Pact, calling for unity of revolutionary forces in Las Villas province.

December 19 – Rebel Army's Second Eastern Front attacks and captures Caimanera in Oriente province.

December 21 – In a joint operation under the command of Ernesto Che Guevara, Rebel Army Column 8 and forces of the Revolutionary Directorate begin a drive that rapidly liberates Fomento, Placetas, Cabaiguán, Sancti Spíritus, Remedios, and Caibarién in Las Villas province.

December 26 – Rebel Army captures Palma Soriano in Oriente.

December 28 – Battle of Santa Clara begins, under the command of Ernesto Che Guevara. The city's population mobilizes in massive show of support to Rebel Army.

– Fidel Castro meets with General Eulogio Cantillo, where the latter agrees to the unconditional surrender of the dictatorship's army and pledges not to make contact with U.S. embassy. Cantillo betrays the agreement.

December 31 – Yaguajay, last army bastion in northern Las Villas, falls to Camilo Cienfuegos's column.

1959

January 1 – Batista flees Cuba at 2:00 a.m. Defeated by the Rebel Army, he cedes power to a military junta headed by General Cantillo and Supreme Court Justice Carlos Piedra.

– Speaking over Radio Rebelde, Fidel Castro calls for a revolutionary general strike to crush the attempt by Cantillo and other of-

ficers to block the revolutionary victory. The population responds
and takes to the streets.

– The rebel columns led by commanders Camilo Cienfuegos and
Ernesto Che Guevara are ordered to march on Havana. The forces
under the command of Fidel Castro, Juan Almeida, and Raúl Castro
advance on Santiago de Cuba. The military leader of Santiago de
Cuba agrees to unconditional surrender. Santiago is declared provisional capital of Cuba.

– The political prisoners at the Model Prison on the Isle of Pines
take over the prison and then the entire island

January 2 – Cuban workers respond to call for revolutionary general
strike with massive uprising.

– Rebel columns led by Cienfuegos and Guevara enter Havana and
occupy principal army garrisons.

– Military junta collapses.

January 5 – A new government is formed, with Manuel Urrutia as president.

January 8 – After the Liberty Caravan triumphantly crosses the coun-
try, the Rebel Army columns commanded by Fidel Castro enter
Havana. Castro addresses the Cuban people that night from Camp
Columbia.

January 21 – More than one million Cubans rally in front of Havana's
Presidential Palace to support the revolutionary government and
its actions in bringing Batista's war criminals to justice. They are
responding to a campaign against these actions by the U.S. government and mass media.

February 16 – Fidel Castro takes over as Cuba's prime minister.

Glossary

Abreu, Gerardo *(Fontán)* (1931–1958) – A member of the Orthodox Youth, he joined the July 26 Movement and was active in the urban underground. Murdered by the dictatorship February 6, 1958.

Action for Liberty – Founded 1952 under leadership of Justo Carrillo. It advocated armed action against the regime, aimed at encouraging disaffected army officers to carry out a coup against Batista. Between the arrests and exile of many of its members, the organization disappeared by early 1955. Many of its members joined the July 26 Movement.

Agostini, Jorge (1910–1955) – An officer in the Cuban navy, who headed the Secret Service at the Presidential Palace 1945–52. He resigned following Batista's coup and engaged in anti-Batista conspiratorial activity within the armed forces. In June 1955 he was murdered by Batista thugs.

Agramonte, Ignacio (1841–1873) – A major general in the Army of Liberation during Cuba's first independence war against Spain, based in Camagüey province. He was killed in battle at Jimaguayú.

Aguilera, Pedro (1925–1998) – A participant in the July 26, 1953, attack on the Bayamo garrison, he was arrested but acquitted. In 1955 he became a member of the first National Directorate of the July 26 Movement and a leader in Havana province. During the revolutionary war he worked in the urban underground. After 1959 he served in the Revolutionary Armed Forces and Ministry of the Interior, obtaining the rank of general.

Aguilera Maceiras, José (d. 1972) – July 26 Movement member from Santiago de Cuba and general secretary of the Civic Resistance Movement in that region. From 1962 until his death he held various leadership positions in the Ministry of Education.

Aldabonazo – In June 1951 Orthodox Party leader Eduardo Chibás, whose political program focused on ending government corruption, was denounced as a slanderer by minister of education Aureliano Sánchez Arango. Chibás responded to the provocation by claiming widespread embezzlement of government funds by Sánchez Arango. When the latter demanded proof, Chibás replied that he would supply it during his weekly radio address on August 5. Unable to show the proof, Chibás closed his speech with the words, "People of Cuba, awake! *Este es mi último aldabonazo*" [This is my final knock on the door]. He then shot himself in the abdomen and died eleven days later. The term *Aldabonazo* became a rallying cry for youth who opposed the Prío regime as well as the Batista dictatorship that replaced it.

Almeida, Juan (1927–) – A bricklayer, he lived in Havana and was a member of the Orthodox Party at the time of Batista's 1952 coup. He was recruited to the movement led by Fidel Castro and participated in the 1953 Moncada attack. He was sentenced to ten years in prison. Released with the other Moncada prisoners in May 1955 following a successful national amnesty campaign, he participated in the *Granma* expedition of November–December 1956. In February 1958 he was promoted to commander and later headed the Third Eastern Front. Since 1959 Almeida's responsibilities have included head of the air force, vice minister of the Revolutionary Armed Forces, and vice president of the Council of State. Together with Guillermo García and Ramiro Valdés, he is one of three Sierra combatants to hold the rank of Commander of the Revolution. He has been a member of the Communist Party Central Committee and Political Bureau since its founding in 1965. He is a Hero of the Republic of Cuba and is president of the Association of Combatants of the Cuban Revolution.

Alomá, Tony (1932–1956) – Member of the July 26 Movement underground in Santiago de Cuba led by Frank País. He was killed in battle during the November 30, 1956, Santiago uprising.

Álvarez, María Angélica (1934–) – A graduate of the University of Havana in the field of education, a teacher, and a member of the July 26 Movement. Her home became a meeting place for Movement combatants, and Haydée Santamaría hid out there at various times. Following 1959 she worked in the Ministry of Education and then the University of Havana. She was rector of the Higher Institute of Art of Cuba (ISA).

Álvarez, Odón – A leader of the Cuban trade unions. After January 1, 1959, he was a member of the Confederation of Cuban Workers' presidium and was its secretary of foreign relations. He later betrayed the revolution while working in Cuba's embassy in Spain.

Amador, Casto (1930–) – A member of Action for Liberty beginning in 1952, in early 1956 he joined the July 26 Movement and participated in the November 30, 1956, Santiago uprising. Arrested, he was imprisoned on the Isle of Pines until January 1, 1959. After the triumph he headed the Military Police in Santiago de Cuba, and was provincial coordinator of the July 26 Movement in 1959–60. He later worked in the revolutionary navy with the rank of captain.

Amat, Carlos (1930–) – Member of the July 26 Movement underground in Santiago de Cuba. After 1959 he held a number of posts, including minister of justice and ambassador at Cuba's Permanent Mission to the UN in Geneva. He is director general of the Cuban Association of the United Nations.

Antuña, Vicentina (1909–1992) – Noted Cuban intellectual and prominent member of the Orthodox Party. After 1959 she was a faculty member and professor emeritus at the University of Havana, and president of the Cuban National Commission of UNESCO.

April 9, 1958, strike – Announced without adequate preparation, a general strike throughout Cuba called by the July 26 Movement on this date failed. In response, the Batista forces stepped up repression and launched a general counteroffensive. The following month the July 26 Movement national leadership convened a meeting in the Sierra to assess the reasons for the strike's failure.

Arango y Parreño, Francisco de (1765–1837) – Cuban-born Creole landowner and cofounder of the Economic Society of Friends of the Country. He sought to improve the profitable cultivation of sugar and obtained for Cuba a reduction of Spanish monopolies, trade barriers, and restrictions on the importation of slaves.

Araújo, Leocadia "Cayita" (1884–1983) – A school teacher and member of the July 26 Movement, she provided important assistance to the fighters in the Sierra. Her home was a meeting place for underground combatants and those from the Sierra.

Arbenz, Jacobo (1914–1971) – President of Guatemala 1951–54. See Guatemala, 1954.

Aróstegui, Mario (1926–1953) – A railroad worker and member of the Orthodox Party, following March 1952 he joined the anti-Batista underground in his native Camagüey and in Oriente province. In November 1953 he was picked up in Santiago de Cuba by Batista thugs. After savage torture, he was murdered.

Arteaga, José *(Pitute)* (1926–1995) – A noted fighter in the July 26 Movement underground, he became part of a small guerrilla unit in Pinar del Río province. Following 1959 he worked in the National Institute of Agrarian Reform (INRA) and was Cuba's ambassador to a number of countries.

Authentic Party (Cuban Revolutionary Party) – Bourgeois-nationalist party (popularly known as *auténticos*) formed in 1934, claiming to be authentic followers of José Martí's Cuban Revolutionary Party. Held the presidency from 1944 until 1952, under Ramón Grau and then Carlos Prío. Part of the bourgeois opposition to Batista in 1952–58. The majority of its leaders left Cuba as the revolution deepened in 1959–60 and joined the counterrevolutionary forces.

Autonomism – A political current in Cuba that sought autonomy as opposed to independence from Spain at the end of the nineteenth century. During the 1895–98 war of independence, the Autonomist Party, led by Rafael Montoro, participated in the Spanish colonial regime, in open opposition to the revolutionary forces.

Baliño, Carlos (1848–1926) – A leader of the socialist and labor movement in Cuba at the turn of the century, he had been a founder of José Martí's Cuban Revolutionary Party in 1892. A founder of the Communist Party of Cuba in 1925, he was a member of its first Central Committee.

Barba, Álvaro (1923–1962) – President of the Federation of University Students (FEU), 1951–52, he became a leader of Action for Liberty. In 1954 he was forced into exile. After the revolution's triumph he became an official in Cuba's National Institute of Agrarian Reform. He died in a plane crash.

Barquín, Ramón (1914–) – Colonel in the Cuban army and Cuba's military attaché in Washington. A leader of an anti-Batista military conspiracy known as "Los Puros" [the pure ones], he was arrested in April 1956 and imprisoned. He was released January 1, 1959, as part of a U.S.-backed attempt to replace Batista with a military junta to forestall a Rebel Army victory. The maneuver failed in face of a revolutionary general strike and Rebel Army advances. Named a special ambassador in Europe by the revolutionary government, he soon broke with the revolution and left Cuba.

Batista, Fulgencio (1901–1973) – Former army sergeant who helped lead the Sergeants' Revolt in September 1933. This was a military coup by junior officers growing out of the popular uprising that had overturned the dictatorship of Gerardo Machado a few weeks earlier. (*See also* Sergeants' Revolt) He was promoted to colonel and chief of staff. In January 1934 he organized a second coup unleashing repression against workers, peasants, and revolutionary forces. After dominating several governments as head of the army, with the rank of major general, Batista was elected president in 1940. He did not run for reelection in 1944, but retained a base of support within the army officer corps, living in Florida until 1948. On March 10, 1952, a Batista-led coup established a brutal military dictatorship that collaborated closely with Washington. He fled to the Dominican Republic on January 1, 1959.

Batista Rubio, Rubén (1933–1953) – A student of architecture at the

University of Havana shot by police during an anti-Batista protest January 15, 1953. He died a month later, the first student martyr in the struggle against the Batista tyranny. His burial was a militant, mass demonstration against the regime.

Bisbé, Manuel (1906–1961) – A member of the Orthodox Party's National Leadership Council and its whip in the House of Representatives during the Authentic Party governments. A professor at the University of Havana, after Batista closed the university in November 1956, he went to the United States. He returned to Cuba after the triumph of the revolution and was named Cuba's permanent representative to the United Nations, holding that position from January 1959 until his death in March 1961.

Bonito, Luis (d. 1985) – A participant in sugar workers' struggles, he joined the July 26 Movement in Havana. He participated in the assault on the Goicuría garrison in Matanzas province in April 1956, and lived in exile in Mexico until 1959. After the revolution he held various responsibilities in Havana until his death.

Borbonet, Enrique (1921–1979) – Central organizer of the 1956 "Los Puros" conspiracy within the armed forces against the Batista regime, he was jailed on the Isle of Pines until January 1, 1959. He held a number of posts within the revolutionary government, including first vice minister of education.

Buch, Luis (1913–2001) – A participant in the anti-Machado movement and Young Cuba during the 1930s together with Guiteras. In 1955 he joined the July 26 Movement, and in May 1958 he was sent abroad to become head of public relations for the July 26 Movement in exile, based in Caracas. He was minister of the presidency and secretary of the Council of Ministers 1959–63. From 1963 to 1987 he was a justice on Cuba's Supreme Court.

Buch, Tony (1927–) – Doctor and July 26 Movement combatant in the urban underground and then the Sierra. Arrested in January 1958 together with Armando Hart and Felipe Pazos, he was imprisoned in the Boniato jail. He left Cuba after the triumph of the revolution.

Buehlman, Victor (1940–) – Son of a member of the U.S. Navy stationed at the Guantánamo naval base, he joined the Rebel Army in March 1957 and served with it for several months before returning to the United States.

Cabrera Infante, Guillermo (1929–) – A Cuban novelist and essayist, he was editor of the literary magazine *Lunes de Revolución* from 1959 until 1961. Named Cuba's cultural attaché in Brussels, he broke with the revolution in 1965.

Camacho Aguilera, Julio (1924–) – A member of the Orthodox Party, Action for Liberty, and the Revolutionary National Movement, he became a founder of the July 26 Movement in 1955 in Guantánamo, where he was the organization's coordinator and action chief. A leader of the November 30, 1956, uprising in that city. On instructions from the July 26 Movement, he helped lead the September 5, 1957, uprising in Cienfuegos and subsequently joined the Rebel Army in the Sierra. A member of the Communist Party Central Committee since its founding in 1965. His responsibilities have included minister of transportation; leadership positions in the Revolutionary Armed Forces; first secretary of the Communist Party's provincial committees in Pinar del Río, City of Havana, and Santiago de Cuba; and ambassador to the Soviet Union.

Carbó, Juan Pedro (1926–1957) – A leader of the Federation of University Students and Revolutionary Directorate at the University of Havana, he participated in the March 13, 1957, attack on the Presidential Palace. He was killed by Batista's police in the 7 Humboldt Street massacre on April 20, 1957.

Cárdenas, Lázaro (1895–1970) – President of Mexico 1934–40. During his administration Mexico nationalized its oil and railroad industries. He gave assistance to the Cuban revolutionaries when they were in Mexico preparing the *Granma* expedition. Following 1959 he gave public support to the Cuban Revolution.

Carratalá Ugalde, Conrado – Police colonel and one of the most notorious assassins of the Batista regime. He fled Cuba January 1, 1959.

Castro Ruz, Fidel (1926–) – A student leader at the University of Havana from 1945 on. He was one of the central organizers of the Orthodox Party youth after the party's founding in 1947. He was Orthodox Party candidate for House of Representatives in the 1952 elections canceled by Batista following the March 10 coup that year. He organized and led a revolutionary movement against the Batista dictatorship that carried out the July 26, 1953, attack on the Moncada garrison in Santiago de Cuba and the Carlos Manuel de Céspedes garrison in Bayamo. Captured, tried, and sentenced to fifteen years in prison, his courtroom defense speech, *History Will Absolve Me*, was distributed in tens of thousands of copies across Cuba, becoming the program of the revolutionary movement. Released in 1955 after a national amnesty campaign, Castro led the founding of the July 26 Revolutionary Movement. He organized the *Granma* expedition from Mexico in late 1956 and commanded the Rebel Army during the revolutionary war. Following the triumph of the revolution, Fidel Castro was Cuba's prime minister from February 1959 to 1976, and has been president of the Council of State and Council of Ministers since then. He is commander in chief of the Revolutionary Armed Forces and, since 1965, the first secretary of the Communist Party of Cuba.

Castro Ruz, Raúl (1931–) – An organizer of student protests at the University of Havana against the Batista dictatorship, he joined in the 1953 Moncada attack, where he headed the attack on the Palace of Justice in Santiago de Cuba. Captured and sentenced to thirteen years in prison. He was released in May 1955 following a national amnesty campaign. A founding member of the July 26 Movement, he was a participant in the 1956 *Granma* expedition. In February 1958 he was promoted to commander in the Rebel Army and headed the Second Eastern Front. Since October 1959 he has been minister of the Revolutionary Armed Forces. He is General of the Army, the second-ranking officer of the Revolutionary Armed Forces. He was vice premier from 1959 until 1976, when he became first vice president of the Council of State and Council of Ministers. Since 1965 he has been second secretary of the Communist Party of Cuba and a member of the Political Bureau.

Centennial Generation, Centennial Youth – Terms broadly used to designate the revolutionary movement of young working people and students seeking to overturn the Batista dictatorship. The name referred to the fact that 1953 was the centennial of José Martí's birth. Cadres of this movement organized and carried out the attack on the Moncada garrison on July 26, 1953.

Céspedes, Carlos Manuel de (1819–1874) – A lawyer and wealthy landowner in Oriente province, on October 10, 1868, he freed his slaves, proclaimed the Republic of Cuba, and launched Cuba's first war against Spanish colonialism, attacking the Spanish garrison in the nearby town of Yara in what became known as the Cry of Yara. He was supreme commander of the Cuban independence army and later first president of the Republic in Arms until October 1873. Killed in battle on February 27, 1874. He is regarded by Cubans as Father of the Country.

Céspedes, Carlos Manuel de (1871–1939) – Son of the initiator in 1868 of Cuba's war for independence, he became a prominent bourgeois politician. In August 1933 he was named Cuba's president in a deal brokered by the U.S. embassy to replace U.S.-backed dictator Gerardo Machado, who had been ousted by a popular uprising. Céspedes was deposed three weeks later in a coup by junior officers known as the Sergeants' Revolt.

Chaviano. See Río Chaviano, Alberto del

Chibás, Eduardo (1907–1951) – A leader of the Student Directorate in the fight against the Machado dictatorship in the 1920s and 1930s. A member of the Authentic Party, in 1947 he was founding leader of the opposition Cuban People's Party *(ortodoxos)* and was elected senator in 1950. On August 5, 1951, in an act of protest against government corruption, he shot himself. See *Aldabonazo*.

Chibás, Raúl (1916–2002) – An Orthodox Party leader and the brother of Eduardo Chibás. In June 1957 he signed the Sierra Manifesto with Fidel Castro and subsequently was treasurer of the July 26 Movement Committee in Exile. He went to the U.S. after the triumph of the revolution.

Chomón, Faure (1929–) – Leader of the Revolutionary Directorate and survivor of the March 13, 1957, attack on the Presidential Palace. He organized a February 1958 expedition that landed in northern Camagüey and established a guerrilla front in the Escambray mountains. Was part of the Las Villas front under Che Guevara's command after the latter's column arrived in October. A member of the Communist Party Central Committee since 1965, he has served as Cuba's ambassador to the Soviet Union, Vietnam, and Ecuador.

Cienfuegos, Camilo (1932–1959) – A *Granma* expeditionary, he became a captain in Che Guevara's Rebel Army column in late 1957. He was promoted to commander in 1958 and from August to October 1958 led the "Antonio Maceo" Column 2 westward from the Sierra Maestra en route to Pinar del Río. He operated in northern Las Villas until the end of the war and became Rebel Army chief of staff in January 1959. He was killed when his plane was lost at sea while returning to Havana on October 28, 1959.

Civic Resistance Movement – Broad opposition formation, predominantly of professionals and businessmen, initiated inside Cuba in early 1957 by July 26 Movement. Its mission was to offer logistical support to the insurrectional movement.

Constitution of 1940 – A bourgeois constitution that assured the dominance of the capitalist class and also reflected the anti-imperialist objectives fought for by broad layers of the Cuban population in the years following the revolutionary upsurge of 1933 that toppled the dictatorship of Gerardo Machado. Some of its provisions included land reform and other democratic measures, but these remained a dead letter under the successive pro-imperialist regimes. Batista abrogated the 1940 constitution when he seized power in 1952. Its restitution was a demand of the forces fighting Batista.

Cowley, Fermín (1907–1957) – A lieutenant colonel in the Cuban army, he was a notorious henchman and murderer under Batista. In December 1956, as military chief of the Holguín regiment, he directed the kidnapping and murder of 23 opponents of the dictatorship in the "Bloody Christmas" massacre. In May 1957 he ordered the killing of 15 captured survivors of the *Corynthia* expedition organized by the Authentic Organization. He was executed by a July 26 Movement commando squad on November 23, 1957.

Creoles – Term used for native-born Cubans of Spanish descent during the colonial period. A Creole landowning class developed in the 19th century, but Spanish colonial policy reserved positions of government and administration for Spanish-born colonists, known as *peninsulares*.

Crespo, Abelardo (1924–) – A participant in the 1953 Moncada attack, he was tried and sentenced to 10 years imprisonment on the Isle of Pines. Released in 1955 following a national amnesty campaign. After 1959 he held various state responsibilities and served many years as national chief of Cuba's corps of firefighters.

Cruz Vidal, Ramón (b. 1906) – A colonel in the Cuban army, following Batista's coup he was commander of the garrison in La Cabaña in Havana. In October 1954 he became inspector of the army general staff.

CTC – Founded in 1939 as the Confederation of Cuban Workers. Prominent Popular Socialist Party leader Lázaro Peña was founding general secretary. In 1947 right-wing forces led by Eusebio Mujal gained dominance. The CTC officialdom supported the Batista dictatorship after 1952. It was reorganized after the revolution and known as CTC-Revolutionary. In 1961 it changed its name to Central Organization of Cuban Workers, retaining the same initials.

Cuadras, Gloria (1911–1987) – A veteran of the anti-Machado fight in the early 1930s, she became a leader of the national amnesty campaign for the imprisoned Moncadistas. In 1955 she was a founder of the July 26 Movement and became its head of propaganda in Oriente province. During the revolutionary war she was active in the underground. After 1959 she held a number of responsibilities and served on the Oriente Provincial Committee of the Communist Party of Cuba.

Cuervo Navarro, Pelayo (1901–1957) – A leader of the Orthodox Party, following Batista's 1952 coup, he supported the wing of the party that advocated a military coup to oust Batista. On March 13, 1957, following the attack on the Presidential Palace by the Revolutionary Directorate, he was picked up by Havana cops and murdered.

Derridá, Jacques (1930–) – French philosopher and founder of the school of "deconstructionism."

Díaz-Balart, Rafael (1926–) – Leader of the youth wing of Batista's United Action Party (PAU), he became undersecretary of the interior after the coup and was elected to congress in 1954. Left Cuba in late December 1958 and founded the first Cuban counterrevolutionary organization in the United States, the Rosa Blanca [White Rose], serving as its president for more than four decades. He is the brother of Fidel Castro's first wife and the father of U.S. congressman Lincoln Díaz-Balart.

Díaz Tamayo, Martín (b. 1904) – A brigadier general in the Cuban army, on July 26, 1953, he traveled to Santiago de Cuba to personally relay Batista's order to kill all the captured Moncada attackers. In July 1955 he became director of the Bureau for the Repression of Communist Activities (BRAC) police unit. In April 1956 he was named head of the military garrison in Santiago de Cuba. The following year he was promoted to major general and became head of the army's intelligence service. He fled Cuba in January 1959.

Directorate, University Student. See Student Directorate, University

Domitro, Taras (1930–1972) – A member of the July 26 Movement in Santiago de Cuba, in March 1957 he was part of the first group of reinforcements to the Rebel Army in the Sierra. He was later sent back to Santiago de Cuba and helped organize armed actions until he was taken prisoner. After 1959 he had leadership responsibilities in the Santiago de Cuba municipal government and the Revolutionary Armed Forces, holding the rank of captain at the time of his death.

Duque de Estrada, Arturo (1928–1994) – An organizer of the July 26 Movement in Oriente, he functioned as Frank País's secretary.

After 1959 he held a number of responsibilities in the revolutionary government. In later years he conducted historical research into Cuba's eastern region.

Echeverría, José Antonio (1932–1957) – President of Federation of University Students from 1954 until his death. He was the principal leader of the Revolutionary Directorate; killed March 13, 1957, by henchmen of the Batista dictatorship during the Directorate-organized attack on the Presidential Palace and Radio Reloj.

Entralgo, Elías (1903–1966) – Assistant dean of the School of Philosophy and Letters at the University of Havana. In 1953 he taught history at the University of Oriente. Following the victory of the revolution he was a dean at the University of Havana. At the time of his death he was also president of the Cuban National Commission of UNESCO.

Espín, Vilma (1930–) – A founding member of the July 26 Movement in Santiago de Cuba. A close collaborator of Frank País, she helped organize the November 30, 1956, uprising and later served as July 26 Movement coordinator in Oriente province. She joined the Rebel Army in July 1958, serving in Second Eastern Front. President of Federation of Cuban Women since 1960. A member of Communist Party Central Committee since 1965 and of its Political Bureau 1980–91, she has been a member of Council of State since 1976.

Esteva, Tina (1912–) – A schoolteacher before 1959, she was an active member of the July 26 Movement who helped collect supplies for the Rebel Army. From 1959 on, she held important positions in the Ministry of Education.

Federation of University Students (FEU) – Organization founded at the University of Havana in 1922 by Julio Antonio Mella and others. It opposed the 1952 Batista coup and advocated military struggle against the dictatorship. From 1954 to 1957 the FEU's president was José Antonio Echeverría. Following 1959 the organization was broadened to encompass all university students throughout the country.

Fernández, José Ramón (1923–) – A first lieutenant in the Cuban army, he opposed the Batista dictatorship and helped organize the "Los Puros" conspiracy of officers opposed to the regime. Court-martialed in April 1956, Fernández was sentenced to six years imprisonment on the Isle of Pines. There he established political relations with the July 26 Movement prisoners, and trained their militia unit. On January 1, 1959, following Batista's flight, he helped lead the July 26 Movement takeover of the prison and the Isle of Pines. Incorporated into the Rebel Army, he served as director of the Militia Leadership School. He led the main column of the revolutionary forces that repelled the U.S.-organized invasion at the Bay of Pigs in April 1961. He was deputy minister of the FAR until 1970, and minister of education 1972–91. Since 1978 he has been vice president of the Council of Ministers.

Fernández, María de la Concepción "Conchita" (1912–1998) – A leader of the Orthodox Party, she was secretary to Fernando Ortiz, Eduardo Chibás, and Fidel Castro. After 1959 she worked in the National Institute of Agrarian Reform (INRA) and later in the Ministry of Agriculture.

Fernández, Marcelo *(Zoilo)* (1932–) – A leader of the July 26 Movement's urban underground, he was national coordinator of the organization from March 1958 to 1960. He was later minister of foreign trade, head of the National Bank, and economic adviser to the Central Planning Commission. A member of the Communist Party Central Committee 1965–86, he is currently an official of Cubanacán corporation.

Fernández Rueda, Luisín (1920–) – An accountant, he was provincial leader of the July 26 Movement in Pinar del Río, arrested on a number of occasions. After 1959 he worked in the Ministry of Foreign Affairs and later the Ministry of Education.

Fernández Sánchez, Leonardo (1907–1965) – Founder and president of the Student Association at the Institute of Havana during the Machado dictatorship. Together with Julio Antonio Mella, he was part of the National Federation of Students. A founder of the Orthodox Party in 1947. An opponent of the Batista regime, he was harassed and arrested under the dictatorship. After 1959 his responsibilities included Cuba's representative in the UN Food and Agriculture Organization and ambassador to Italy.

Ferrer, Nilda (d. 1990) – Member of the July 26 Movement in Santiago de Cuba. Together with María Antonia Figueroa, she carried out the first public demonstration of support for the imprisoned Moncadistas as they arrived for their trial in September 1953. After 1959 she held various responsibilities.

Figueroa Araújo, María Antonia (1918–) – Joining the Authentic Party in 1940, she became a founding member of the Orthodox Party in 1947. A member of the National Directorate of the July 26 Movement in Santiago de Cuba, she helped organize the uprising of November 30, 1956. She later helped organize supplies for the Rebel Army's Third Front. After 1959 she was a professor at the Universities of Oriente and Havana.

Figueroa Araújo, Max (1913–1996) – A university professor and member of the July 26 Movement in Santiago de Cuba. After 1959 he held various responsibilities in the Ministry of Education.

Fortuny, Mario (1911–1953) – A veteran of the anti-Machado movement of the 1930s. Following Batista's 1952 coup, he helped found the Triple A, an organization affiliated to the Authentic Party that advocated armed action against Batista. In November 1953 he was picked up by the police, tortured, and murdered.

Foucault, Michel (1926–1984) – French philosopher and skeptic of science and reason.

Fraga, Gustavo (1902–1957) – A veteran of the anti-Machado struggle, he belonged to Young Cuba beginning in 1934. During the revolutionary war he was an organizer of the July 26 Movement underground and a workers leader in Guantánamo. He was killed when a bomb he was preparing accidentally went off August 4, 1957.

Francia, José Gaspar Rodríguez de (1766–1840) – Dictator of Paraguay 1814–40.

Franqui, Carlos (1921–) – Until 1946 a member of Popular Socialist Party, he joined the July 26 Movement and helped edit its underground newspaper *Revolución*. In 1958 he went to the Sierra Maestra, where he edited the Rebel Army newspaper *El*

Cubano Libre and headed Radio Rebelde in late 1958. He was editor of the daily *Revolución* 1959–63 and later director of Council of State Office of Historical Affairs. He left Cuba in 1968 and became an outspoken opponent of the revolution.

Frías, Ciro (1928–1958) – A peasant from the Sierra Maestra, he joined the Rebel Army in January 1957 and became a captain. A member of Column 18 of the Second Eastern Front led by Raúl Castro, he was killed in battle April 10, 1958, and was posthumously promoted to commander.

Gangsterism – After the reversal of the revolutionary upsurge that toppled the Machado dictatorship, during the 1940s a number of armed "action groups" were formed, composed initially of militant and revolutionary-minded youth. In the absence of a revolutionary leadership, these groups degenerated into rival gangs that served the interests of various bourgeois currents. Violent conflicts between the different bands reached a peak in the years before Batista's coup. The main gangs were Guiteras Revolutionary Action (ARG), the Revolutionary Socialist Movement (MSR), and the Revolutionary Insurrectional Union (UIR).

García, Guillermo (1928–) – A peasant from the Sierra Maestra, he was a member of a July 26 Movement cell. In December 1956 he helped organize the regroupment of rebel forces who had been scattered following the *Granma* landing by the assault of Batista's forces. He became a Rebel Army combatant in early 1957, and by late 1958 was promoted to commander in the Third Eastern Front led by Juan Almeida. He has been a member of the Communist Party Central Committee since 1965 and served on the Political Bureau 1965–86. He is one of three Sierra combatants, together with Juan Almeida and Ramiro Valdés, to hold the rank of Commander of the Revolution.

García, Pilar (1896–1960) – Army brigadier and one of the most notorious murderers of the Batista dictatorship. He personally tortured and murdered the attackers of the Goicuría garrison in 1956. As chief of police in Matanzas and later Havana, he implemented what became known as the "García method," a euphemism for openly murdering prisoners. Head of the national police from March 1958, he fled Cuba in January 1959.

García Bárcena, Rafael (1907–1961) – A veteran of the anti-Machado struggle of the 1920s and 1930s, he became a university professor and member of the Orthodox Party. After Batista's 1952 coup he founded the Revolutionary National Movement (MNR), seeking to promote a military coup by anti-Batista officers. He was arrested, tortured, and imprisoned in April 1953. He was named Cuba's ambassador to Brazil in 1959.

García Gil, Carlos (d. 1958) – Active in the July 26 Movement underground struggle in Matanzas. He was killed April 21, 1958, together with Enrique Hart and Juan González when a bomb they were preparing accidentally exploded.

García Oliveras, Julio (1931–) – A member of the Revolutionary Directorate, he participated in the March 13, 1957, attacks on the Presidential Palace and Radio Reloj. He escaped and went into exile in Costa Rica and the U.S. He returned to Cuba in February 1958 and participated in the clandestine struggle in Camagüey and Havana. He was a member of the Communist Party Central Committee 1965–86, and was Cuba's ambassador to a number of countries.

García Peláez, Raúl (1927–) – A July 26 Movement combatant in Camagüey province. After 1959 he held various positions in the government and Communist Party, including head of the Communist Party's Department of Revolutionary Orientation.

Gardner, Arthur (1889–1967) – U.S. ambassador to Cuba 1953–57. Noted for his close relations with Fulgencio Batista.

Garvey, Michael (1942–) – Son of a member of the U.S. Navy stationed at the Guantánamo naval base, he joined the Rebel Army in March 1957 and served with it for several months, before returning to the United States.

Gómez, Juan Vicente (1859–1935) – Dictator of Venezuela 1908–35.

Gómez, Máximo (1836–1905) – Born in the Dominican Republic, he went to Cuba in 1865. Joining the 1868 pro-independence uprising, by the end of the war in 1878 he had become major general of the Liberation Army. After the independence war was relaunched in 1895, he returned to Cuba as general in chief of the Cuban independence army.

González, Cándido (1929–1956) – General secretary of the Orthodox Youth in Camagüey, he became provincial coordinator of the July 26 Movement. A member of the *Granma* expedition, he was captured and murdered December 8, 1956.

González, María Antonia (d. 1987) – A Cuban living in Mexico City, she was a supporter of July 26 Movement who gave assistance and refuge to those preparing for the *Granma* expedition. She returned to Cuba in 1959.

González, Ricardo (1925–) – A member of the faculty at the Teachers College in Matanzas, he was a leader of the MNR and then of the July 26 Movement there, becoming Movement coordinator in that province. He later became its coordinator in Oriente. In October 1958 he joined the Rebel Army in Fidel Castro's column. In 1959 he was named provisional representative of the revolutionary government in Matanzas. He later held various responsibilities in the government.

González, Sergio *(El Curita)* (1922–1958) – A former member of the Orthodox Youth, he joined the July 26 Movement and in February 1958 he became head of its action and sabotage activities in Havana. Arrested and imprisoned in Príncipe Castle prison, he escaped and was murdered in Havana, March 18, 1958.

Granma – Name of yacht used by revolutionaries to travel from Mexico to Cuba, from November 25 to December 2, 1956. Taken as name of daily newspaper of Communist Party of Cuba in 1965.

Grau San Martín, Ramón (1889–1969) – President in the Hundred Days Government 1933–34, which was overthrown in a U.S.-backed coup by Batista. Later that year Grau became founding leader of the Cuban Revolutionary (Authentic) Party. President in 1944–48, his administration was marked by a proimperialist stance, corruption, and repression against the labor movement. During the Batista dictatorship of 1952–58, Grau advocated an "electoral solution" and opposed the July 26 Movement's course. Retired from political activity, he remained in Cuba after 1959.

Guantánamo naval base – U.S. naval base located in Caimanera on

Guantánamo Bay in the southeastern part of Cuba. Established shortly after the U.S. military occupation of Cuba in 1898, since 1959 it has been held against the demand of the Cuban government that it be returned.

Guatemala, 1954 – U.S.-backed mercenaries invaded Guatemala in 1954, seeking to crush broadening political and social struggle accompanying a land reform initiated by the regime of Jacobo Arbenz that affected the substantial holdings of United Fruit and other U.S. corporations. Among those volunteering to fight the imperialist-organized attack was Ernesto Guevara, a young doctor who had been drawn to Guatemala by his support for the struggle unfolding there. Arbenz refused to arm those ready to resist and resigned. A right-wing military dictatorship replaced him.

Guerra, Eutimio (d. 1957) – Peasant Rebel Army collaborator who became a traitor and was involved in a plot to kill Fidel Castro. He was executed by rebels February 17, 1957.

Guevara, Ernesto Che (1928–1967) – Argentine-born leader of the Cuban Revolution. A physician, he participated in the *Granma* expedition, and was the first combatant to be promoted to the rank of commander during Cuba's revolutionary war. In 1958 he led a Rebel Army column from Oriente to the Escambray mountains, from which he united various revolutionary organizations in Las Villas province under his command and led them in the capture of Santa Clara, central Cuba's most important city. Following the 1959 triumph, in addition to ongoing military tasks, Guevara held a number of responsibilities in the revolutionary government including head of the National Bank and minister of industry; he often represented the revolutionary leadership internationally. In April 1965 he led the Cuban column that fought for several months alongside anti-imperialist forces in the Congo. In late 1966 he led a vanguard detachment of internationalist volunteers to Bolivia. Wounded and captured by the Bolivian army in a CIA-organized operation on October 8, 1967, he was murdered the following day.

Guitart Rosell, René "Renato" (1930–1953) – A member of the leadership committee of the movement led by Fidel Castro prior to the Moncada attack, he was killed in battle during the action.

Guiteras Holmes, Antonio (1906–1935) – Student leader of the fight against the dictatorship of Gerardo Machado in the 1920s and 1930s. A leader of anti-imperialist forces during the 1933 revolutionary upsurge that overthrew the Machado regime, he became interior minister in the Hundred Days Government, which was overthrown in January 1934 in a coup by Batista. Founder of the revolutionary organization Young Cuba, he was killed May 8, 1935, while leading the clandestine struggle against the regime.

Gutiérrez, José Manuel – A leader of the Orthodox Party who in 1953 used his law business to help the Moncada combatants. Haydée Santamaría, following her release from prison for her part in the attack, worked in his office, where she helped prepare false passports for the Moncadistas and other combatants to go to Mexico to join the *Granma* expedition. He left Cuba after 1959 and died abroad.

Gutiérrez Otaño, Reinaldo (1938–1958) – A July 26 Movement member in Havana, he was murdered in the Príncipe Castle prison massacre of August 1, 1958.

Hart Dávalos, Enrique (1929–1958) – A member of the Revolutionary National Movement, he joined the July 26 Movement and was in charge of action and sabotage in Havana during the revolutionary war. Sent to Matanzas, he organized the militias of the July 26 Movement there. During the April 9, 1958, strike attempt, he helped seize a radio station and addressed the population. He and two other revolutionaries were killed April 21, 1958, when a bomb they were preparing accidentally exploded. Brother of Armando Hart.

Henríquez Ureña, Max (1885–1969) – Dominican writer and novelist, he is the author of *Panorama histórico de literatura cubana* [Historical overview of Cuban literature].

Hernández, Melba (1921–) – One of two women to participate in the Moncada attack. Captured, she was sentenced to seven months in prison. When the July 26 Movement was founded in June

1955, she became a member of its National Directorate. Returning to Cuba from Mexico after the *Granma* landing, she carried out intensive underground activity and later joined the Rebel Army. Since 1959 she has held a number of leadership and diplomatic positions. She is vice president of the Anti-Imperialist Tribunal of Our America and a member of the Central Committee of the Communist Party. In 2001 she was named Heroine of the Republic of Cuba.

Hidalgo, Alonso "Bebo" (1926–1994) – A member of the Revolutionary National Movement (MNR) following Batista's coup, he later was a founder of the July 26 Movement in Havana. He collaborated with Frank País in Santiago in organizing the first group of Rebel Army reinforcements to the Sierra in 1957. He subsequently became a Rebel Army captain and second in command of Column 16. After the revolution's victory he was Cuba's consul in Miami, and later held leadership positions in the Ministry of Industry under Che Guevara and in the Revolutionary Armed Forces.

Hidalgo, Mario (1924–) – Belonging to the Revolutionary National Movement (MNR) following Batista's coup, he later was a member of the July 26 Movement's National Directorate and head of its Youth Brigades August–October 1956. A member of the *Granma* expedition, he was captured December 1956 and imprisoned until January 1, 1959.

Hundred Days Government – In September 1933 a coup by junior officers led by Fulgencio Batista—in an action known as the Sergeants' Revolt—established a coalition government led by Ramón Grau San Martín. The new government included anti-imperialist leaders, among them Antonio Guiteras, who became minister of the interior. During this period, some of the demands long fought for by working people were realized, such as annulment of the U.S.-imposed Platt Amendment, the eight-hour day, and seizure of the U.S.-owned Electricity Company. In January 1934 Batista carried out a second coup with U.S. backing and put an end to the Hundred Days Government, installing a regime compliant to capitalist interests in the United States and

Cuba. Batista, who had been appointed head of the army and dominated the new government, sought to buy off former opponents of the Machado dictatorship, while carrying out murderous repression against those who refused to buckle, such as Guiteras.

Iglesias, Carlos *(Nicaragua)* (1930–) – A leader of the July 26 Movement in Santiago, he was arrested May 1957 and later freed by a July 26 Movement commando raid. Joining the Rebel Army, he finished the revolutionary war as commander of Column 16. Following the revolutionary victory he served as head of education for Cuba's Western Army, director of the National Pork Industry Plan, and municipal delegate to People's Power in Havana.

Infante, Enzo *(Bruno)* (1930–) – A member of the July 26 Movement National Directorate, he was its provincial coordinator in Oriente and Camagüey. He was later head of propaganda for the National Directorate until the failed general strike of April 9, 1958, after which he became July 26 Movement coordinator in Havana province. He was imprisoned July 1958 to January 1, 1959. After the revolution's victory he served as adviser in the Ministry of Labor, an official in the armed forces' Political Directorate, and a leader of the Association of Combatants of the Cuban Revolution.

Jiménez Ruiz, Eva (1906–1996) – A former member of the Orthodox Party and founder of the Martí Civic Front of Women. A member of the Revolutionary National Movement, she was arrested and imprisoned in April 1953. Joining the July 26 Movement after her release, she went into exile in Mexico, where she collaborated with the future *Granma* expeditionaries. She returned to Cuba in 1957 and worked with the Revolutionary Directorate.

July 26 Revolutionary Movement – Founded June 1955 by Fidel Castro and other participants in the Moncada attack, along with youth activists from the left wing of the Orthodox Party and other forces, including National Revolutionary Action led by Frank País in Santiago and cadres of the Revolutionary National Movement such as Armando Hart and Faustino Pérez in Havana. During the revolutionary war it was composed of the Rebel Army in the mountains *(Sierra)* and the underground network in the cities and countryside (*Llano*—"plains"). Following the meeting of the July 26 Movement's National Directorate in Altos de Mompié in the Sierra Maestra, the center of the Movement's national leadership was transferred from Havana and Santiago to the Sierra Maestra, under the direct command of Fidel Castro. It began publishing the clandestine newspaper *Revolución* during the revolutionary war.

Leiseca, Marcia (1934–) – A student at the University of Havana and a member of the July 26 Movement. She assisted Armando Hart and Haydée Santamaría in the underground in Havana. After 1959 she worked in Casa de las Américas and later the Ministry of Culture.

Lemus, Orlando León (d. 1954) – a leading member of Guiteras Revolutionary Action, an armed gang that functioned under the protection of the Authentic Party. He was murdered on a Havana street by Batista cops.

Lezama Lima, José (1910–1976) – Cuban poet, novelist, and essayist, in 1944 he became founding leader of the literary trend around the journal *Orígenes*. In 1961 he became one of the founding vice presidents of the Union of Writers and Artists of Cuba (UNEAC). From 1969 he was literary adviser to Casa de las Américas.

Llano (plains) – See July 26 Revolutionary Movement

Llerena, Mario (1913–) – Chairman and public relations director of the U.S.-based July 26 Movement Committee in Exile during the revolutionary war. He quit the organization in August 1958. An opponent of the revolution, he moved to the U.S. in June 1960.

López, Antonio "Ñico" (1934–1956) – A participant in the July 26, 1953, attack on the Bayamo garrison. He escaped arrest and lived in exile in Guatemala, where he became friends with Ernesto Guevara in 1954 and helped win him in Guatemala and Mexico to the ranks of the July 26 Movement. In 1955–56 he served as a member of the July 26 Movement's National Directorate and head of its youth brigades. He participated in the *Granma* expedition in December 1956 and was captured and murdered by the army shortly after the landing.

Louit, Octavio *(Cabrera)* (1925–2001) – Railroad mechanic from Guantánamo, he headed the July 26 Movement's National Workers Front in Oriente. After 1959 he became a leader of the Central Organization of Cuban Workers (CTC).

Luz y Caballero, José de la (1800–1862) – A nineteenth century opponent of slavery and an advocate of independence from Spain.

Maceo, Antonio (1845–1896) – Military leader and strategist in Cuba's wars of independence from Spain in the nineteenth century. He was a leader of the 1895–96 westward march from Oriente that culminated in the invasion of Pinar del Río province. At the conclusion of Cuba's first independence war in 1878, he became a symbol of revolutionary intransigence when he refused to put down his arms against the colonial regime in what became known as the Baraguá Protest. Popularly known in Cuba as the Bronze Titan, he was killed in battle December 7, 1896.

Machado, Gerardo (1871–1939) – Elected Cuba's president in 1924, three years later he forced through a constitutional change extending his term in office, unleashing a wave of protest around the country. These protests were brutally suppressed. In August 1933 a revolutionary upsurge against the bloody U.S.-backed dictatorship forced him from office and into exile.

Machado, Margot – Founder of the July 26 Movement in Las Villas, she was active in the clandestine struggle and head of the Civic Resistance Movement there. Mother of revolutionary martyr Julio Pino Machado. Following 1959 she was vice minister of education.

Machado Rodríguez, José Ramón (1932–1957) – A founder of the Revolutionary Directorate, he participated in the March 13, 1957, attack on the Presidential Palace. He was killed in the 7 Humboldt Street massacre of April 20, 1957.

Machado Ventura, José Ramón (1930–) – Member of the July 26 Movement and a physician, he joined the Rebel Army during the revolutionary war and served under Raúl Castro, attaining the rank of commander. He was minister of public health 1960–

68, and first secretary of the Havana provincial committee of the Communist Party 1971–76. He has been a member of the Central Committee of the Communist Party since 1965. A long-time member of the Political Bureau, he has been on the Central Committee Secretariat since 1976.

Mambí – Fighters in Cuba's wars of independence from Spain, many of them freed slaves, peasants, and agricultural workers. These wars took place during 1868–78 and 1895–98. The term *mambí* originated in the 1840s during the fight for independence from Spain in the nearby colony of Santo Domingo. After a black Spanish officer of Haitian origin named Juan Ethninius Mamby joined the Dominican independence fighters, Spanish forces began referring to the guerrillas by the derogatory term *mambíes*. Later the related term *mambises* was applied to the freedom fighters in Cuba, who adopted it as a badge of honor.

Mañach, Jorge (1898–1961) – A Cuban writer, essayist, journalist, he was a veteran of the anti-Machado struggles of the 1930s. During the 1940s and 1950s he directed the University of the Air radio program. In 1952 he founded the television program Meet the Press, which he led until it was shut down in 1957. After leaving the Orthodox Party, in March 1955 he founded the Movement of the Nation and became its president. Following 1959, he opposed the deepening revolution and left the country.

Márquez, Juan Manuel (1915–1956) – Imprisoned in the 1930s for his activities opposing the Machado dictatorship, in 1947 he was a founding leader of the Orthodox Party and a leader of its left wing. He joined the July 26 Movement in 1955. Second in command of the *Granma* expedition, he was captured days after it landed and was murdered.

Martí, José (1853–1895) – Noted revolutionary, poet, writer, speaker, and journalist, he is Cuba's national hero. He founded the Cuban Revolutionary Party in 1892 to fight Spanish colonial rule and oppose U.S. designs on Cuba. He organized and planned the 1895 independence war and was killed in battle at Dos Ríos in Oriente province. His revolutionary anti-imperialist program is part of the internationalist traditions and political heritage of the Cuban Revolution.

Martínez, Narciso (d. 1955) – Youth kidnapped and murdered by the army in Santiago de Cuba.

Martínez Páez, Julio (1908–1999) – Rebel Army commander, he was a combatant and physician. A well-known scientist and orthopedic surgeon, after the revolution's triumph, he served as minister of public health, and director of the Fructuoso Rodríguez Orthopedic Hospital.

Martínez Villena, Rubén (1899–1934) – A poet, he joined the Communist Party of Cuba in 1927 and became its central leader. Forced into exile in 1930 by the Machado dictatorship, he returned secretly in May 1933 and died of tuberculosis the following January.

Mas, Joaquín (1932–2001) – Leader of the FEU at the University of Havana during Batista's dictatorship, he became a leader of the Revolutionary Directorate. Arrested for his activities, he was imprisoned for two and a half years on the Isle of Pines. After 1959 he was vice president of the FEU, a leader of the Union of Young Communists, and worked in the International Relations Department of the Communist Party. He was later Cuba's ambassador to various countries.

Matthews, Herbert (1900–1977) – A *New York Times* correspondent, on February 17, 1957, he was the first journalist to interview and photograph Fidel Castro in the Sierra Maestra, disproving the Batista regime's lie that the rebels had been wiped out.

Mella, Julio Antonio (1903–1929) – Founding president of the Federation of University Students (FEU) and leader of the university reform movement in Cuba in 1923. He was a founding leader of the Communist Party of Cuba in 1925. Arrested by Machado's police, he escaped to Mexico in 1926, where he organized against the dictatorship and joined in the international campaigns to defend Sacco and Vanzetti, Augusto César Sandino, and others. Hounded by Machado's agents, he was assassinated on a Mexico City street in January 1929.

Méndez Cominches, Joaquín (1934–1991) – A member of the July 26 Movement in Santiago de Cuba led by Frank País. A participant in the November 30, 1956, uprising, he later became a Rebel Army combatant in the Sierra. After the revolution's victory he reached the rank of division general in the Revolutionary Armed Forces, was head of intelligence for the Ministry of the Interior, and later assistant to the minister of the FAR until his death.

Méndez, Marta (1934–) – Sister of Moncada martyr Ramón Méndez Cabezón, she worked closely with Armando Hart and Ñico López in producing the Movement's propaganda materials. Following Hart's escape from prison in 1957, she helped hide him. After 1959 she worked in the Ministry of Transportation. In 1965 she became Hart's assistant in the Central Committee of the Communist Party and later in the Ministry of Culture.

Mendoza, Jorge Enrique (1930–1994) – Student leader from Camagüey, he was a member of the Orthodox Youth. Joining the July 26 Movement, he became an announcer for Radio Rebelde in the Sierra Maestra from July 1958, and was judge advocate in the regions of La Plata, La Miel, and Charco Redondo. His responsibilities after 1959 included editor of *Granma* for over 20 years, and then president of the Institute of Cuban History. A deputy to the National Assembly beginning 1976, and member of the Communist Party Central Committee from 1975 until his death.

Menéndez, Jesús (1911–1948) – General secretary of the National Federation of Sugar Workers and a leader of the Popular Socialist Party. He was murdered at the Manzanillo train station by army captain Joaquín Casillas in January 1948.

Miret, Pedro (1927–) – A leader of the 1953 Moncada attack, he was sentenced to 13 years in prison. Released by the May 1955 amnesty, he became a founding leader of the July 26 Movement. During the revolutionary war he became a Rebel Army commander. He has been a member of the Communist Party Central Committee since 1965. Currently he is a member of the Council of State and vice president of the Council of Ministers.

Miró Cardona, José (1902–1974) – A prominent figure in the bourgeois opposition to Batista in the 1950s, he was Cuba's prime minister from January 5 to February 13, 1959, when he was replaced by Fidel Castro. Subsequently ambassador to Spain, he resigned in July and left Cuba in November. In March 1961 he became president of the newly formed Cuban Revolutionary Council, set up at the initiative of the CIA to become a "provisional government" following the Bay of Pigs invasion.

MNR (Revolutionary National Movement) – Insurrectional organization founded by Rafael García Bárcena in May 1952, it attracted support from many Cuban youth. Its political goal was to encourage a coup by forces within the military, with popular backing. The MNR went into decline after the failure of an attempted putsch in Havana in April 1953. Most of its youth cadres, including Armando Hart and Faustino Pérez, later joined the July 26 Movement.

Moncada garrison attack – On July 26, 1953, some 160 revolutionaries under the command of Fidel Castro launched an insurrectionary attack on the Moncada army garrison in Santiago de Cuba together with a simultaneous attack on the garrison in Bayamo, opening the revolutionary armed struggle against the Batista dictatorship. After the attack's failure, Batista's forces massacred more than fifty of the captured revolutionaries. Fidel Castro and twenty-seven others, including Raúl Castro and Juan Almeida, were tried and sentenced to up to fifteen years in prison. They were released on May 15, 1955, after a broad national campaign forced Batista's regime to issue a general amnesty for political prisoners.

Montané, Jesús (1923–1999) – A leader of the 1953 Moncada attack, he was sentenced to ten years in prison, and released in the May 1955 amnesty. A participant in the *Granma* expedition, he was captured in December 1956 and held prisoner for the remainder of the war. Responsibilities he held after 1959 included head of the Central Committee's International Department; organizer of the Central Committee; minister of communication. He was a member of Communist Party Central Committee from 1965 until his death.

Montseny, Demetrio (1925–) – A member of Oriente Revolutionary

Action and the National Revolutionary Movement in Guantánamo, he joined the July 26 Movement there. Joining the Rebel Army, he became head of its Column 20 in 1958. After 1959 he was military attaché in Czechoslovakia and the Soviet Union; head of the foreign relations directorate of the Ministry of the Revolutionary Armed Forces; and later head of the Eastern Army. He is a brigadier general and heads the Association of Combatants of the Cuban Revolution in Santiago de Cuba.

Morales, Calixto (1929–) – A *Granma* expeditionary and Rebel Army combatant, he was assigned to work in the Santiago underground from September 1957 to March 1958. He subsequently became a captain in Che Guevara's column. In the early 1960s he worked with Guevara in the Ministry of Industry.

Morán, José (1929–1957) – A *Granma* expeditionary, he left the Rebel Army in February 1957. Becoming a traitor, he worked for Batista and was executed in Guantánamo by revolutionary fighters.

National Workers Front (FON) – Formed in Havana in December 1957 at initiative of July 26 Movement and its workers section. It raised a series of demands around wages, jobs, pensions, and union rights, and called for a general strike to help bring down the Batista regime. In November 1958, it was succeeded by the United National Workers Front (FONU), which included trade union cadres belonging to the July 26 Movement, the Popular Socialist Party, the Revolutionary Directorate, and other unionists.

Navarrete, Agustín – Member of July 26 Movement underground in Havana and Santiago de Cuba. Named Rebel Army commander in 1959. He later served as vice minister of the steel industry.

Oltuski, Enrique (1930–) – Coordinator of July 26 Movement underground in Las Villas province. He was named minister of communications in 1959. He is currently vice minister of the fishing industry.

Orthodox Party (Cuban People's Party) – Known as the *ortodoxos*, it was formed in 1947 as a radical-democratic bourgeois movement on a platform of opposition to U.S. imperialist domination of Cuba and government corruption. Its principal leader was Eduardo Chibás. The party's youth wing provided the initial cadres for the revolutionary movement Fidel Castro organized after Batista's 1952 coup. Its leadership moved rightward after Chibás's death in 1951, and following Batista's 1952 coup the party fragmented.

País García, Frank (1934–1957) – Vice president of the Federation of University Students in Oriente, he was the central leader of Oriente Revolutionary Action, later renamed Revolutionary National Action, and became a leader in Oriente of the Revolutionary National Movement (MNR). In June 1955 he was a founder of the July 26 Movement. He was the central leader of July 26 Movement in Oriente province, its national action coordinator, and head of its urban militias. He was murdered by the dictatorship's forces July 30, 1957.

País García, Josué (1937–1957) – Active in the Revolutionary National Association and Martí Student Bloc in Havana, he joined the July 26 Movement and participated in the Santiago de Cuba uprising of November 30, 1956. Captain in the July 26 Movement urban militia in Santiago, he was murdered by government troops June 30, 1957. Brother of Frank País.

Palacios, Juan – A member of the July 26 Movement guerrilla unit in Pinar del Río during 1958. After 1959 he held various responsibilities in the revolutionary government.

Parellada, Otto (1928–1956) – A member of Action for Liberty, he worked closely with Frank País. A founding member of the July 26 Movement, he was killed in the Santiago de Cuba uprising of November 30, 1956.

Paz, Ramón (1924–1958) – Member of July 26 Movement and Rebel Army commander in Column 1. Killed in battle, July 28, 1958.

Pazos, Felipe (1912–2001) – Head of Cuba's National Bank during the Prío administration, he opposed Batista's coup in 1952 and was replaced. He signed the Sierra Manifesto in 1957 with Fidel Castro, and later the Miami Pact in November 1957. He was president of the National Bank, January–October 1959. He was replaced by Che Guevara. An opponent of the deepening revolution, he left Cuba and moved to the U.S.

Pazos, Javier (1936–) – A member of July 26 Movement and son of Felipe Pazos. He joined the Rebel Army in July 1957. Captured January 1958 together with Armando Hart, he was released in July. He moved to the U.S. in September 1960.

Peña, Lázaro (1911–1974) – A leader of the Popular Socialist Party for several decades before 1959. General secretary of Cuba's trade union federation, 1939–49, 1961–66, 1973–74. A member of the Communist Party Central Committee at the time of his death.

Pérez, Faustino (1920–1992) – A member of the Orthodox Party, following Batista's 1952 coup he joined the Revolutionary National Movement (MNR), and in 1954 together with Armando Hart became a leader of it. He was jailed in October 1954 for planning a sabotage action but was freed by the national amnesty of May 1955. A founder of the July 26 Movement in June 1955, he was part of its first National Directorate. A *Granma* expeditionary, he headed the July 26 Movement underground in Havana until April 1958. Returning to the Sierra, he became a Rebel Army commander. After 1959 he occupied numerous posts, including minister for the recovery of stolen property; organizer of the National Institute of Hydraulic Resources; first secretary of the Communist Party in Sancti Spíritus; Cuba's ambassador to Bulgaria. He was a member of the Communist Party Central Committee from 1965 until his death.

Pérez Almaguer, Waldo (b. 1907) – Authentic Party leader from Holguín. After March 10, 1952, he went over to Batista and was named governor of Oriente province. After being deposed, in 1955 he went public with a denunciation of the 1953 murder of the captured Moncadistas.

Pérez Jiménez, Marcos (1914–2001) – Military dictator of Venezuela from 1952 until he was toppled in a popular rebellion in January 1958.

Pino Machado, Julio Rafael (1933–1957) – Founding member of the July 26 Movement in Las Villas, he and other comrades were killed in Santa Clara May 1957 when a bomb they were carrying in their car exploded.

Pino Machado, Quintín (1931–1986) – Member of the July 26 Movement in Las Villas. Responsibilities after 1959 included Cuba's ambassador to Nicaragua, its representative to the Organization of American States, and vice minister of culture.

Piñeiro, Manuel (1933–1998) – A participant in student protests against Batista's 1952 coup, in 1955 he became a founding member of the July 26 Movement. He joined the Rebel Army in 1957, and by January 1959 had become a commander. After the victory he helped organize State Security and became first vice minister of the interior. As head of its Technical subministry during the 1960s, he coordinated Cuba's support to revolutionary movements around the world, including support for Che Guevara's columns in the Congo and Bolivia. He was longtime head of the Communist Party's Department of the Americas and a member of the party's Central Committee from 1965 until 1997.

Platt Amendment – Named after U.S. Senator Orville Platt (Republican, Connecticut), this provision was imposed on Cuba in 1901 during the U.S. military occupation. Under the terms of the amendment—incorporated in Cuba's new constitution—Washington was given the "right" to intervene in Cuban affairs at any time and to establish military bases on Cuban soil. The Platt Amendment was eliminated from the Cuban constitution in the wake of the 1933 revolutionary upsurge, but Washington continued to claim "rights" to its naval base in Guantánamo, and institutionalized other forms of political and economic exploitation of Cuba.

Playa Girón – On April 17, 1961, an expeditionary force of 1,500 Cuban mercenaries organized, financed, and deployed by Washington invaded Cuba at the Bay of Pigs on the southern coast. The counterrevolutionaries aimed to spark an antigovernment uprising while trying to hold a beachhead on Cuban territory long enough to install a provisional government that would appeal for Washington's support and for direct military intervention. In less than seventy-two hours of intense combat, however, the mercenaries were defeated by Cuba's militias, Revolutionary Armed Forces, Revolutionary Air Force, and Revolutionary National Police. On April 19 the remaining invaders were captured at Playa Girón (Girón Beach), which is the name Cubans use to designate the battle.

Ponce Carrasco, Vicente (1933–1958) – Member of July 26 Movement in Havana, he was arrested in an attack on an armory during the April 9, 1958, strike attempt. He was murdered in the Príncipe Castle prison massacre of August 1, 1958.

Popper, Karl (1902–1994) – Austrian-born positivist philosopher and political opponent of Marxism.

Popular Socialist Party (PSP) – Name taken in 1944 by the Communist Party of Cuba. The PSP opposed the 1952 Batista coup and dictatorship but rejected the political course of the Moncada assault, and of the July 26 Movement and Rebel Army in launching the revolutionary war in 1956–57. The PSP collaborated with the July 26 Movement in the final months of the struggle to bring down the Batista dictatorship. After the revolution's victory, the PSP fused with the July 26 Movement and Revolutionary Directorate in 1961 to form the Integrated Revolutionary Organizations, and later the Communist Party of Cuba in 1965.

Prieto, José "Pepe" (1928–1958) – A member of the Revolutionary National Movement (MNR) after Batista's coup, he was head of the July 26 Movement's propaganda work in Havana in 1958. A participant in the April 9, 1958, strike, he was murdered the following day.

Prío Socarrás, Carlos (1903–1977) – Leader of the Authentic Party and president of Cuba from 1948 until Batista's 1952 coup. He was a leading figure in the bourgeois opposition during Cuba's revolutionary war. In early 1961 he left Cuba and went to the U.S.

Pujol, Raúl (1918–1957) – Member of the Civic Resistance Movement in Santiago de Cuba. He was murdered together with Frank País on July 30, 1957.

Ramos Latour, René *(Daniel)* (1932–1958) – July 26 Movement national action coordinator after Frank País's death, heading its urban militias. Joining the Rebel Army as a commander in May 1958, he was killed in battle July 30, 1958, at the end of the

Batista army's offensive in the Sierra Maestra.

Ravelo, Héctor – Member of the Orthodox Youth who joined the July 26 Movement and was active in the underground struggle. A participant in the hunger strike at Príncipe Castle prison in early 1958.

Revolutionary Directorate – Formed in 1955 by José Antonio Echeverría and other leaders of the Federation of University Students. Cadres of the Revolutionary Directorate carried out the attack on the Presidential Palace and Radio Reloj on March 13, 1957, in which a number of central leaders, including Echeverría, were killed. Adding "March 13" to its name, the Directorate organized a guerrilla column in the Escambray mountains in Las Villas in February 1958 led by Faure Chomón that subsequently put itself under the command of Che Guevara. The Revolutionary Directorate fused with the July 26 Movement and PSP in 1961 to form the Integrated Revolutionary Organizations and later the Communist Party of Cuba.

Riera, Santiago (d. 1984) – Member of the Orthodox Party who joined the July 26 Movement in Las Villas. After the revolution's triumph he worked with Che Guevara in the Ministry of Industry. He later served as vice minister of commerce and of military supplies, and minister of the State Committee on Prices.

Río Chaviano, Alberto del (b. 1911) – Commanding officer of the First Regiment in Santiago de Cuba based at the Moncada garrison. Following the defeat of the Moncada attack of July 26, 1953, he personally directed the massacre, under Batista's orders, of some 50 of the captured revolutionaries. He was later promoted to brigadier general. He fled Cuba in January 1959.

Roa, Raúl (1907–1982) – Student leader and opponent of U.S.-backed regimes in Cuba in the 1920s and 1930s; later dean of social sciences at the University of Havana. In 1959 he became Cuba's foreign minister, serving until 1976, during which time he became known as the "chancellor of dignity." He was a member of the Central Committee of the Communist Party and was vice president of the National Assembly at the time of his death.

Rodríguez, Carlos Rafael (1913–1997) – A leader of the first Cuban

Communist Party (later renamed Popular Socialist Party) from the 1930s, in 1944 he became a minister without portfolio in Batista's wartime government. Went to the Sierra Maestra in 1958 on behalf of the PSP leadership for discussion with July 26 Movement leadership. He was editor of the PSP's daily *Noticias de Hoy*, 1959–62, and president of National Institute of Agrarian Reform 1963–65. He was a member of the Communist Party Central Committee and Political Bureau from 1965, and vice president of the Council of State and Council of Ministers from 1976.

Rodríguez, Fructuoso (1933–1957) – One of the most prominent leaders of the Revolutionary Directorate after José Antonio Echeverría, and vice president of the Federation of University Students. A participant in the March 13, 1957, attack on the Presidential Palace. He was murdered by Batista's police in the 7 Humboldt Street massacre of April 20, 1957.

Rodríguez, Guillermo (1929–) – Member of July 26 Movement in Las Villas. After 1959 he held various responsibilities in the Revolutionary Armed Forces, being promoted to brigadier general in 1989. Works in the Ministry of Foreign Relations.

Rodríguez, Léster (1927–1998) – A participant in the Moncada attack, he escaped into exile, returning clandestinely in April 1955. When the July 26 Movement was founded in 1955, he became coordinator in Oriente province. He helped organize the Santiago uprising of November 30, 1956. Arrested following that action, he was acquitted in April 1957 and went into exile again, where he was July 26 Movement war delegate in the United States through October 1957. He signed the Miami Pact without authorization. In 1958 he returned to Cuba and joined the Rebel Army, becoming a captain. After 1959 he held various responsibilities in the government, among them in the iron and steel industry.

Rodríguez, Luis Orlando (1917–1989) – A veteran of the anti-Machado movement of the 1930s. He founded the newspaper *La Calle*, which was closed by the dictatorship in 1952, relaunched in 1955, and closed again that same year. In 1956 he joined the July 26 Movement. Joining the Rebel Army in 1957, he became the first editor of its newspaper *El Cubano Libre* and director of Radio Rebelde. Following the revolution's victory he served as home minister and spent over twenty years in the diplomatic service.

Rodríguez, Osvaldo – Head of action and sabotage for the July 26 Movement in Las Villas province. After 1959 he was named director of the telegraph system for the Ministry of Communications, a position he held until his retirement.

Rodríguez, René (1931–1990) – Worked with Fidel Castro in preparations for the Moncada attack, in 1956 he was a *Granma* expeditionary. He later served in Che Guevara's column in Las Villas. After 1959 he was head of Cuban Institute for Friendship with the Peoples (ICAP) for many years. He was a member of Communist Party Central Committee from 1980 until his death.

Rodríguez Llompart, Héctor – Head of a group of July 26 Movement underground combatants in the Regla neighborhood of Havana during the revolutionary war. Following 1959, his responsibilities included ambassador to the German Democratic Republic, minister for foreign collaboration, and president of the National Bank. He is executive chairman of FINCOMEX, a Havana-based enterprise facilitating trade and mixed-venture companies in Cuba.

Rojas, Marta (1931–) – Journalist who covered the 1953 trial of the Moncada combatants for *Bohemia*. Since 1959 she has been a prominent Cuban journalist.

Rosa Valdés, Roberto de la (1919–1958) – Member of the July 26 Movement in Havana who participated in actions around the April 9, 1958, strike. Arrested and jailed, he was killed in the Príncipe Castle prison massacre of August 1, 1958.

Rosas, Juan Manuel de (1793–1877) – Governor of Buenos Aires province 1829–32, 1835–52. He assumed dictatorial power over the entire country in 1842, ruling until being toppled in 1852.

Rosell, Allan – A member of the Revolutionary National Movement (MNR) after the Batista coup, and later a leader of July 26 Movement in Las Villas. A doctor in the Rebel Army, he served with Che Guevara's column in Las Villas.

Ryan, Charles "Chuck" (1938–) – Son of a member of the U.S. Navy stationed at the Guantánamo naval base, he joined the Rebel Army in March 1957 and served with it for several months, participating in the battle of Uvero. After returning to the United States, he helped raise funds for the July 26 Movement.

Salas Cañizares, José María – Lieutenant colonel and SIM (Military Intelligence Service) commander in Santiago de Cuba. One of the most notorious of Batista's henchmen, he commanded the police squad that assassinated Frank País in July 1957.

Salvador, David (1923–) – Headed July 26 Movement workers section 1957–58. He was general secretary of Cuban Workers Confederation (CTC) 1959–60. He was arrested and imprisoned for counterrevolutionary actions in 1960.

Sánchez, Celia (1920–1980) – Born in Manzanillo in Oriente, Cuba, she was a founding member of the Orthodox Party in 1947 and a leader of its youth. She became a leader in Oriente province of the amnesty campaign for the political prisoners. In 1955 she was a founding member of the July 26 Movement and its central organizer in Manzanillo. She organized the urban supply and recruitment network for the Rebel Army, and was the first woman to become a combatant in the Rebel Army, serving on its general command beginning October 1957. At her death she was a member of the Communist Party Central Committee and secretary of the Council of State and Council of Ministers.

Santamaría Cuadrado, Abel (1927–1953) – A member of the Orthodox Party at the time of Batista's 1952 coup, he organized a revolutionary group that fused with the movement led by Fidel Castro, becoming Castro's closest collaborator and second in command of the July 26, 1953, Moncada attack. He was captured, tortured, and murdered following the action. The brother of Haydée and Aldo Santamaría.

Santamaría Cuadrado, Aldo (1926–2003) – A leader of the July 26 Movement, he was imprisoned in late 1956. He joined the Rebel Army 1958, serving in Fidel Castro's command post. He was a member of Communist Party Central Committee 1965–86 and a vice admiral in the Cuban navy. Brother of Haydée and Abel Santamaría.

Santamaría Cuadrado, Haydée "Yeyé" (1923–1980) – Born in Encrucijada, Las Villas, in 1950 she moved to Havana. Following Batista's 1952 coup, she helped publish and distribute the underground newspapers *Son los mismos* and *El Acusador*, and became part of the movement led by Fidel Castro. A participant in the Moncada attack, she was captured and sentenced to seven months in prison. Released in February 1954, she helped reorganize the movement and coordinate the distribution of *History Will Absolve Me*. She became a founding member of the National Directorate of the July 26 Movement in 1955. A participant in the November 30, 1956, uprising in Santiago de Cuba, she undertook extensive underground and international responsibilities during the course of the war. After 1959, she served as director of Casa de las Américas and was a member of the Central Committee of the Communist Party of Cuba, posts she held at the time of her death.

Santos, Asela de los (1929–) – Founding member of the July 26 Movement in Santiago de Cuba and collaborator of Frank País and Vilma Espín, she later became a member of the Rebel Army Second Eastern Front's Column 6, where she organized the department of education. She was later deputy minister and minister of education, and is currently adviser to the president of the Cuban Institute of Radio and Television (ICRT).

Santos Buch, Ángel María – Research physician in Santiago de Cuba, he was a founder of the July 26 Movement. First president of the Civic Resistance Movement in Santiago de Cuba. He left Cuba in 1960.

Sarría, Pedro (1900–1972) – Lieutenant in Cuban army who captured Fidel Castro and other Moncadistas days after July 26, 1953. Defying orders to murder them, Sarría brought the prisoners unharmed to the city jail in Santiago de Cuba. During the revolutionary war he refused to fight against the rebels and was court-martialed. In January 1959 he was incorporated into the Rebel Army as a captain.

Sergeants' Revolt – On September 4, 1933, in the midst of the revolutionary upsurge that ousted dictator Gerardo Machado a month earlier, a group of junior army officers led by Sgt. Fulgencio Batista staged a coup against the regime of Carlos Manuel de Céspedes, who was supported by Washington. A coalition government that included anti-imperialist leaders was set up, later known as the Hundred Days Government. It was ousted in a second coup led by Batista, with Washington's support, in January 1934.

Smith, Earl (1903–1991) – U.S. ambassador to Cuba 1957–59. An ardent defender of the Batista dictatorship, he eventually entered into conflict with members of the U.S. State Department, for whom Batista was becoming an obstacle.

Somoza García, Anastasio (1896–1956) – Made head of Nicaragua's National Guard in 1933 by U.S. occupying forces, he was dictator from 1937 until his assassination in 1956. His sons Luis and then Anastasio succeeded him as rulers of the country until 1979, when the U.S.-backed dictatorship was overthrown in a revolutionary struggle led by the Sandinista National Liberation Front.

Sorí Marín, Humberto (1935–1961) – Authentic Party politician. Joined Rebel Army in Sierra Maestra 1957, ending war with rank of commander. Minister of agriculture after revolution. Later joined counterrevolutionary bands; captured and executed in 1961.

Student Directorate, University – Formed 1927 by students at the University of Havana to oppose Machado's assumption of dictatorial powers . The majority of its leaders were expelled from the university. A new Directorate was formed in September 1930. Some of its leaders played prominent roles in the Hundred Days Government of 1933–34, during which time the organization dissolved.

Student Left Wing – Formed 1931 by members of the University Student Directorate who were supporters of the Communist Party at the University of Havana.

Suárez Blanco, José "Pepe" (1927–1991) – Participated in the Moncada attack of July 26, 1953. Captured, he was tried and sentenced to ten years in prison, serving 22 months on the Isle of Pines. Freed by the May 1955 amnesty, he became a member of the first National Directorate of the July 26 Movement, in charge of the organization in Pinar del Río. At the beginning of the revolutionary war he left Cuba to obtain armaments for the Rebel Army. Following 1959 he carried out a number of responsibilities in the revolutionary government.

Suárez Gayol, Jesús (1936–1967) – A student leader in Camagüey following Batista's 1952 coup, he participated in numerous demonstrations against the dictatorship. When the July 26 Movement was founded in 1955, he became head of its Youth Brigade in Camagüey province. During the revolutionary war he joined the Rebel Army. After 1959, he was vice minister of production in the Sugar Ministry. A volunteer *(Rubio)* in the revolutionary effort in Bolivia led by Guevara in 1966–67, he was killed in battle in April 1967.

Taber, Robert (1919–1981) – A U.S. journalist, he interviewed Fidel Castro for CBS-TV in the Sierra Maestra in 1957. Author of *M-26: The Biography of a Revolution,* he was one of the initiators of the U.S. Fair Play for Cuba Committee.

Tabernilla Dolz, Francisco (b. 1888) – A general in the Cuban army who participated in Batista's 1952 coup, he subsequently became army chief of staff with the rank of major general. He fled Cuba January 1, 1959.

Tabernilla Palmero, Carlos – Head of the Cuban air force under Batista, by 1958 he reached the rank of brigadier general. During the revolutionary war, the air force was notorious for its bombing and strafing of peasant villages in the Sierra Maestra and throughout Oriente province. Son of Francisco Tabernilla.

Tanquistas (Tank corps members) – The nickname of a group of army officers who had initially supported Batista's coup but who came to advocate the elimination of even the fig leaf of constitutional rule that Batista retained as cover for his dictatorship. Working in collaboration with the Trujillo regime in the Dominican Republic and bringing in Dominican weapons, the *tanquistas* conspired to oust Batista by carrying out a new coup. They eventually made their peace with Batista as the struggle against the rebel forces escalated.

Tasende, José Luis (1925–1953) – A participant in the 1953 Moncada attack, he was captured and murdered following the action.

Tey, José "Pepito" (1932–1956) – Student leader in Santiago de Cuba, he was a close collaborator of Frank País. Together with País, he belonged to Action for Liberty (1952–53), the Revolutionary National Movement (1953–54), Oriente Revolutionary Action (1954), Revolutionary National Action (1955), and the July 26 Movement (1955–56). He was killed during the November 30, 1956, uprising in Santiago de Cuba in an attack on the police station.

Torres, Antonio "Ñico" (d. 1991) – A railroad worker from Guantánamo, he was a leader of July 26 Movement's workers section. He joined the Rebel Army Second Eastern Front, under Raúl Castro, heading its Workers Bureau. After 1959 he was an officer in the Revolutionary Armed Forces.

Torriente, Cosme de la (1872–1956) – A colonel in the Liberation Army that fought for Cuba's independence from Spain, he became a prominent judge and bourgeois politician in the neocolonial republic established under the U.S. occupation. During the Batista dictatorship established in 1952, he was a leader of the accomodationist bourgeois opposition, heading the Society of Friends of the Republic (SAR).

Torriente Brau, Pablo de la (1901–1936) – Cuban journalist and fighter against the Machado dictatorship. A volunteer for the Spanish republic in that country's civil war, he was killed in battle December 1936.

Trejo, Rafael (1910–1930) – President of the University of Havana Law School, he was killed by cops September 30, 1930, during a demonstration against the Machado dictatorship.

Trujillo, Rafael Leónidas (1891–1961) – Dictator in the Dominican Republic from 1930 until his death. After 1959, backed by Washington, he organized attacks against the Cuban Revolution. He was assassinated on May 30, 1961.

Ubico, Jorge (1878–1946) – Elected president of Guatemala in 1931, he established a U.S.-backed dictatorship. He was overthrown in 1944.

Ugalde Carrillo, Manuel – Colonel in Batista army and head of the Bureau for the Repression of Communist Activities (BRAC), a secret police unit notorious for the torture and murder of political prisoners. He fled Cuba on January 1, 1959.

Urgency courts – Formed in June 1934 under the first Batista regime, these were set up to try political offenders, and were used against Batista's opponents, primarily members of Young Cuba and the Authentic Party. The urgency courts continued to be used up until the triumph of the revolution, when they were abolished.

Urrutia Lleó, Manuel (1901–1981) – A judge at the Santiago de Cuba trial of captured *Granma* expeditionaries, where he publicly criticized the Batista regime. On the initiative of the July 26 Movement, he became Cuban president January 5, 1959. An opponent of land reform and other revolutionary measures, he resigned July 17, 1959, in face of mounting popular opposition. He later moved to the U.S.

Valdés, Ramiro (1932–) – Participant in 1953 Moncada attack, he was sentenced to ten years in prison. Released May 1955 following amnesty campaign. A *Granma* expeditionary, he became second in command of Guevara's Rebel Army Column 4 in the Sierra, later becoming its commander, and was second in command of Guevara's column in Las Villas. He was interior minister 1961–68, 1979–85. A member of Communist Party Central Committee since 1965, and of Political Bureau 1965–86. He is one of three Sierra combatants with the rank of Commander of the Revolution.

Varela, Félix (1787–1853) – A Catholic priest and opponent of slavery and champion of women's education, he is considered the first prominent Cuban to advocate complete separation from Spain. His life and work are a cornerstone of Cuban national culture. From the age of 35 until his death he lived in the United States, where he had a prominent career in the church.

Varela Castro, Manuel – A lieutenant colonel serving in the military academy during the Batista dictatorship. He was part of the "Los Puros" conspiracy of military officers opposed to the dictatorship who were arrested in April 1956 and jailed until the triumph of the revolution.

Vargas Llosa, Mario (1936–) – Peruvian-born novelist. From 1965 until 1971, he was on the editorial board of *Casa de las Américas* published in Cuba. In 1971 he broke with the revolution and has since been a well-known opponent of the Cuban Revolution and of popular struggles throughout the region. Entering bourgeois politics, he was an unsuccessful candidate for president of Peru in 1990. He currently lives in Spain.

Varona, Enrique José (1849–1933) – A poet, writer, and activist for Cuba's independence from Spain. Vice president of Cuba 1913–21.

Ventura Novo, Esteban (1913–2001) – Colonel in Batista police, he was a notorious torturer and murderer. He fled to the U.S. on January 1, 1959.

Vera, Aldo (d. 1976) – A leader of the July 26 Movement's underground in Havana. He was named acting chief of police in January 1959. In 1960 he left Cuba and went to Puerto Rico, where he formed the counterrevolutionary Fourth Republic organization.

Viera, Arístedes (1926–1958) – A leader of the July 26 Movement's urban underground in Havana. In March 1958 he led an attack on a police car. Although outnumbered, in order to allow two co-fighters to escape, he and another revolutionary kept fighting and were killed in battle.

Welles, Benjamin Sumner (1892–1962) – U.S. assistant secretary of state sent by Roosevelt as ambassador to Cuba in 1933 to organize the transfer of power from dictator Gerardo Machado and put an end to the revolutionary upsurge. His efforts led to the creation of the openly proimperialist Céspedes government, which was toppled a few weeks later.

Westbrook, Joe (1937–1957) – A youth leader of the Revolutionary Directorate and survivor of the March 13, 1957, attack on the Presidential Palace. He was murdered by Batista's police in the massacre at 7 Humboldt Street on April 20.

Young Cuba – Revolutionary organization founded May 1934 by Antonio Guiteras to fight the regime established earlier that year by Fulgencio Batista. Adopting an anti-imperialist and pro-socialist program, the organization became a rallying point for revolutionary-minded workers and youth. In 1937, after the death of Guiteras, it fused with the Authentic Party.

Zayas, Alfredo (1861–1934) – A leading politician in the neocolonial regime coming out of the U.S. occupation. President of Cuba 1921–24.

Index

384 / INDEX

THE CUBAN REVOLUTION

Episodes of the Cuban Revolutionary War, 1956–58

ERNESTO CHE GUEVARA

A firsthand account of the political events and military campaigns that culminated in the January 1959 popular insurrection that overthrew the U.S.-backed dictatorship in Cuba. With clarity and humor, Guevara describes his own political education. He explains how the struggle transformed the men and women of the Rebel Army and July 26 Movement, opening the door to the first socialist revolution in the Americas. $23.95 Also in Spanish.

Cuba and the Coming American Revolution

JACK BARNES

"There will be a victorious revolution in the United States before there will be a victorious counterrevolution in Cuba." That statement, made by Fidel Castro in 1961, remains as accurate today as when it was spoken. This is a book about the class struggle in the United States, where the revolutionary capacities of workers and farmers are today as utterly discounted by the ruling powers as were those of the Cuban toilers. And just as wrongly. $13 Also in Spanish and French.

Making History
Interviews with Four Generals of Cuba's Revolutionary Armed Forces

Through the stories of four outstanding Cuban generals—Néstor López Cuba, Enrique Carreras, José Ramón Fernández, and Harry Villegas—each with close to half a century of revolutionary activity, we can see the class dynamics that shaped the Cuban Revolution and our entire epoch. $15.95 Also in Spanish.

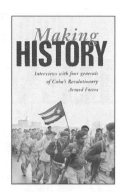

The Second Declaration of Havana

In 1962 the workers and farmers who carried out a socialist revolution in Cuba refused to back down in face of the rapidly escalating military, economic, and political attack by the U.S. government. Instead, they pointed to the example of the Cuban revolution as the way forward for the oppressed and exploited throughout Latin America. Their ringing indictment of imperialist rule, read by Fidel Castro at a rally of a million people in Havana, remains a manifesto of revolutionary struggle for working people everywhere. $4.50 Also in Spanish and French.

From the Escambray to the Congo
In the Whirlwind of the Cuban Revolution
VÍCTOR DREKE

In this participant's account, Víctor Dreke describes how easy it became after the Cuban Revolution to take down a rope segregating blacks from whites at a dance in the town square, yet how enormous was the battle to transform social relations underlying all the "ropes" inherited from capitalism and Yankee domination. $17 Also in Spanish.

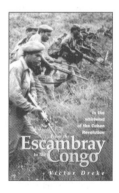

Dynamics of the Cuban Revolution
A Marxist Appreciation
JOSEPH HANSEN

How did the Cuban Revolution come about? Why does it represent, as Hansen puts it, an "unbearable challenge" to U.S. imperialism? What political obstacles has it overcome? Written as the revolution advanced from its earliest days. $22.95

FROM THE ARSENAL OF MARXISM

The Communist Manifesto
Karl Marx, Frederick Engels
Founding document of the modern working-class movement, published in 1848. Explains why communism is derived not from preconceived principles but from *facts* and from proletarian movements that are the product of the workings of capitalism itself. $3.95
Also in Spanish and French.

Socialism: Utopian and Scientific
Frederick Engels
"The task of scientific socialism," wrote Frederick Engels in 1877, is "to impart to the now oppressed proletarian class a full knowledge of the momentous [revolution] it is called upon to accomplish." $4

Lenin's Final Fight
SPEECHES AND WRITINGS, 1922–23
V.I. Lenin
In the early 1920s Lenin waged a political battle in the Communist Party leadership in the USSR to maintain the course that had enabled workers and peasants to overthrow the tsarist empire, carry out the first socialist revolution, and begin building a world communist movement. The issues posed in this fight—from the leadership's class composition, to the worker-peasant alliance and battle against national oppression—remain central to world politics today. $19.95
Also in Spanish.

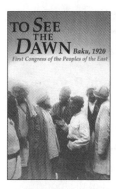

To See the Dawn

BAKU, 1920—FIRST CONGRESS OF THE
PEOPLES OF THE EAST

How can peasants and workers in the colonial
world achieve freedom from imperialist
exploitation? By what means can working people
overcome national, religious, and other divisions
incited by their own ruling classes and act
together for their common class interests? These
questions were addressed by 2,000 delegates to the
1920 Congress of the Peoples of the East. $19.95

History of the Russian Revolution

Leon Trotsky

The social, economic, and political dynamics of
the first socialist revolution as told by one of its
central leaders. "The history of a revolution is for
us first of all a history of the forcible entrance of
the masses into the realm of rulership over their
own destiny," Trotsky writes. Unabridged edition,
3 volumes in one. $35.95

Fascism: What It Is and How to Fight It

Leon Trotsky

Writing in the heat of struggle against the rise of fascism in Germany,
France, and Spain in the 1930s, communist leader Leon Trotsky examines
the class origins and character of fascist movements. Building on
foundations laid by the Communist International in Lenin's time, Trotsky
advances a working-class strategy to combat and defeat this malignant
danger to the labor movement and human civilization. $4

Rosa Luxemburg Speaks

Edited by Mary-Alice Waters

From her political awakening as a high school
student in tsarist-occupied Poland until her
murder in 1919 during the German revolution,
Rosa Luxemburg acted and wrote as a proletarian
revolutionist. This collection of her writings and
speeches takes us inside the political battles
between revolution and class collaboration that
still shape the modern workers movement. $26.95

Also from PATHFINDER

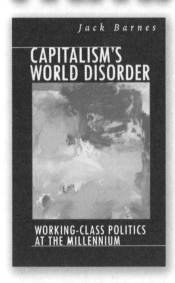

Jack Barnes

CAPITALISM'S WORLD DISORDER

WORKING-CLASS POLITICS AT THE MILLENNIUM

Capitalism's World Disorder
Working-Class Politics at the Millennium
JACK BARNES

The social devastation and financial panic, the coarsening of politics, the cop brutality and acts of imperialist aggression accelerating around us—all are the product not of something gone wrong with capitalism but of its lawful workings. Yet the future can be changed by the united struggle and selfless action of workers and farmers conscious of their power to transform the world. $23.95 Also in Spanish and French.

The Long View of History
GEORGE NOVACK

Revolutionary change is fundamental to social and cultural progress. This pamphlet explains why—and how the struggle by working people to end oppression and exploitation is a realistic perspective built on sound scientific foundations. $5

The Struggle for a Proletarian Party
JAMES P. CANNON

"The workers of America have power enough to topple the structure of capitalism at home and to lift the whole world with them when they rise," Cannon asserts. On the eve of World War II, a founder of the communist movement in the U.S. and leader of the Communist International in Lenin's time defends the program and party-building norms of Bolshevism. $21.95

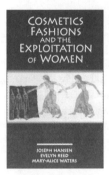

COSMETICS FASHIONS AND THE EXPLOITATION OF WOMEN

JOSEPH HANSEN
EVELYN REED
MARY-ALICE WATERS

Cosmetics, Fashions, and the Exploitation of Women
JOSEPH HANSEN, EVELYN REED, MARY-ALICE WATERS

How big business plays on women's second-class status and social insecurities to market cosmetics and rake in profits. The introduction by Waters explains how the entry of millions of women into the workforce during and after World War II irreversibly changed U.S. society and laid the basis for a renewed rise of struggles for women's emancipation. $14.95

www.pathfinderpress.com

To Speak the Truth
Why Washington's 'Cold War' against Cuba Doesn't End
FIDEL CASTRO, ERNESTO CHE GUEVARA

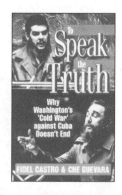

"In the coming year, our country intends to wage its great battle against illiteracy, with the ambitious goal of teaching every single illiterate person to read and write," Fidel Castro told the UN General Assembly in September 1960. A year later that task was done. In speeches before UN assemblies, two leaders of Cuba's socialist revolution present its political gains and internationalist course. They explain why Washington so hates Cuba's example and why its effort to destroy the revolution will fail. $16.95

Politics of Chicano Liberation
OLGA RODRIGUEZ AND OTHERS

Lessons from the rise of the Chicano movement in the United States in the 1960s and 1970s, which transformed consciousness and dealt lasting blows against the oppression of the Chicano people. Presents a fighting program for those determined to combat divisions within the working class based on language and national origin. $15.95

The Jewish Question
A Marxist Interpretation
ABRAM LEON

Traces the historical rationalizations of anti-Semitism to the fact that Jews—in the centuries preceding the domination of industrial capitalism—emerged as a "people-class" of merchants and moneylenders. Leon explains why the propertied rulers incite renewed Jew-hatred in the epoch of capitalism's decline. $17.95

Their Trotsky and Ours
JACK BARNES

"History has shown that small revolutionary organizations will face not only the stern test of wars and repression, but also potentially shattering opportunities that emerge unexpectedly when strikes and social struggles explode. As that happens, communist parties not only recruit. They also fuse with other workers organizations and grow into mass proletarian parties contesting to lead workers and farmers to power. This assumes that well beforehand their cadres have absorbed a world communist program and strategy, are proletarian in life and work, derive deep satisfaction from—have fun—doing politics, and have forged a leadership with an acute sense of what to do next. *Their Trotsky and Ours* is about building such a party." $15 Also in Spanish and French.

EXPAND *Your Revolutionary Library*

Malcolm X Talks to Young People

Four talks and an interview given to young people in Ghana, the United Kingdom, and the United States in the last months of Malcolm's life. This new edition contains the full 1964 talk to the Oxford Union in the UK, in print for the first time anywhere. The collection concludes with two memorial tributes by a young socialist leader to this great revolutionary. With a new preface and expanded photo display. $15 Also in Spanish.

Thomas Sankara Speaks
The Burkina Faso Revolution, 1983–87

Peasants and workers in the West African country of Burkina Faso established a popular revolutionary government and began to combat hunger, illiteracy, and economic backwardness imposed by imperialist domination. Thomas Sankara, who led that struggle, explains the example set for all of Africa. $19.95

What Is Surrealism?
ANDRÉ BRETON

Writings of the best-known leader of the Surrealist movement. Includes a facsimile reproduction of the 1942 Surrealist Album by André Breton. $34.95

Puerto Rico: Independence Is a Necessity
RAFAEL CANCEL MIRANDA

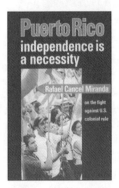

Rafael Cancel Miranda is one of five Puerto Rican Nationalists imprisoned by Washington for more than 25 years until 1979. In two interviews, he speaks out on the brutal reality of U.S. colonial domination, the campaign to free Puerto Rican political prisoners, the example of Cuba's socialist revolution, and the resurgence of the independence movement today. $3 Also in Spanish.

www.pathfinderpress.com

Che Talks to Young People

"If this revolution is Marxist, it is because it discovered, by its own methods, the road pointed out by Marx." —*Che Guevara, 1960.* Eight speeches from 1960 to 1964 by the legendary Argentine-born leader of the Cuban Revolution. With a preface by Armando Hart and introduction by Mary-Alice Waters. $14.95 Also in Spanish.

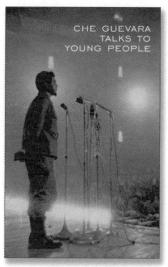

Fighting Racism in World War II

BY C.L.R. JAMES, EDGAR KEEMER, GEORGE BREITMAN

A week-by-week account of the struggle against lynch-mob terror and racist discrimination in U.S. war industries, the armed forces, and society as a whole from 1939 to 1945, taken from the pages of the socialist newsweekly, the *Militant.* These struggles helped lay the basis for the rise of the mass civil rights movement in the subsequent two decades. $21.95

Socialism on Trial

JAMES P. CANNON

The basic ideas of socialism, explained in testimony during the trial of 18 leaders of the Minneapolis Teamsters union and the Socialist Workers Party framed up and imprisoned under the notorious Smith "Gag" Act at the beginning of World War II. $15.95 Also in Spanish.

Pathfinder Was Born with the October Revolution

MARY-ALICE WATERS

From the writings of Marx, Engels, Lenin, and Trotsky, to the speeches of Malcolm X, Fidel Castro, and Che Guevara, to the words of James P. Cannon, Farrell Dobbs, and leaders of the communist movement in the U.S. today, Pathfinder books aim to "advance the understanding, confidence, and combativity of working people." $3 Also in Spanish and French.

"Without revolutionary theory,

Each issue of this magazine of Marxist politics and theory features articles by leaders of the communist movement analyzing today's world of capitalist economic crisis, sharpening interimperialist conflict, and accelerated drive toward war. Among the questions of revolutionary working-class strategy discussed in its pages are…

U.S. IMPERIALISM HAS LOST THE COLD WAR

by Jack Barnes

Contrary to imperialist expectations in the wake of the collapse of regimes across Eastern Europe and the USSR claiming to be communist, the working class there has not been crushed. It remains an intractable obstacle to stabilizing capitalist relations, one the exploiters will have to confront in class battles and war. In *New International* no. 11. $14 Also in Spanish, French, and Swedish.

OPENING GUNS OF WORLD WAR III: WASHINGTON'S ASSAULT ON IRAQ

by Jack Barnes

"Washington's slaughter in the Gulf in 1991 is the first in a number of conflicts and wars that will be initiated by the U.S. rulers in the 1990s…. Never has the gap been greater in the Middle East between toilers' aspirations for national sovereignty, democracy, and social justice and the political course of bourgeois misleaderships. That fact marks the dead end of advancing these goals today in the name of 'pan-Arab' or 'pan-Islamic' unity." In *New International* no. 7. $12 Also in Spanish, French, and Swedish.

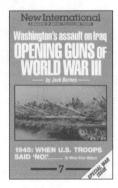

there can be no revolutionary movement."

DEFENDING CUBA, DEFENDING CUBA'S SOCIALIST REVOLUTION

by Mary-Alice Waters

"As working people enter into struggle with the employing class and its political representatives in Washington, the most combative and class-conscious workers will increasingly understand the stakes in standing shoulder to shoulder with the working class in Cuba, which is fighting in similar trenches against a common class enemy." In *New International* no. 10. $14 Also in Spanish, French, and Swedish.

THE RISE AND FALL OF THE NICARAGUAN REVOLUTION

by Jack Barnes, Steve Clark, and Larry Seigle

Recounts the achievements and worldwide impact of the 1979 Nicaraguan revolution and traces the political retreat of the Sandinista National Liberation Front leadership that led to the downfall of the workers and farmers government in the closing years of the 1980s. In *New International* no. 9. $14 Also in Spanish.

WASHINGTON'S 50-YEAR DOMESTIC CONTRA OPERATION

by Larry Seigle

As the U.S. rulers prepared to smash working-class resistance and join the interimperialist slaughter of World War II, the federal political police apparatus as it exists today was born, together with vastly expanded executive powers of the imperial presidency. This article describes the consequences for the labor, Black, antiwar, and other social movements and how communists have fought over the past fifty years to defend workers rights against government and employer attacks. In *New International* no. 6. $15 Available in Spanish as booklet. $7